T0339027

Praise for *Persuade*

"These guys are brilliant. They have taken the fun, interactive and information packed experience that SNI has imparted to my Business Mastery folks for years and translated it into this book that delivers all of that and more. Jeff Cochran and Andres Lares are experts at taking common sense approaches to impactful skills but delivering them with a playfulness that is unique in this industry. These guys take their topic seriously, but never make the mistake of taking themselves any other way than with a grain of salt."

Tony Robbins - NYT best-selling author, philanthropist, world renowned life and business strategist

"*Persuade* is great for leaders and aspiring leaders. It opens your eyes to the incredible science and research available around influencing others in a way that you can seamlessly implement in business and life, thanks to the authors' decades of experience and practical approach. For those of us looking to learn about persuasion and influencing, you will become better at both by reading this book."

Howie Roseman, EVP and General Manager for the Philadelphia Eagles

"The principles outlined in *Persuade* are simple, easy to implement, and ultimately game-changing. After having worked with the authors, I have seen firsthand what an impact they had on our organization. This book will make you better at persuasion and provide the catalyst for real change that sticks. You will thoroughly enjoy reading this book and be glad you did!"

Julie Kadnar, Divisional President, Great American Insurance Group, Property & Inland Marine

"While the business landscape is crowded with advice about decision making, it is rare to find a simple, yet impactful process outlined so clearly. What makes *Persuade* so valuable is the unique perspective provided by authors Lares, Cochran, and Digan. They balance a deep base of research with a wealth of practical experience. This book will be an invaluable resource for anyone looking to improve personal and business outcomes through more effective strategies with persuasion at the core."

Mark Shapiro, President & CEO, Toronto Blue Jays

This book is a must read for anyone in business. As a former c-level executive who then ran a graduate school business program, I've read a lot of books on persuasion and influence and there is simply nothing quite like this one. *Persuade* provides the perfect mix of research and scientifically supported information with practical tools and skills, all while leveraging the authors' stories from their extensive experience in the field. I will not only recommend this book to all my students I will also recommend it to every leader that I know, regardless of industry and job function."

Jim Kahler, Executive in Residence at Ohio University and Former SVP of Sales & Marketing, Cleveland Cavaliers

"We have brought in the Shapiro Negotiations Institute for my programs domestically and abroad because of their thought leadership and expertise in the areas of influencing, persuasion, and negotiation. This book is based on decades of experience training. It will instantly become your go-to bible for influencing others and getting things done."

Alisia Genzler, President and Chief Client Officer, Randstad Technologies

Persuade

Persuade

The Four-Step Process to Influence People and Decisions

Andres Lares and Jeff Cochran
with Shaun Digan, PhD

WILEY

Published by John Wiley & Sons, Inc., Hoboken, New Jersey.

Published simultaneously in Canada.

For general information on our other products and services or for technical support, please contact our Customer Care Department within the United States at (800) 762-2974, outside the United States at (317) 572-3993 or fax (317) 572-4002.

Wiley publishes in a variety of print and electronic formats and by print-on-demand. Some material included with standard print versions of this book may not be included in e-books or in print-on-demand. If this book refers to media such as a CD or DVD that is not included in the version you purchased, you may download this material at http://booksupport.wiley.com. For more information about Wiley products, visit www.wiley.com.

Library of Congress Cataloging-in-Publication Data:

ISBN 978-1-119-77851-6 (Hardback)
ISBN 978-1-119-77873-8 (ePDF)
ISBN 978-1-119-77872-1 (ePub)

Cover image: ©rudall30/Getty Images
Cover design: Wiley

SKY10027172_052521

Contents

1 The Art of Influence and Persuasion

Why did you buy this book?

If you are like most of the people and organizations that have come to us for assistance over the last few decades, you likely bought this book because you want to persuade colleagues, sell more, convince bosses for more budget, motivate your staff, or communicate more effectively. Perhaps you are frustrated that you missed out on landing a huge account, were passed over for a promotion, or are having trouble getting colleagues to prioritize your projects. You know how important persuasion is, yet until now, you did not know your success in this area was limited by your not having a process. Stick with us, all the way through this book, and we promise, guarantee even, you will become more persuasive. And, unlike any other book before it, your newly found persuasiveness will not be the result of memorizing a few tactics but instead actually understanding why and how the brain works to improve performance in any future situation you may face.

Humans have been studying the art of influence and persuasion for thousands of years. From ancient philosophers like Plato, Aristotle, and Cicero to the thought leaders of today, such as Carnegie, Cialdini, and Shapiro, the craft of influence and persuasion has fascinated humankind for centuries. Though there is likely more that we do not know than we do know, we have collected a wealth of knowledge on the power and process of influence and persuasion. This wealth of knowledge has come from philosophers, psychologists, economists, medicine, sociology, and other domains, all constantly wanting to better understand why people do what they do.

To accomplish our promise, meaning to improve the way you persuade others, we will summarize the most relevant and supported research over the last two centuries, add the findings of our own extensive research and experience, and convert it all into a practical process, tools, and habits. What you are reading is the result of the following:

1. Over a decade of extensive research in this field by the three authors.
2. A pilot study and research study conducted by the authors that involved more than 1000 decision makers from all over the world, testing the various persuasion and influencing techniques referenced throughout the book.
3. Countless iterations to our model, tactics, and tools through training tens of thousands of people via various academic institutions and our corporate training firm, the Shapiro Negotiations Institute (SNI).

Given the above, and as you will quickly notice beyond this chapter, a tremendous amount of information is packed into this book. *As a result, we recommend reading it in chunks, one chapter at a time, with the expectations that you will refer back to it when needed.* Almost as if each chapter is its own short book. Though it will be an enjoyable read, it will also be challenging. To make this easier, we have included summaries at the end of each chapter and one at the end of the book to refer to again.

Finally, to conclude this introduction and before we go any further, we need to get one administrative item out of the way. Importantly, what is influence and persuasion? According to the *Oxford Dictionary*, influence is "the capacity to have an effect on the character, development, or behavior of someone or something, or the effect itself." Persuasion is "to cause (someone) to do something through reasoning or argument." Though both terms are not completely synonymous, we will use them fairly interchangeably and will refer to our definition, which is to cause someone to do or say something.

So, without further ado, Jeff, Shaun, and I hope you enjoy the book and find it helps you improve your communication, persuasion, and influencing skills, professionally and personally.

Ethics of Influencing

You are negotiating with a terrorist and the only way you can prevent him from setting off a bomb is to deceive him. Do you do it?

Hopefully, you are not faced with this situation; however, this question is an example of many tough questions we face when dealing with the ethics of influencing and persuasion. Does the end justify the means? What role does intention play? Will this decision impact others? These are a few of the many fair questions we need to ask when we are working through the ethics of persuasion.

This book will improve your ability to influence and persuade others, but with this improved skill comes a responsibility. Our hope, or more directly stated, our request, is that you use the information in this book with positive intentions, in a truthful manner, and respecting all of the other parties involved. A fine line exists between "white hat" and "black hat" uses for these tools, but we trust you will decide where that line belongs. This is a dynamic decision, one that you should think about while reading this book, as opportunities arise, and continuously address as needed. We cannot tell you where to draw an ethical line but your being aware and thoughtful of this aspect will increase the likelihood the knowledge, tools, and tactics in this book are used the right way.

The Tenets of Ethical Principles

The five tenets of the Ethical Principles of Psychology[1] is a simple method you could use to determine the ethical use of the concepts covered in this book:

1. **Beneficence:** Approach influence and persuasion with the intent to benefit others and do no harm. To do this, you must be alert to the wants and needs of others and balance these against your own motives and self-interest.
2. **Responsibility:** Your obligation to be loyal and faithful and do what you say. You must hold your end of any agreement and accept your own responsibility for the outcomes.

3. **Integrity:** Your dedication to use accuracy, honesty, and truthfulness in your pitches and arguments. You should not lie, use fraud, or deceive to elicit self-serving interests, and you should strive to correct any misconceptions that lead to mistrust.
4. **Justice:** The sense of fairness behind your outcome or intended outcome. In your attempts to influence and persuade, you should be looking for the win-win, where everyone benefits and there is no loser.
5. **Respect:** People have the right to privacy, confidentiality, and to their own self-determination. This means not taking advantage of people and allowing them to come to their decision without being manipulative or forceful.

The Influence and Persuasion Process

As we previously mentioned, the study of influence and persuasion has been around for a long, long time. In approximately 350 B.C., Aristotle, one of the most famous and impactful philosophers in human history, introduced the concepts of Ethos, Pathos, and Logos, three elements of rhetorical persuasion, which are the basis for many models we continue to use.

Ethos is about a person's credibility and character.

Pathos is about appealing to the audience's emotion.

Logos is about using logic and reason.

Since then, for thousands of years, philosophers, businesspeople, marketers, entrepreneurs, agencies, negotiators, politicians, and many other professionals and organizations have used these concepts to persuade audiences. Today, one can find the triangle shown in Figure 1.1 in many offices, textbooks, and websites.

Since the early 2000s, our sales, negotiation, and influence training company, Shapiro Negotiations Institute (SNI), has studied and taught this concept. In 2005, SNI developed its own model, based upon these principles, which you will see in this book. Since its first iteration, many aspects of the model have evolved, and rightfully so. Through our decades of experience, the growing body of scientific studies, and our own research, we have tweaked our tools and techniques,

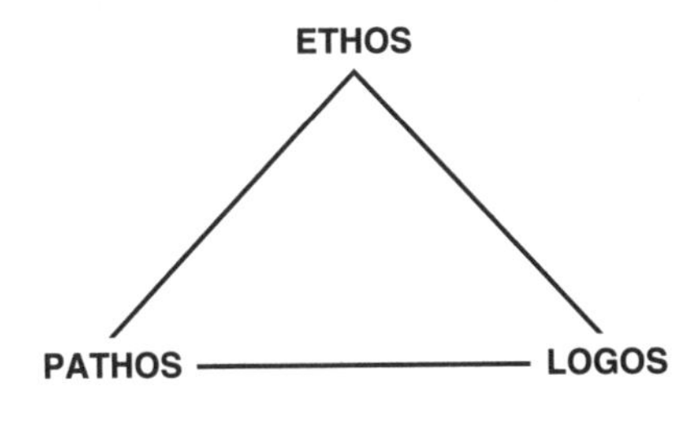

Figure 1.1

developed new exercises, and evolved our methods and model, using this knowledge to advise people and organizations all over the world. All of this has led Jeff, my partner in the business, Shaun, a friend and fellow researcher, and myself to write this book.

We chose to base our influence and persuasion model and our Influence Without Authority™ training program on Aristotle's concepts because they are strong, simple, and actionable. However, we felt compelled to update this model for two key reasons:

1. The world, and how we understand it, had changed. Around the time that Aristotle proposed these concepts, Alexander the Great was in his prime. Wars were constant, and if you were a man of age, you would almost certainly be drafted into the army. When not at war, you might attend symposia, which were drinking parties that lasted for days. Attending public trials commonly ended with the execution of those found guilty. Gender and socioeconomic status defined who you were. If you were poor, you were unable to vote or get an education. If you were a woman, you probably did not control your life; instead, your father, brother, husband, or son controlled it. Since that time, we have evolved in the way we interact and in our knowledge of the most effective ways to communicate, influence, and persuade.
2. Aristotle's philosophies needed adaptation to become a practical process. Aristotle did not address when to use ethos, pathos, or logos. When are they appropriate? Is there an order? How do I build credibility? What emotions should I engage? These were all the questions we felt needed to be answered more specifically in a model people and organizations could implement to improve their influencing abilities and performance in a sustained and repeatable fashion.

Figure 1.2 shows the Four-Step Process of Influence and Persuasion based on over 15 years of research, analysis, and experience.

In 1943, American psychologist Dr. Abraham Maslow famously published his controversial hierarchy of needs, in the form of a pyramid, which described how humans are motivated by basic needs first and then work their way up from there. Similar to Maslow's hierarchy of needs, we use a pyramid to represent the hierarchy of the influence and persuasion process. The pyramid is built in such a way where each layer is built upon what comes below. In our case, building credibility is the first step in persuading someone. Without it, the other party will not care enough or not put enough stock in whatever you do or say to be influenced. Second, engaging the other party's emotion is what allows you to impact the way they think or behave. Though difficult to do, you can do it, and we will show you how. Third, and only then does logic play a role in the influencing process. Our years of research and experience have shown us that the timing and the way logic is used is the most common mistake people make when persuading others. Finally, Facilitating Action; this was not in Aristotle's notes but a product of the research and many iterations of development we discussed above. This is the extra step that allows you to reap the fruits of your influencing labor.

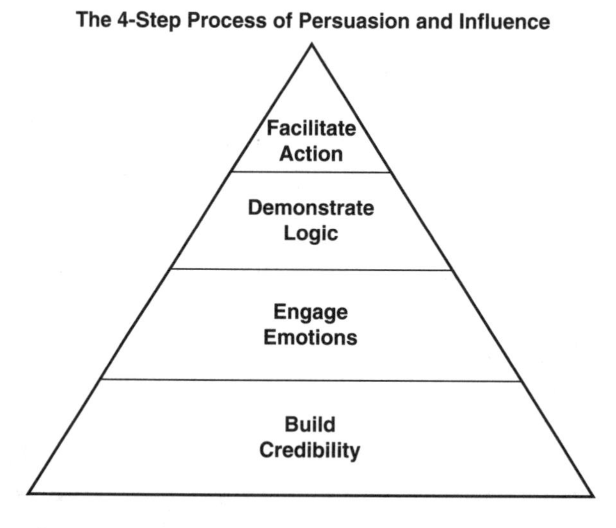

Figure 1.2

Our book will use some of these principles to influence you into using this process. We will share countless sources to support our claims as well the results of our own research to demonstrate our expertise in the field. We will leverage stories to engage you emotionally and give you a sense of the practical nature of this process. We will provide our evidence in a succinct and persuasive manner so you can see how it works and easily use it yourself. Finally, we will provide you with summaries and other tools throughout the book to make it easy for you to use it to obtain results quickly.

2 Building Credibility

"People want an authority to tell them how to value things, but they choose this authority not based on facts or results."
– Michael Burry, Hedge fund manager featured in the movie The Big Short

Michelin restaurant

New York Times bestseller

Directed by Steven Spielberg

If that is all you knew about a restaurant, book, or movie, would you be inclined to pay for it? Notice how quickly you can establish credibility. By the same token, put the words felon, discredited, or disbarred before a description and see what happens.

Before any attempt to influence people or before any decisions are made, you must establish you are credible, that you are believable and people can trust you. It does not matter how logical your reasoning is; if you are not credible, then you are unlikely to be convincing. In other words, without credibility, the message will not get through. This is because people are often persuaded not by the logic but by whom it is coming from and how it is communicated.

Thus, Building Credibility is the first step in the Four-Step Process of Influence and Persuasion. In this chapter, you will learn how credibility is built along with tips and tactics to establish your trustworthiness and expertise.

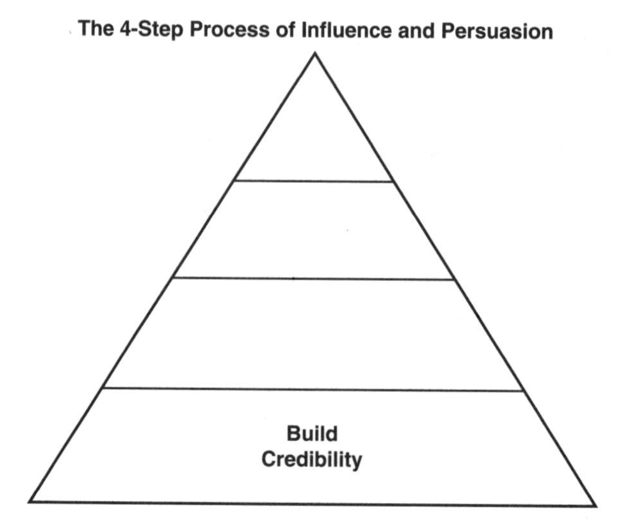

Figure 2.1

Credibility: Trust and Expertise

To learn how credibility is established, we need to understand what it is. Credibility refers to the quality or power of being trusted and believable. Establishing credibility entails someone having faith in you as a person, your intentions and integrity, and believing in your ideas and suggestions.

To establish trustworthiness and faith in you as a person, you must show you warrant it, that you are honest and can be trusted, are genuine, sincere, and consistent, and will do what you say you will do.

Though trust is required to be credible, it alone is not usually enough to persuade. You can be a trustworthy person, but that does not mean your ideas are worth listening to and, even less, worth meriting action. The second core aspect of credibility is being deemed to have sufficient related knowledge or skills about the topic.

The importance of credibility and expertise can be seen in the credibility equation:

Credibility = Trust + Expertise

How important are trust and expertise? One recent study by scientists at City, University of London, found that trustworthiness, expertise (organizational role and experience), and approachability were the three top factors in who one deemed as credible and someone he or she would go to for advice. In their study, among Australian intensive care unit nurses, they found that even when making the type of life-or-death decisions facing them in the critical care settings in which they work every day, these nurses relied on the credibility of the person providing them information more highly than on the information itself.[2]

Building Trust

Have you ever wondered why we are so quick to trust one person and not another? For example, why is it that we might walk into a retail store and say "Just browsing" before the staff members even open their mouths, yet we will drop off our car at a repair shop and not question the mechanic when we pick it up? Ultimately, this comes down to trust.

At a company level, this can play the same role. Think of how much time and money Apple, Gucci, Coca-Cola, and other companies spend creating a brand you trust. You buy the next iPhone expecting it to be powerful and easy to use, you drink a Coke expecting to know the taste, and you assume the Gucci handbag will last forever because of its branding.

This same is done on a personal level. People can and will Google you to gain their first impression of you based on your online presence, positive or negative, before you meet.

Now that we know what credibility is, we need to further delve into the trust component that drives it. The impact of trust cannot be overstated as it relates to influencing and persuading others. In fact, research suggests that trustworthiness is the most important characteristic that someone would describe in an "ideal person."[3]

So, how do you build trust? Over our years of experience and advising others, we have seen some consistency around how people build trust, identifying four key components: connection, value, reliability, and self-interest. From these components, we came up with the trust equation shown in Figure 2.2.

$$\text{Trust} = \frac{\text{Connection} + \text{Value} + \text{Reliability}}{\text{Self-Interest}}$$

Figure 2.2

Let us dig into each of these further.

People often determine how much they trust others, in part, because of their ***connection*** with the other person. Connection has to do with the strength of the relationship. In everyday language, it could be described as whether you gel with someone. This comes from mutual understanding, shared interests, alignment in priorities, etc. Research tells us that spending more time with someone makes a connection more likely to develop. The more often you engage and the more personal those engagements tend to be will determine how much trust is derived from your connection with others. While knowing this is helpful, we will share various ways to speed up and shortcut this process throughout this book.

To gauge your connection with someone, think about how you would rate the overall connection and ask yourself, "Do I communicate often? Do they reach out or am I always the instigator of conversations? Who typically ends conversations? Do they smile when they speak with me?"

The ***value*** you bring to the relationship is another strong determinant of trust. The higher the value that someone perceives you bring to the relationship, the more they will trust you.

To assess the value you bring to a relationship, ask yourself, "Do I freely offer your expertise and advice? Does the other party use or reference any ideas or resources I have shared? Is the value I provide consistent?"

Another important determinant of trust is ***reliability***. Reliability refers to the belief that you will do what you say you will do. Simply put, if you cannot be counted on to do what you say you will do, the other person is unlikely to trust you.

To gauge others' perception of your reliability, consider whether you have a history of following through on what you say, finishing projects on time, and generally being consistent.

Finally, these factors are balanced by others' views of your own ***self-interest***.

To gauge this, ask yourself, "Does the other person feel I am only seeking self-gain? Have I demonstrated interest in their wants and needs? Would I be willing to make any sacrifices for their benefit?"

As a final note about trust, other characteristics are associated with trustworthy people. Here is a list of the most common that you can tap into to develop trust from others.

Characteristics Associated Trustworthiness

Honesty	Respectfulness	Caring
Responsibleness	Reliability	Benevolence
Optimism	Authenticity	Kindness
Sincerity	Humility	Gratefulness
Consistency	Dependability	
Selflessness	Generosity	

The Nonverbal Communication Signals of Trustworthiness

In addition to the behavior and traits you display, how you say something matters. Research has found that nonverbal communication signals, such as the pacing of speech, eye contact, whether or not you smile, and appropriate attire are all related to how trustworthy someone is seen. We will talk more about nonverbal communication (i.e., body language) in Chapter 7, where we devote the entire chapter to body language and nonverbal communication. For now, here are some tips on building trust through nonverbal communication:

- Pay attention to your speech. If you are a fast speaker, you will want to slow down. Research has shown that speaking quickly can make the other person feel pressured. Also, pay attention to your pitch. While lowering one's pitch is a common way to attempt to convey authority, speaking in your natural pitch is seen as more authentic and a communicator of trust.
- Maintain more eye contact. Studies have shown that eye contact evokes feelings of trust by showing you like the other person and are actively listening.
- Smile. Smiling is another useful way to cultivate trust. Smiling conveys liking, especially while maintaining eye contact, and research shows that authentic and genuine smiles impart the perception of trustworthiness.
- Mirror the other person's body language. Matching the other person's stance, gestures, and facial expressions has been shown to convey empathy and trustworthiness. We will discuss mirroring in more depth in the next chapter.

The Neuroscience of Trust

Trust appears to be hardwired into our brains. Research has found that the hormone oxytocin increases your impulse to trust others. Oxytocin, or the "love drug," is a hormone that acts as a chemical messenger in the brain. Oxytocin has been found to play an important role in mating, childbirth, and breast feeding and has been associated with empathy, trust, happiness, generosity, intimacy, and relationship building.

Neuroscientist Dr. Paul J. Zak has been studying the role of oxytocin on trust for the past two decades.

In one experiment, Zak developed an exercise called the trust game, in which participants were assigned one of two roles: senders or receivers. The senders were given $100 of hypothetical money and asked to send it to anonymous recipients via computer. Senders were also told the recipients would receive three times the amount that was sent, and the receivers would then choose whether, and how much, to share with the senders.

Zak found that the more money people received, denoting the more the senders trusted them, the more oxytocin was produced in the receiver's brain. It was a confounding process as that led those recipients to share more, living up to the trust the senders bestowed on them.

According to Zak, "the biological basis for social connections—oxytocin—is part of the brain mechanisms that serve to make us happy." In other words, interacting with others, building connections, and being trusted makes us happy. In turn, this increases the oxytocin in our brains, leading to an increase in our own willingness to trust.[4]

However, the influence of oxytocin on trust is not always the same. Dr. Moira Mikolajczak, of the Catholic University of Louvain, believes that "Oxytocin is not the magical 'trust elixir' described in the news, on the Internet, or by some influential researchers." The relationship between oxytocin and trust is highly contextual.

When Mikolajczak conducted a modified version of the trust game, she found that though oxytocin increased trust when participants were given cues recipients were trustworthy, oxytocin did not increase trust when the participants were given cues recipients might be untrustworthy. Mikolajczak's takeaway was that "Oxytocin makes people trusting, not gullible."[5]

Trust Equation Score

Try calculating your Trust Equation Score. Think of someone with whom you have a real business relationship. Consider the connection, reliability, and value that each of you bring to the relationship, and then assess the level of your trust by calculating your Trust Equation Score.

To calculate your Trust Equation Score, rate yourself on a scale of one to five points on the Connection, Value, and Reliability that you believe the other party would describe you as bringing to this relationship. For each of Connection, Value, and Reliability, a low score represents your belief the other party would rate you low in the amount of connection, value you bring to the relationship, or reliability; a higher score represents your belief that the other party would rate you high in these areas.

Now, give yourself a rating on a scale of one to five as to where the other party would rate you in terms of your self-interests. Here, a low rating means you believe you would be perceived as less self-interested and/or concerned about the other person's best interests, and a high score means you believe you would be perceived as highly self-interested. To summarize, for each of the three aspects, above the line a higher score is better, and for the one below the line, lower is better.

Now, go ahead and calculate your Trust Equation Score as shown in Figure 2.3.

> 0-5: Low Trust signals a weak relationship where connection, reliability, and value all may be low, and perceptions of your own self-interest may be high.
>
> 6-10: Medium Trust signals a relationship with a moderate amount of trust, but where some trust factors could be improved.
>
> 11-15: High Trust represents a strong relationship with a high amount of trust. One or two areas may exist for improvement, but you are likely perceived as highly trustworthy.

$$\text{Trust} = \frac{\underset{\text{(Connection)}}{\underline{\qquad}} + \underset{\text{(Value)}}{\underline{\qquad}} + \underset{\text{(Reliability)}}{\underline{\qquad}}}{\underset{\text{(Self-Interest)}}{\underline{\qquad}}}$$

Figure 2.3

To get the most out of this exercise, notice where you scored the lowest with this person and work on improving those aspects of your relationship. To improve your overall relationships, repeat this exercise for several people you know and look for any common trends. Perhaps you will see one or two areas where you are consistently low, and you can focus on those aspects of your perception to change your image.

The Liking Effect

Have you ever noticed that most people tend to typically "like" people who are similar to themselves? It is true. Birds of feather do flock together. Study after study has found we are more inclined to like people who look like us and share our interests, attitudes, or other commonalities.

Finding similarities is the bridge that brings people together. Although there are several explanations for this, part of the reason is because we are attracted to familiarity. We tend to know and understand things familiar to us. There is less uncertainty, more of a feeling of safety, which, in turn, leads to a greater willingness to trust.

Similarities also help us validate ourselves and our own interests and attitudes about the world. They confirm and verify our self-concepts and make us feel good about ourselves. Thus, to increase liking and increase trust, look for similarities.

Want to know another secret to get someone to like you? Like them. In psychology, this is known as the "reciprocity of liking." When we believe people like us, we are more likely to like them back. This is part of the reason warm greetings and positive first impressions are so important. Showing people you like them paves the way for them to like you, and, in doing so, to trust you more and act more trustworthy.

PRO TIP Another way to build trust is by telling a personal story. Personal stories make you seem more human and likeable. Stories give you an opportunity to find ways to connect with your audience. They make you seem authentic. In one study by researchers from the University of Missouri, they found people were most receptive to information when someone communicated a personal story. In their study, they asked participants to judge the credibility of scientists communicating information on plant science, a noncontroversial subject. What they found was that when the hypothetical scientists included a personal story on how they became interested in plant science, they were deemed more credible and authentic than when the information presented contained no personal backstory.[6] We discuss storytelling more deeply in Chapter 3. Until then, think about how you can use stories to highlight your own trustworthiness.

TAPPING INTO NOSTALGIA

Jeff has a story on increasing liking by invoking one special emotion: nostalgia. Here is Jeff's learning experience using a rather odd smell to increase his credibility:

> *In thinking about the research that indicates how the sense of smell is the sense most associated with memory and emotion, I thought about a time when, while customizing a program, I unknowingly tapped into it.*

In preparing for programs, we will often do whatever is necessary to relate to the individuals to whom we will be presenting. If we are speaking to salespeople, we will go on a ride-along with a few of them to get a sense of the real-life challenges they face. That approach has given me the opportunity to enjoy different experiences. I have stood in clean rooms where they manufactured pharmaceuticals. I have tested outerwear equipped with a special tracking sensor that is activated in an avalanche. I toured a family-owned operation that processed three million hogs per year. But the smell that allowed me to connect with participants the most was formaldehyde.

I was about to present a program on persuasion and negotiation to a group of medical device salespeople who convinced surgeons to use their device during surgery for the hemostatic sealing of tissue at the surgical site. Part of their job was to gain enough credibility that they were allowed into the Operating Room; at the critical moment, they would interrupt the surgeon and suggest not using the device on which they had learned their skills and pick up the rep's company's device for a preferred patient outcome. I had gone on multiple ride-alongs and one thing was obvious: The confidence a rep needed to be so bold as to tell a surgeon what tools to use during surgery precluded a lot of input from individuals who had never done the same. But I needed to bond and establish credibility with these folks if I were to have any chance of leading a learning session for them. I could not imagine how I was going to connect. Until I had a perfect stroke of good luck.

Six weeks before the session, I received a call from the logistics contact in Portsmouth, New Hampshire. She was calling to let me know that rather than meet at her home office in Portsmouth, we would instead be meeting in Indianapolis, Indiana. "Why the change?"

I asked. She said the members of the training session were going to be attending a cadaver lab the day before the training started in Indianapolis. "Cadaver lab?" I asked. She explained they had two teaching orthopedic surgeons and 12 salespeople who would attend the cadaver lab all day to simulate an authentic sales call. She heard the interest in my voice and offered me the chance to join them. I leapt at it.

The morning of the mock-surgeries, I think that I was the first one at the lab. We would be in two groups of six and one group would perform an anterior hip replacement with Dr. So-n-so, and the other group would perform a routine back surgery on the lumbar section. In the second round, we would switch.

So, the doctors led us through the whole routine. We scrubbed in, gowned up, donned masks (before they were fashionable circa 2020), and went to work. There were a lot of memorable parts to it. I remember the surgeon coaxing the reluctant participants to take their turn incising the skin. I remember the sound of the special medical power drill (sounded like my Stanley) whirring as it prepared the socket to receive the artificial hip's ball joint. But the sense we remember was the smell.

Six weeks later when we assembled for the training sessions with the salespeople who had been through the cadaver lab, the common bonding point was the smell. In the first five minutes of the first day and, reflecting on what they had done weeks before at the cadaver lab, I would look at participants and comment, "How about that smell?" Noses would wrinkle and memory banks would flood, and I would have instant credibility based on the scent of formaldehyde. All in the session would begin to buzz about THEIR personal experiences in the lab. Sure, we would talk about the blue scrubs and the awkward gloves, but the one thing over which we all bonded was the smell. The smell was the evidence we had experienced the same thing. For credibility, smell was the litmus test because hardly anyone can fake the memory of a smell.

Later, as we researched to prepare for this book, we discovered why. It turns out that smells are related to parts of the brain associated with long-term memory and emotion, one of the reasons scents evoke the feeling of nostalgia.[7]

So, there you have it. Smells evoke nostalgia, and nostalgia is a strong, pleasant emotion, which leads to bonding. If you are ever in a fix for bonding with someone find out what smell they remember best to increase linking.

PRO TIP To establish rapport more quickly, ask about people's interests. Find out what energizes them and what irritates them. What makes them tick? Ask about what they do in their free time, their hobbies, or their favorite movies. These types of questions allow you to get to know someone more quickly, and find similarities, research has shown that (1) talking about oneself makes people happy,[8] and (2) these types of questions are likely to make people feel closer.[9] This can be especially useful in the virtual world where establishing rapport and closeness is more challenging.

The Four Key Components for Building Trust

As we discussed at the beginning of the "Building Trust" section, four key components exist for building trust: connection, value, reliability, and self-interest. Now that you've learned about how nonverbal signals, neuroscience, the liking effect, and nostalgia are related to trust, let's revisit the four key components:

1. Focus on building a connection. Make sure you focus on the person when providing your solutions.
2. Be reliable. Do what you say you will do and even give yourself extra opportunities to do so.
3. Provide value. Every time you speak with someone, seek out ways you can increase the value you bring to the relationship.
4. Be selfless. Always remember the best interests of everyone at the table.

Putting these core components into action is the key to building trust with people in every relationship.

Establishing Expertise

"Blueberries are good for you," says the cashier at your local grocery store.

"Blueberries are good for you," says the Head of Internal Medicine at Johns Hopkins Hospital

Whose opinion impacts you more? Though you do not know either, the expertise you believe a person has in the content domain makes a world of difference in how much credibility they have. The cashier's opinion is fine, but it does not carry the same weight as someone you likely deem to be an expert in the field. So, the question becomes, how do you put yourself in the position to be more like the latter than the former when influencing others?

This is why the second major factor in building credibility is establishing knowledge and expertise. However, general knowledge and expertise will not suffice. Though trustworthiness may translate as an important part of credibility in all social situations, the knowledge and expertise you display must be directly relevant to the situations and decisions you are building credibility to influence.

1. **Identify Your Expertise.** The first step in establishing your expertise is identifying how your knowledge is relevant to your ideas, solutions, and proposals. Think about the types of projects you are drawn to, what you are good at, and the type of advice people come to you for.

   For example, Jeff, Shaun, and I have been working in the fields of influence, persuasion, negotiation, and communication for decades. These are our areas of expertise.
2. **Claim Your Expertise.** The next step in beginning to establish your expertise is to claim your expertise. Claiming your expertise is telling yourself and others where your expertise lies and how it is related. An important part of claiming your expertise is believing in yourself. Confidence sells, and how you introduce, describe, and carry yourself matters in establishing your expertise.

   For example, over the last decade, Jeff, Shaun, and I have been claiming our expertise in the areas above, conducting research, publishing articles, and working to develop our expertise in these areas.
3. **Show Your Expertise.** Now that you have claimed expertise you need to support it by demonstrating your expertise. One way is to generously give advice in your area of expertise. Being a "part of the conversation" is important. This could include joining industry groups or associations, professional groups, and groups on social media. Another way to show your expertise and join the conversation is to create, curate, or share valuable content in your domain.

For example, as members of various organizations, teaching and guest speaking at academic institutions all over the world, training and consulting with global leading companies, and consistently being sourced by various publications such as Forbes, CNBC, Harvard Business Review, and the Sports Business Journal, Jeff, Shaun, and I have many examples we can use to show our expertise.

4. **Develop Social Credibility.** Once you have claimed and shown it, the next step is to get some social verification. This means gaining acknowledgment and support from others who agree you are credible in your domain.

   Depending on your field and expertise, you may build social credibility through formal acknowledgment. Formal acknowledgment can take the form of accreditations, awards, certificates, degrees, or other former acknowledgment of your accomplishments or knowledge.

   For example, all of our hard work has paid off and we have developed a depth of social credibility thanks to teaching awards, best presenter awards, testimonials from clients, and many other sources of social credibility where others vouch for the quality of our work.

5. **Be a Thought Leader.** The final step in establishing expertise over your domain is to become a thought leader. Thought leaders have accomplished all the aforementioned steps, and their social verification grows due to their actual expertise and ability to communicate it. Make sure to not lose sight of this point: A thought leader is an expert in the field who is also successful in communicating that expertise with others.

   For example, companies and individuals actively seeking our training and consulting and a respected publishing company like Wiley publishing this book are two examples of our hard work being valued and considered thought leadership.

Evidence from Decision Makers: Credibility

To dig deeper into the factors influencing the perceptions of one's credibility, we asked decision makers in our study to rate the importance of factors related to trust and expertise in their assessments of the credibility of others.

Decision makers affirm that signals related to trust and expertise are important in their assessments of credibility. These decision makers rated all 11 signals we believed to be important to credibility as being moderately to extremely important in assessments of the credibility of others. In order of least important to most, here is how decision makers rated signals of trust and expertise in their assessments of others' credibility:

11. The endorsement of a major sports star (4.0/7)
10. The endorsement of social media influencers (4.35/7)
9. They wrote a white paper on their proposed solution (4.76/7)
8. They have a lot of things in common with you (4.94/7)
7. Customer reviews on independent third-party websites (5.23/7)
6. They are a member of the Better Business Bureau and local Chamber of Commerce (5.26/7)
5. They are someone you feel you would like (5.38/7)
4. Customer reviews on their company website (5.47/7)
3. They have the endorsement of experts in their industry (5.59/7)
2. They are approachable and easy to talk to (5.60/7)
1. They are someone you feel that you would work well with (5.77/7)

Test Your Knowledge

What are the two components of credibility?

Credibility = ________________ + ________________

Fill in the Trust Equation:

Trust = ____________ + ____________ + ____________

The Influencer's Toolbox

Borrowing Credibility

Did you review the testimonials for this book before buying it? You likely did. How do we know? According to writer Gigi Griffis and the study she conducted in 2017, 82% of readers read the back cover, which includes the testimonials, when making their buying decision. Why? Because the author(s) borrow credibility from people you likely know and/or respect to convince you their book is worth reading. I hope they did their job.

So, how do we build credibility? It can take time but you can use some shortcuts. For example, one way to expedite increasing your credibility is to borrow it. Borrowing credibility means using the credibility of others to increase your own credibility. This is a great way to build your own credibility and authority.

In psychology, borrowing credibility is associated with the association fallacy. The association fallacy refers to our penchant to assume the qualities of one thing are related to the qualities of another due to their proximity or association.

You have probably heard of the common bias of guilt by association. The guilt by association fallacy points out a common tendency is to assume people are guilty of something because they are associated with a person or group who is guilty or viewed in a negative light.

However, the association fallacy can work in the opposite way. The counterpart to guilt by association is honor by association. When you associate or surround yourself with people who are highly regarded, people see you as more credible. Hence, borrowing credibility through your associations with others is possible.

People and organizations have various ways to borrow credibility:

Borrow credibility by associating and comparing yourself to those with credibility.

In a way, your associations act as endorsements of you or your company. One way to do this is joining or aligning yourself with professional groups and organizations with credibility in your industry or field. Membership in organizations, such as trade organizations, the Better Business Bureau, the local Chamber of Commerce, or other organizations or industry groups send strong signals of trustworthiness and credibility.

One common way companies do this is using trustmarks, such as security seals and seals of approval. Trustmarks have been proven to work. Numerous studies have found most consumers rely on trustmarks to judge a company's credibility, and many report they have used trustmarks to determine whether to make a purchase.

Think about a trip to the grocery store. Do you pay attention to any trustmarks? Maybe you have noticed the REAL seal on a gallon of milk, 100% organic vegetables, or USDA grades for beef. They often make us feel more comfortable with our purchases and consumption, but do we understand these marks?

Borrow credibility by partnering with an expert or with trusted companies or brands.

These kinds of partnerships could range from soliciting recommendations and endorsements by trusted people or brands to full-fledged partnerships. The closer your associations are with those who are credible, the more credibility you and your organization receive.

Borrow credibility by showcasing your achievements and recognition.

If you, your company, or your company's products or services have earned certifications, won awards, received designations, or have been featured on or in any notable media outlets, showcasing these achievements is a good way to build credibility.

One place you can find a plethora of examples of borrowing credibility is company websites. Businesses often borrow credibility by telling the story of their company or highlighting their team's background, education, and experience. Many highlight membership associations and partnerships with other respected firms. Some display a list or the logos of their prominent and well-known customers. Others highlight their achievements, awards, and recognition.

IT DOESN'T MATTER WHAT YOU THINK!

As a brief aside and crash course on online marketing, perhaps the most powerful support of borrowing credibility for me came from Conversion Optimization. Conversation Optimization is conducted by A/B testing, which is testing different variations of the same website page to see which version performs better. This is done to reverse engineer what visitors want to see, what they have no interest in, what compels them to read or act, and what will increase "conversions," which refers to whatever behavior you wish to achieve.

When I took over online marketing at Shapiro Negotiation Institute (SNI) several years ago, I immediately began battling with everyone, including my bosses, on the best strategies to use for our marketing and campaigns. Most of my colleagues and bosses felt that, based on their extensive experience in the industry, they knew what people wanted. I valued their experience but would constantly rebut with what later became a famous line: "It doesn't matter what you think." I do not recommend saying this to your bosses, and I learned to be more diplomatic how I communicated, but in this case, this phrase was correct, and the concept worked.

Though the senior members of the team had incredible knowledge and expertise in the industry and their intuition was right in some cases, they were wrong in more cases. I will be the first to admit that I was wrong a lot, too. Of course, it did not matter what I thought.

At this point, you may be wondering, what were the two most impactful takeaways from the entire Conversion Optimization experiment? First, we did better when, even before explaining what we did, we shared a few of our client's logos. Think about that for a moment. That says visitors to our page were saying to themselves, "I want to know who you work with before I even know what you do." The second was that a longer page filled with more content performed better as long as readers could get the gist quickly and decide whether to continue reading or pick up the phone and call us, which was the desired outcome.

The next time you visit a new website, take a few minutes, and look for the ways that organization borrows credibility from others. If they are companies that rely on their online presence (e.g., think Amazon, eBay, Zappos, *The New York Times*), notice how everything is laid out. You can bet it is not a coincidence and is the result of constant Conversion Optimization.

Now, use that for yourself. The next time you are communicating with people who do not know you well, whether adding a page to your website or speaking to an audience, think about who or what you will reference that the audience knows, values, and trusts, and use that association to borrow your own credibility. Think about using client logos, published articles, testimonials, case studies, awards, association membership, etc. Or, simply put, make sure you consider the ways you can borrow credibility.

Nathan's Five-cent Hot Dog Problem

One good example of borrowing credibility can be found in the story of Nathan's Famous Hot Dogs. Nathan Handwerker, a Polish-American who immigrated to America in 1912, was working at the famed Coney Island eatery Feltman's, which introduced the hot dog to America nearly 50 years earlier. But Nathan had a dream of launching his own hot dog eatery someday. Saving up $300, from his meager $11 per week paycheck, Nathan opened up shop in 1916 right across the street from his former employer.

Initially, sales were slow. During the first week, Nathan charged 10 cents per hot dog, the same price as his former employer; however, sales struggled as customers balked at paying the same price charged by his former employer right across the street. He lacked the credibility of Feltman's, and New Yorkers may have been apprehensive about paying the same price for his unknown product.

By the next week, he had dropped the price to five cents each, figuring a lower price might convince potential customers to buy his hot dogs. However, the lower price came with credibility issues of its own. How could a five-cent hot dog be of any quality?

Time was ticking for Nathan. He needed to do something to turn his business around, but he could not figure out what. He made what he thought was a better hot dog, he chose a successful location, and he was pricing his product lower than the competition.

He thought long and hard and decided his problem was one of credibility. Feltman's had been there for years, but he had been there for weeks. So, Nathan decided to borrow credibility. As the story goes, Nathan went to local hospitals and offered free hot dogs at his stand to doctors, nurses, administrators, and lab techs wearing their lab coats. Some even say he hired additional people to come stand around his eatery in white lab coats. His logic was that if his hot dogs were good enough for "doctors," they would be good enough for anyone. The gimmick worked. Nathan's Famous Hot Dogs became a Coney Island staple, with the original store still standing today.

Next time you need to influence someone, ask yourself, who are your lab coats?

Show Vulnerability

Another way to build trust and credibility is to show vulnerability. One way to do this is to make acknowledgments that, at their face value, may not be aligned with your own self interests. Allow yourself to be vulnerable.

This may seem counterintuitive; however, vulnerability and trust go hand-in-hand. Think about it. When you trust people, you make yourself vulnerable to them. Even trusting that people will do what they say, you allow yourself to be vulnerable to any consequences that may occur if they do not follow through. Thus, vulnerability is a central aspect of trust.

One of the most successful salespeople I have ever met was also one of the most unlikely top performers. As part of our standard customization work for training salespeople, we like to schedule video or phone calls with some low, average, and top performers. This top performer, Mike, on paper did not have the experience or education to set him apart. Even on our customization call, he did not set himself apart or impress me. However, when I could not figure out how he was so successful and decided to tag along on a day's worth of sales calls, I realized what he did that was unique: He asked every client for help. He did this naturally, whether asking for an education on their business to craft his proposal assistance reaching the decision maker or hitting his lofty sales quota only a few days before his deadline. In all cases, I could see how his request changed the tone of the conversation: from you versus me to we. It worked so well because, unbeknown to him, he was showing vulnerability in many of the different ways outlined below.

As you can imagine, we made sure to include a section in our training around called "Asking for help, like Mike" that referred to the power of using vulnerability. But that was one of many tools we provided participants because, to maximize your success in persuasion, you need to be able to adjust your tactic and strategy depending on the person and situation.

Though vulnerability is often thought of as a weakness, showing vulnerability is a sign of strength. Showing vulnerability takes courage, and it shows you are confident enough to know and admit the things you may not be good at. University of Houston researcher Dr. Brene Brown says, "vulnerability is the core of shame and fear and our struggle for worthiness, but it appears that it's also the birthplace of joy, of creativity, of belonging, of love."[10]

Many people believe trust must be earned before making themselves vulnerable. However, trust does not have to precede vulnerability. Rather, the opposite can be more effective.

One final note about vulnerability: It can be contagious in what is known as a "vulnerability loop." After all, from an influencing perspective, vulnerability often creates a new routine of openness. One goal of telling people about a weakness or opening up with a vulnerability is to get them to return in kind and open up about a vulnerability of their own. This can go back and forth. As parties detect vulnerability, they respond with vulnerability in return. Each time vulnerability is detected, it creates more trust.

So, if vulnerability is so important, how do I use it?

Statements Against Self-Interest

Using statements against self-interest can help you appear trustworthy. Think of the Canadian cough syrup Buckley's with the motto "It tastes awful. And it works"; Heinz Ketchup, "It's Slow Good"; and Smucker's, "With a name like Smucker's, it has to be good." These are examples of two important concepts in influencing people: "If you can't fix it, feature it" and using statements against self-interest. Let's focus on the latter. Pointing out something negative in yourself (e.g., how bad it tastes) demonstrates vulnerability and signals to the other side you are not purely driven by self-interest. As a result, whatever you say next (e.g., it works) is more likely to be trusted.

Share a Weakness

Sharing weaknesses is a deviation of statements against self-interest. According to business author Daniel Coyle, sharing a weakness is a key way to build trust within groups. The major difference between these two methods is that in the former, you immediately follow it with something of value; in the latter, it is banked for later.

An easy way to share a weakness is to discuss a weakness that you are working on improving. For instance, "I know I am not great at answering my email as quickly as I should be, but I am working on it." There is no positive statement after; however, sharing that you are working on it, makes sharing easier and gives it an additional element of vulnerability.

How powerful is this concept? Self-deprecating stories is one of the most impactful tools a public speaker can use. The vulnerability helps the audience develop trust and a connection with the speaker.

Ask for Help

The final way that you can make yourself vulnerable is to ask for help or advice. According to Dr. Jeff Polzer, a Harvard University professor of organizational behavior, asking for help is "about sending a really clear signal that you have weaknesses, that you could use help. And if that behavior becomes a model for others, then you can set the insecurities aside and get to work, start to trust each other, and help each other. If you never have that vulnerable moment, on the other hand, then people will try to cover up their weaknesses, and every little microtask becomes a place where insecurities manifest themselves."[11]

Thus, once again, counterintuitively, the courage to ask for help is a strength. Asking for help fosters trust and creates an atmosphere for collaboration. As they say, if you want to make a friend, ask someone for a favor. What you ask for can be small. Whether you ask for help, advice, or a suggestion, your comfortableness being "indebted" to another is a signal of trust.

NOT JUST ANY ICE BREAKERS

Shaun often uses the concept of showing vulnerability in his teaching. Here is his story on establishing trust and credibility in the classroom:

> As an educator, one of my goals is to get my students to tap into their creative side to come up with innovative ideas. One problem I often run into is getting students to share their ideas. Sharing your ideas requires trust. This is especially true when sharing creative or innovative ideas. Innovation comes with risk. For students, one of the biggest risks is looking foolish in front of their peers.
>
> Over the years, I have developed many approaches and exercises to show my own vulnerability. One of these is to not be afraid to look silly. For example, I often use an ice breaker exercise on the first day of class where I have my students fold a sheet of notebook paper into a boat.
>
> Once they have folded their boats, I walk them through a story about a boat at sea, exploring the ocean among calm and storm. For the first minute or so, I hold up my boat and rock it with the imaginary waves. Soon after, I ask my students to hold up their paper boat and make it rock on the waves as well. This little act embarks us on what is meant to be a little vulnerability loop.

When they get comfortable rocking the boat, I start adding sound effects to my story like waves crashing and bird cawing. Then I ask them to help me with the sound effects as well. At each step, it takes a while between my willingness to look silly and their willingness to give a little more. But, by the end of the exercise, we normally have a laugh at the lesson. This and other lessons go a long way toward building credibility and showing students being wrong is all right, and sharing their ideas in a trusting environment is safe.

Companies and organizations use tools like this all the time. We have all probably participated in ice breaker activities with silly goals or that required us to reveal something personal about ourselves. Aside from learning the names of the others in the group, these activities are designed to build trust and credibility among the group. In my experience, when done right, they often work.

Become a Trusted Advisor

The pinnacle of building credibility is to attain the elusive status of trusted advisor. Trusted advisors are the people, typically seen as experts in their domain, that someone goes to for advice. Trusted advisors typically have a seat at the table and are often involved in the decision-making process in some way.

Becoming a trusted advisor does not happen overnight. To become one, it takes time to build a relationship and garner trust; therefore, becoming a trusted advisor is emotional and logical at the same time. But ways to accelerate the process exist, which we will examine shortly.

First, however, let's explore some factors that go into what makes one a trusted advisor. We have discussed the factors that go into building trust: consistency, value, and reliability. The other factor that goes into becoming a trusted *advisor* is offering valuable *advice*.

Let's say that again: To be a trusted advisor, you must provide valuable advice. This means taking the time to understand the wants and needs of the other party, putting its interests ahead of your own and offering your knowledge generously.

Several clues tell where you stand and whether someone considers you a trusted advisor. To assess your standing as a trusted advisor, consider the following questions: Is there a personal connection that goes beyond business? How frequently do you communicate? Do they ask you for advice? Do you ask them for advice? How quickly does the person get back to you?

Trusted Advisor Quick Score

Are you a trusted advisor? For the same person that you completed the Trust Equation Score, assess the level of your status as a trusted advisor by calculating your Trusted Advisor Quick Score.

To calculate your Trusted Advisor Quick Score, answer these four questions to rate where you stand as a trusted advisor:

1. Do you discuss personal topics? If so, who brings it up?
2. Does this person ask you for advice? Has it happened more than once?
3. When you reach out to people, how quickly do they get back to you?
4. Have you sought their advice? And if so, have they given it to you?

Score each of these on a scale of one through five in all cases with the higher the number being the more often it occurs.

The first question assesses the connection. The more personal the conversations become and the more the other party leads the conversation in a personal direction, the higher the score.

The second question assesses the value you provide. If they have asked you for advice, the more they have asked, the higher the score.

The third question assesses reliability. When you reach out to these people, the quicker they respond, on average, the higher the score.

The fourth question assesses their level of self-interest. If you have asked for feedback or advice (do not force it!) and they have been comfortable providing it, the higher the score.

Now total your score. As a simple scoring system, consider the various tiers to be a Stranger, Acquaintance, Preferred Peer, and finally a Trusted Advisor. Examine where you score lowest and focus on that area to improve your relationship. Compare it to the following list to find your standing as a trusted advisor.

0-5: Stranger shows little evidence of a connection as a trust advisor. Neither party has a seat at the table nor is a consistent source of advice.

6-10: Acquaintance shows some connection and sharing of advice may exist, and you are unlikely to be the first source of advice sought nor have a seat at the table.

11-15: Preferred Peer shows you are on your way to becoming a trusted advisor.

16-20: Trusted Advisor indicates you are likely considered a trusted advisor, recognized as a valuable, reliable, and consistent source of advice.

Though this is not a perfect scoring system, it is a quick and easy way to gauge where your business relationship stands and is a good refresher on what some of the key drivers are to reaching a stronger relationship level and achieving trusted advisor status.

To accelerate building your relationship and become a trusted advisor, you can do three things. First, you can ask the parties you are building a relationship with for a small favor or advice. Asking for their advice is a great way to advance a relationship. Ideally, asking for advice can lead to the other party asking you for advice as well, which typically means you have reached the elusive Trusted Advisor status.

Second, create opportunities where you can make a commitment, and do what you say you will do. By consistently fulfilling your commitments, you will become seen as someone who can be trusted.

Third, use the trust equation. Remember, trust is a combination of connection, reliability, and value, all balanced by the perceptions of your character and level of self-interests.

BUILDING MY CREDIBILITY

I had been working at SNI for about five years. I was advising sports teams on huge negotiations, supporting training of some of the leading companies in the world, and had learned a tremendous amount by my own effort and by working with some incredible people. However, when I advised a client to do X or Y, it did not have the same power as when other senior members of our team would do it.

I spent time thinking about this, asked a few colleagues for advice, and created a plan to develop myself in this area. The plan was to develop credibility in three ways:

1. Learn more about subject matter to develop additional expertise.
2. Expand my resume to be able to have more proof of my experience and knowledge.
3. Gain more confidence in myself, which in turn would give me more conviction when I communicated.

Up to that point, I had a seat at the table and was heard because I had borrowed credibility from other team members. Based on this plan, I started teaching a Sports Negotiation class at Johns Hopkins University, I guest lectured at various conferences and universities across the country, and studied furiously additional related topics, in this case Collective Bargaining Agreements for the sports leagues we were involved with, watching our clients' games, etc. Finally, I made it a point to get to know our clients more personally: not just hopping on calls and talking business but spending time with them in person, dinners, golf, and other options.

It was not magic, but a year later, the difference was enormous. There was a tangible difference in the way others perceived me and the way I perceived myself. Before this development effort, I remember one specific situation that captured the situation well. I felt strongly about a client waiting several days before responding to an agent's aggressive first offer. I had tremendous conviction in that strategy, but when I communicated it, I could not instill that same level of confidence in the client, who moved forward with a different strategy which ended up being less successful. But, a year later, that changed. Thereafter, I knew that my voice was heard more, and when I recommended a course of action, it instilled more confidence in our clients, so much so that my suggestion was always considered or followed. This did come with greater responsibility: More than ever, I had to make sure my opinions were fully vetted, but I received a different level of satisfaction from my work, not to mention I got to know our clients much deeper.

Today, we teach this in our influence training and with our internal team. You need to put in the effort to become an expert in something, borrowing credibility along the way. Then you must develop your own credibility from various sources, building a connection with people and being genuine about your interest in them. That combination is what builds trust, maximizes your performance in whatever field you operate in, and gives you a tremendous amount of satisfaction.

How do your credibility and the Trust Equation go hand-in-hand? Back to my story about how I proactively tried to increase my credibility: One of the first steps I took in the process was to diagnose my trust scores with clients. I felt that most of them valued my advice, felt they could count on me, and were confident I cared about them and their goals. Where I was falling short was the connection. I was so careful and thoughtful about what I said and suggested that I was less approachable. In my personal relationships, I often got the feedback that I made deep connections with people, in large part because of my curiosity. However, in wanting to make few recommendations and make each one count, I missed that powerful human aspect that builds relationships. Once I focused on doing that, these relationships soon flourished, and many of these clients have become close friends, well beyond our work together.

Putting It All Together

Step 1: Building Credibility

You now better understand the components of establishing credibility. Let us review the components of credibility, along with the steps you can use to build credibility and accelerate this process.

Credibility

Establishing credibility occurs along two primary fronts: building a trusting relationship with the person with whom you are building credibility and showing the knowledge and expertise behind your ideas and proposals.

> **Building Trust:** Remember to use the trust equation. Trust is the connection, value, and reliability in a relationship, balanced by one's self-interest. Build trust by being honest, trustworthy, and likeable and through finding similarities. People trust people they are similar to and like. Make promises and keep them, and do not make promises you cannot keep.

Establishing Expertise: You must be credible as a person, and your ideas must be credible. You can show the credibility of your ideas by establishing your knowledge and expertise. Do this by identifying and claiming your expertise, showing you know what you are talking about and working to develop social credibility.

The Influencer's Toolbox

Borrow Credibility: Borrow credibility to increase your own credibility more quickly. Many ways exist to borrow credibility, including borrowing credibility through your brand story and through associations, partnering with experts, and showcasing your achievements and recognition.

Show Vulnerability: Showing vulnerability signals to people you trust them. It shows a willingness to trust, which makes the other party more willing to trust you. Consider making statements against self-interest, sharing weaknesses, or asking for help. These tactics display honesty, willingness to cooperate, and selflessness.

Become a Trusted Advisor: Finally, work to earn the elusive status of a Trusted Advisor. You can do this by building a connection, a relationship, understanding the other person's wants and needs, and by generously sharing your knowledge and providing value.

3 Engaging Emotion

"When dealing with people, remember you are not dealing with creatures of logic, but with creatures of emotion."
– Dale Carnegie, How to Win Friends and Influence People

While, as individuals, we may think we are fairly logical beings, research indicates otherwise. We rarely make logical decisions. Rather, we make decisions emotionally and then justify them rationally.

From deeply felt emotions to passing moods, humans are driven by their feelings. Emotions play a role in our thinking, decision making, and behavior and even how we experience the world around us. That is why emotion is such a critical portion of our influence model. In this chapter, you will learn how to harness emotions, your own and others, in the process of influence and persuasion.

The Linda Problem

A good example of the role of emotions in decision making is the conjunction fallacy, also known as the Linda Problem. In 1983, famed scientists Amos Tversky and Daniel Kahneman carried out an experiment providing participants the following description and asking them to answer the related question:

Linda is 31 years old, single, outspoken, and very bright. She majored in philosophy. As a student, she was deeply concerned with issues of discrimination and social justice, and also participated in anti-nuclear demonstrations.

Which is more probable?

1. Linda is a bank teller.
2. Linda is a bank teller and is active in the feminist movement.

Which do you believe is the correct answer?

The majority (an overwhelming 85%) of participants in Tversky and Kahneman's study chose option two, meaning Linda is a bank teller and is active in the feminist movement, and these 85% of participants were, sadly, wrong.[12]

Rationally, the second statement cannot be more probable than the first statement. The first statement, "Linda is a bank teller," does not preclude her from being a feminist. Therefore, if Linda is a bank teller, statement one is correct whether Linda is a feminist or not. Statement two is only correct if Linda is a feminist.

The probability of two things being true can never be greater than the probability of either thing being true alone.

In our most recent study, we retested the Linda problem to see if it holds up after all these years. Indubitably, our results aligned with the findings of Tversky and Kahneman, with more than 70% of decision makers in our study believing that option two was more probable.

So, why do so many people get this question wrong?

One explanation is that individuals make decisions intuitively, relying heavily on their emotions. In this case, the statement that Linda is an active feminist and a bank teller felt more likely and consistent with her description when it was mathematically less likely.

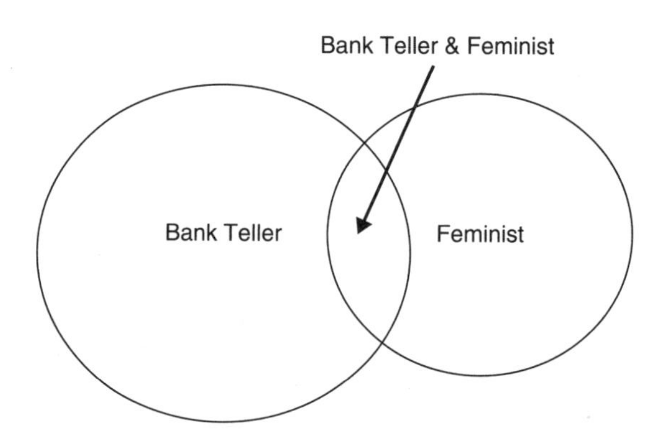

Figure 3.1

Not only did 85% make the logical mistake, there was also countless research to support this is how most humans make decisions most of the time.

Emotions

Engaging Emotions is the second step in the Influence Process (shown in Figure 3.2), for a reason. To maximize your effect on another person's emotion, you must have built credibility. The order matters because if people do not feel you are credible and have their best interest in mind, you may not get the chance to pull their emotional lever. As the saying goes, "No one cares how much you know until they know how much you care."

So, what exactly is emotion? In psychology, emotion is often defined as a "complex reaction pattern involving experiential, behavioral and physiological elements."[13] This means emotions influence (and are influenced by) your subjective experience, behavior, and body.

The expression of emotion communicates useful information both for oneself (i.e., our experience of emotion and how emotion influences our decision making) as well as for others. Our communication of emotions is so powerful that it can affect our emotional state and in turn impact outcomes. For instance, a positive or good mood has been

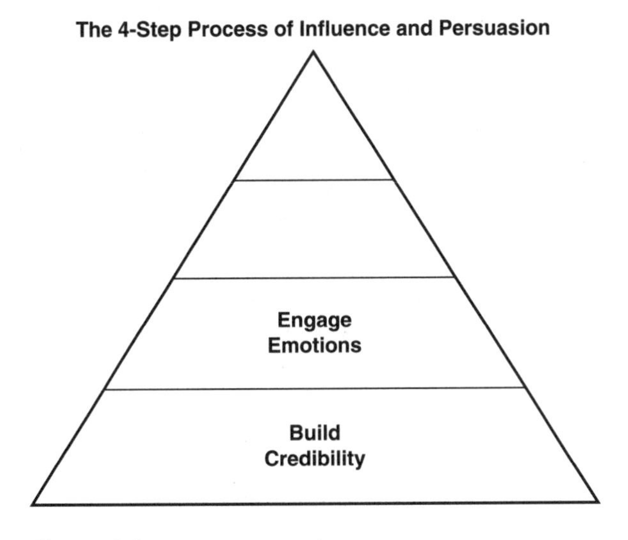

Figure 3.2

shown to have positive impacts on influencing expectations, strategies, and outcomes; a bad mood has been shown to have a negative effect. Dr. Amy Cuddy, from Harvard University, made this concept mainstream when she proved in her research that setting up with a power pose prior to an important meeting increased performance. More specifically, prior to an interview, those who conducted a power pose for two minutes experienced elevations in testosterone, decreases in cortisol, and increased feelings of power and tolerance for risk, which in turn led to improved interview performance.[14] More to come on this and how you can use it in Chapter 7.

In our influence model we focus on engaging three of the most powerful emotions that shape human decision making: the need for achievement, the fear of missing out or avoiding negative consequences, and the sense of obligation toward fairness.

Achievement

Have you ever looked at the faces of runners that come in second at a track meet? Or at a basketball team's bench when they are down 20 points in the fourth quarter? You will likely see disappointment, frustration, and pain. Nobody likes to be wrong, and nobody likes to lose.

The principle of the need for achievement focuses on engaging the emotions surrounding humans' innate desire to win or obtaining something not previously had. The need for achievement has been long studied, first identified by Henry Alexander Murray in the 1930s.[15] The need for achievement has been strongly tied to pride and has even been defined as "a capacity to experience pride in accomplishment."[16] Several emotional experiences may be engaged, surrounding the principle of achievement including satisfaction, interest, and joy.

Want some real-life examples of how achievement is used to influence? Think of the leaderboard within a sales organization or presidents' clubs, tryouts for sports teams, or bonus compensation for a manager based on individual and team performance.

Fear

The second principle, the principle of fear, focuses on emotions surrounding the need to avoid punishment or negative consequences. This desire is often linked to scarcity and the fear of missing out (FOMO). Emotions that may be aroused and are associated with the principle of fear include the emotional experiences of fear, anxiety, disgust, and relief.

The purpose of fear is survival. Therefore, fear is an exceptionally strong motivator, evolutionarily linked to our biology, and is built into our brains. When experiencing fear, our brains create a neurologic response of the medulla oblongata without much ability to turn off the response as long as the fear persists. So, our bodies react to FOMO in much the same way our cave dweller ancestors reacted to the sight of a saber-toothed tiger. Adrenaline rushes, temperatures increase, heart rate quickens, and we are overcome with the thrill of the hunt even if the hunt is for the last Buy One Get One (BOGO) on beach umbrellas.

Real-life examples of the use of fear to influence include do not text and drive campaigns that show a horrible car accident, Amazon Prime Days with a countdown of how many sale items remain available, or a life insurance agent asking what would happen if a client's working spouse died.

Obligation

Have you ever gotten a nickel or complimentary personalized return labels from a charity asking you for money? You know it is softening you up, yet it still works. Why?

The final principle, the principle of obligation, refers to one's need for (perceived) balance or fairness. This emotion is often associated with the need for reciprocity. Obligation can come in different forms. One common form is guilt. For example, fundraisers will often send a penny, a nickel, or a stack of mailing labels as a gift in their request for donations to create the feeling of guilt in the person who does not reciprocate and donate money to their cause. Emotions connected to the principle of obligation include feelings of admiration, satisfaction, and fear.

We often get asked the question, "When is the best time to make the ask?" Many variables exist, but consider taking advantage of obligation, which is why we suggest the best time to ask for something is shortly after you have given something.

Examples of using obligation include a bartender offering a free beer sample to a patron that likely gets a larger tip, a business-to-business (B2B) company providing a free resource to a prospect to get an introductory call, or children saying their parent is the best and then asking for extra allowance.

PRO TIP Speaking of best times to ask for something and how emotions play a role in our decisions, Columbia University professor Jonathan Levav completed a study of judges presiding over parole hearings.[17] He found that prisoners were two and six times as likely to be paroled if they were one of the first three prisoners in the morning, presumably after breakfast or after lunch, than if they were one of the last three prisoners. Think about that for a moment: Perhaps the phrase "Justice is what the judge ate for breakfast" is truer than we thought. Next time you need to influence someone, consider setting up a breakfast or lunch meeting: it provides an informal setting, and the food, change in environment, and break could all help your case. You never want to talk to Frank until he has had two cups of coffee. Know your audience.

ENGAGING EMOTIONS FOR THE WIN-WIN

When Ron Shapiro, the founder of Shapiro Negotiations Institute (SNI), was getting ready to sell it, I had been working with Ron for over 10 years; my potential partners Jeff Cochran and Chip Tames had been there for 15 and 20 years, respectively. We knew he was getting more serious about selling the business. And we knew he was getting some offers for amounts that were higher than we could afford. But we knew that on several occasions he had gotten close to selling, and for different reasons, he didn't complete the deals. Though we did not know all the reasons, we suspected that one reason was because Ron was naturally reluctant to walk away from a business he had built and was special to him.

As it became clearer to us that Ron's willingness to sell the business increased with time, Chip, Jeff, and I got together to build our plan to make the purchase happen and ensure all parties were satisfied. We had worked together for a long time, so we knew Ron well. We knew Ron was an experienced negotiator—he wrote the book on it—but we also knew this sale was a lot more than dollars. There was and would be some emotion involved because he would be letting go of the business he had been devoted to for over 20 years and because it would mean adjusting his lifestyle to no longer running a company.

One of the first things we did was probe for his interests. Though we thought we knew what was important, we did not want to make any assumptions. So, we asked a lot of questions. During this process, we confirmed that selling was emotional for Ron: He was thinking a lot about what would happen to the company after he sold it, and he wanted to make sure his team members were treated well, regardless of the direction the company took next.

Knowing that another deal fell apart because some emotion became part of it, and this was sensitive for Ron, we came up with a strategy to keep our own emotions in check. To do this, we designated one individual to negotiate with Ron instead of approaching him as a team. This way, when the individual or Ron was angry, either could point to the people who were not in the room to vent frustration and diffuse the situation. I became that designated person.

Next, looking to the Aristotle model, we worked through how we could leverage three key emotions that we know influence decision making to convince Ron to sell the business to us: achievement, fear, and obligation.

First, we assessed Ron's fears. Fear is one of the strongest motivators, and we wanted to make sure we were addressing any fears Ron might have been having about selling the business.

Two of his biggest fears were would the business succeed after him and would he continue to have an impact on the business after the deal? We built the team of Chip, Jeff, and me, specifically to address the first fear: Jeff was the world-class facilitator with over 20 years of experience; Chip was a talented facilitator as well, with a thoughtful and methodical approach, and he had extensive experience teaching outside of SNI. I was the day-to-day operator who had done it all, from building SNI's online training and facilitating to managing the marketing, selling, and advising on major negotiations.

The other fear we wanted to make sure we addressed was his legacy. We believed several of the other suitors would buy the intellectual property and roll it up into what they already offered or would remove his name and much of the company history, changing directions. We had the complete opposite intentions, and we wanted to make sure he knew it. We learned under Ron, he had incredible experience and impact on the negotiation field, and we thought keeping and highlighting the company's history and his accomplishments had tremendous value. This was what he hoped for and what we thought was in our and SNI's future best interests.

Finally, as anyone would, Ron wanted to make sure he received a fair deal. We understood that, and given the decades of working together, all agreed early on we would rather walk away from the deal than make one all parties were unhappy with.

The second emotion we wanted to appeal to was that of achievement. By helping us through a succession plan, Ron created a scenario where three guys who have worked for him for 10, 15, and 20 years, respectively, came up through the business and worked themselves into an ownership position. We knew that was something he would be proud of. Ron had always been more concerned about helping and developing others around him than his own personal gain, and no other situation could accomplish this more than his handing over the keys and seeing us flourish.

The third emotion we sought to tap into was Ron's sense of obligation. We had worked together for many years and it was mutually beneficial, but we all felt a sense of obligation to hear the other party out and work through all the options in good faith. Ron could walk away from an outsider more easily than from us because of the sweat equity we had put in working with him. That was the least powerful of the three emotions in this case, but it helped a few times when the conversations were stalling.

This story does not have a surprising ending because as you see on the book cover, Jeff and I are partners at SNI. The deal was a success. However, we are prouder of how we got here. We practiced what we preached, probing, not making assumptions, utilizing the various emotions that affect decision making most, and all in a genuine way to reach an agreement that all parties could be proud of. Now, looking back after three years, this deal was a success, the business is flourishing, Ron remains involved as an advisor, and our relationship is stronger than ever.

As overused as the cliché is, this was truly a win-win deal.

The Influencer's Toolbox

Managing Emotions

To be effective at influence, you must notice and manage emotions. To do this, you can work on increasing your emotional intelligence. Emotional intelligence refers to the ability to notice and manage the emotions of yourself and others. According to Daniel Goleman, a leading expert and the author of several books on emotional intelligence, there are four key domains of emotional intelligence.[18] These key domains are self-awareness, self-management, social awareness, and relationship management.

1. Self-Awareness

The first component in managing emotions is an awareness of your own emotions. You should take note of and label the emotions you feel. By noticing and labeling your emotions, "putting your feelings into words," you recognize them for what they are, emotions, and you feel them less strongly. In one brain imaging study led by Dr. Matthew Lieberman of the University of California, Los Angeles, researchers found that when participants in the study labeled an emotion, such as fear, it even diminished the emotional response in the brain.[19]

I do this with my kids all the time. My oldest son loves to play hockey, but he does not like to lose. So, during the emotional time (when he lost, which does occur sometimes) and when we talk about it later, I label that I think he is feeling sad, frustrated, and/or disappointed. We talk about it. "It looks as if you're frustrated you lost our hockey game" or "Are you disappointed we can't play another game because it's bedtime?" This way, he learns to work through it rather than me letting him win every time or avoiding the topic. He is still emotional, but he understands why and that makes the negative state last less long and be less intensely negative.

2. Self-Management

The second component in managing emotions is self-management. Although awareness of your own emotions will make you feel them less strongly, learning to manage your own emotions goes well beyond awareness. You can utilize tactics to manage your emotions. The first is to accept the emotion is real and you can choose how you respond to it. Accepting the emotion allows you to turn your focus toward figuring out the problem (what is driving this emotion?) and finding a solution. Then, it takes practice to be able to feel the emotion and not act on it. For example, if you get upset in a discussion with your colleague, can you manage the anger by taking a break, redirecting the conversation, or explaining how you feel, without letting the emotion get the best of you?

Keeping negative emotions in check to make logical decisions, let alone to be effective at influence and persuasion, is important. Asking for a break or to resume the conversation later is all right if you notice you are angry, anxious, or upset. If you need to, come up with an excuse, whether it be a coffee break or a bathroom break. Or be honest and let the other party know you are upset and believe it would be a good idea to resume the conversation later.

After labeling the negative emotions, I make sure to explain to my son he gets to control how he reacts to the disappointment of losing. Is he sad and it stops there? Does he think about why he lost and will work to improve? Does it motivate him to play better next time? Practice harder? Be more focused? Although we cannot control results and our initial reactions to things, we can manage what we do with that emotion.

3. Social Awareness

The third step in managing emotions is an awareness of the emotions of others. The emotions of others are often on full display. Even when they try to hide it, most people are incapable of doing so. Emotions are displayed in words and in the speed, volume, pitch, and tone of one's speech, as well as nonverbally in facial expressions, body language, and gestures. Pay attention to the verbal and nonverbal cues of others and be aware of the emotions they are feeling and expressing. Take note of what excites others, what they are passionate about, and what triggers the verbal and nonverbal cues that suggest satisfaction, obligation, or fear.

Next, I try to make my son aware of how his reaction to his emotions impacts others. No one will want to play with him again if he is a sore loser. Although sometimes seeing him in the moment is hard, as he matures and experiences it more, he will notice the impact of his reactions.

4. Relationship Management

The final step in managing emotions is using the knowledge and tools at your disposal to manage the emotions of others. Negative and excessively positive emotions have an adverse effect on decision making. In the example previously discussed in the "Self-Management" section, if you and your colleague are upset in a discussion, can you manage your emotions and his/hers by quickly de-escalating the situation and directing both parties to a mutually acceptable solution?

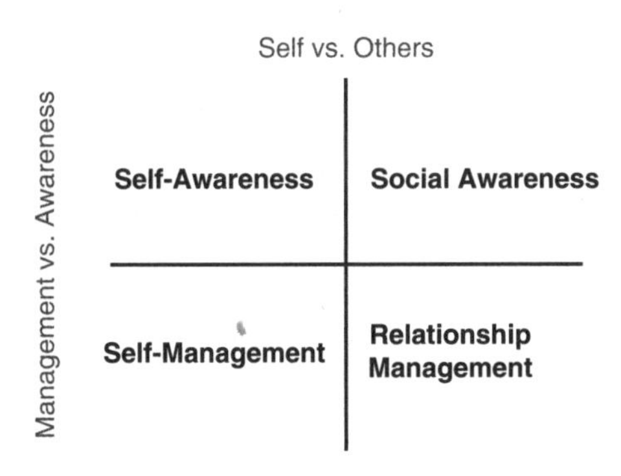

Figure 3.3

Ultimately, emotional intelligence is about having the capacity to manage your own and other emotions. Having this skill works hand-in-hand with the next set of skills we are going to cover. Now is the time to employ tools like storytelling, framing, and mirroring to increase your influence on people and decisions.

Although I want to teach my son to develop more emotional intelligence, my focus is guiding him toward relationship management. When he notices he is getting upset, can he stop himself from saying something he will regret? Can he stop himself from shutting down? Can he notice and adjust before he is fully engulfed by his emotions? Finally, can he adjust his behavior based on the emotions of others? For example, how does he react if his friend is frustrated? Even worse, frustrated at him? Can he talk about it and do so empathetically enough that it helps the other person?

Storytelling

Heard any good stories lately? I bet you can think of at least one or two. Stories are an immensely powerful form of communication. That is why, throughout this book, you will find a myriad of stories and examples to explain the principles behind the Influence Model.

Why are stories so important?

Stories are memorable. Have you ever noticed how much easier it is to remember a story than it is to remember facts and figures? Want to know how much easier? According to famed cognitive scientist Jerome Bruner, you are up to 22 times more likely to remember something when it is wrapped in a story than when it is presented as a fact alone.[20]

Stories convey context. Without stories, facts and figures have no meaning. The story conveys what these facts and figures mean and why they mean what they do. Stories also have the power to convey why the listener should care. I am reminded of the sportscaster who reports the scores from last night's NBA finals and says 102-98 but fails to mention which team had which score. The facts are there, but without context and a picture in your mind of the team's colors, the facts alone are meaningless.

Stories engage emotions. Never underestimate the power of a compelling story. In fact, storytelling is one of the most powerful ways to engage emotion. How? Stories transport us into the perspective of the storyteller, and perspective-taking develops empathy.

We have stories to tell. Good stories capture emotions. However, not all stories are good stories. For a story to be good, it has to have two important elements. First, it must be interesting to the listener. Uninteresting stories do not capture our attention. Second, the story must be relevant to the listener. Listeners must connect with the story to develop empathy and for the story to engage their emotions.

We also believe stories must be directly proportional to the value they deliver. No one likes a long story without a valuable payoff. However, a short story with an equal payoff can be worthwhile. Ideally, a story is short and succinct while delivering a significant impact. "Brevity is the soul of wit," according to William Shakespeare.

Types of Stories

According to Annette Simmons, the author of the book *The Story Factor: Inspiration, Influence, and Persuasion Through the Art of Storytelling*, six types of stories are particularly helpful in influencing others:

- "Who I Am"
- "Why I Am Here"
- "Values-in-Action"
- "Teaching"
- "The Vision"
- "I Know What You're Thinking"

We believe you can distill these down ever further to the following three story types:

1. You Stories: You Stories tell your listener who you are. "Who I Am" stories and "Values-in-Action" stories are good examples of You Stories. You Stories provide opportunities to connect with the listener and are useful for building likability and credibility. Though saying "we value this" or "we value that" may be easier, telling a story exemplifies how you live those values, and it contributes to eliciting emotions surrounding obligation. They are also useful stories for probing, and they can be used to elicit emotions around one's need for achievement and/or fears as well.
2. Why Stories: Why Stories tell your listener why you are you and why you are there. They share your passion and/or intentions, the things that motivate you. "Why I am Here" and "Vision Stories" are examples of Why Stories. "Why I am Here" stories provide opportunities to connect with the listener and are useful for building likability and credibility. Similarly, "Vision Stories" communicate to your listener "what's in it for both of you" and are useful for engaging emotions related to one's need for achievement.
3. Relationship Stories: Relationship Stories are stories meant to build or extend the relationship between two parties. Relationship Stories build commitment or obligation and are meant to move the relationship further. "Teaching Stories" are one example of Relationship Stories. "Teaching Stories" allow a level of connection with the listener useful for building likeability and credibility and eliciting emotions surrounding obligation. On the other hand, "I Know What You're Thinking Stories" are a little more pre-emptive. They are meant to reduce fear by highlighting potential objections and disarming them.

We have covered a lot of information on stories and you may be wondering what to do with all this information. First, think through what important points you need to make most often. It could be demonstrating a key skill at a job interview, differentiating your offering from various competitors, or highlighting why a free agent should come to play for your sports team. Then, work through the list and create a database with your best stories to make those specific points. Try them out a few times in real but low-pressure situations, or share them with friends, until you get comfortable and fine-tune them. The result is succinct, relevant, and impactful stories that make a point much more effectively than any résumé, one-pager, or email could do.

Evidence from Decision Makers: Storytelling

We again turn to decision makers to find out how they use stories and anecdotes in their conversations and communication. We asked decision makers in our study to think about their previous attempts to build personal and professional relationships and, specifically, how they used stories to build and enhance their relationships. We asked them how they viewed storytelling as a strategy to communicate and how often they used stories or anecdotes in a number of contexts.

Overall, decision makers in our study rated storytelling as moderately important to very important in their conversations and communications. Though most decision makers reported using storytelling and anecdotes sometimes or often in their communication, the places and ways in which stories and anecdotes are used the most often included making people feel more comfortable, improving understanding, strengthening trust, strengthening relationships, explaining logic, and reinforcing a point.

Scripting

As you learned in the previous chapter, stories are powerful motivators. As the old saying goes, "Facts tell, but stories sell." An important part of storytelling and messaging is scripting or planning what you are going to say ahead of time. Crafting your pitch.

The Five Canons of Rhetoric

The power of scripting draws on the art of rhetoric. The ability to be persuasive in the use of language. According to the ancient Greek philosopher Cicero, there are Five Canons (or principles) of Rhetoric: Invention, Arrangement, Style, Memory, and Delivery.[21]

Invention is coming up with what to say. It determines the arguments you want or need to make to influence and persuade your audience. According to Aristotle, invention involves "discovering the best available means of persuasion." This involves brainstorming, coming up with alternatives, and thinking through the key points you want to make.

We believe that a key aspect of invention is writing your stories, speeches, and arguments. Writing helps you capture and remember your ideas. Writing your thoughts forces you to focus on your arguments, helping you to clarify your thinking and express your arguments more clearly.

Arrangement refers to how to present your argument. It is the order and structure of your statements or claims. Arrange your arguments so they are clear.

According to current traditional uses of language, rhetoric should be composed of at least three parts: An opening or an introduction, the body of your argument, and a conclusion.

When arranging your argument, remember the steps in the Four-Step Process of Influence and Persuasion. First, build credibility. Second, engage emotion. Third, demonstrate your logic. Finally, facilitate action to make sure you get the result you desire.

According to Cicero, the introduction of an argument can be linked to Ethos. Use this part of your script to build credibility while playing to an emotional appeal (Pathos). The body of your argument can be linked to Logos. Using this part of your argument to demonstrate logic. Finally, the conclusion should be linked to facilitating action, calling on your audience to reach a conclusion or to decide.

Style concerns the wording of what you will say and how you are going to say it. Not only is style related to word choice, sentence structure, and the use of figures of speech, but it also involves considerations of the tone and pace of your voice, your body language, visuals, and other "evidence" that accompanies your rhetoric.

Make sure to use the right language. To do this, first understand your audience. What is it going to take to convince *them*? As important, be simple, clear, and vivid. Ensure your rhetoric has a flow.

Another important part of style is the medium through which your story or message is communicated. In some cases, the medium can make or break a message. For instance, reading a story in print can convey a message different from listening to someone telling you the same story.

Memory regards the preservation of one's rhetoric. It has to do with all means and methods of preserving one's rhetoric. This includes not only writing and committing to memory one's rhetoric to aid in your delivery, but it also concerns the manners and devices used to make it memorable to your audience.

If you want your audience to remember it, you need to determine why and how it will be memorable to your audience. Several factors determine what makes something memorable. Among these are the story's relevance to listeners or readers, how much it captures their attention, and its novelty.

Delivery is the presentation of your story, speech, or argument. It is where, when, and how something is said. A number of important elements are associated with delivery. Your argument needs to be delivered at the right time, in the right place and context, and with the proper body language and voice.

The delivery of a presentation is most prominent in oral presentations. However, the delivery of a story influences its impact in written communication as well.

SCRIPTING FOR THE WIN

Our firm, SNI, was asked to participate in a Request For Proposals (RFPs) for contract consulting with one of the world's largest airplane manufacturers. Although 24 companies submitted proposals, we were able to differentiate ourselves throughout the process and our proposal was well received.

We were chosen to be one of four companies that flew to present our proposal to a large boardroom of decision makers. And, again, we were fortunate enough to do well. Finally, we had the great news the company would award us the project; however, it asked us to make some significant reductions to our pricing structure. Though it was a wonderful opportunity, seven-figure contract, we could not make those concessions.

My partners and I knew we had to be prepared with a reply. So, over the next several days, we scripted everything. We went through exactly what to offer, the concessions we might be willing to make, and how to respond to each possible objection and counter.

We drafted our script, along with questions and replies, and role played it. Did the RFP leaders say what we expected? Did I use the words we had scripted? No. but, by the time I was done with that process, the real thing felt easy. As if I had done it before!

I specifically remember when the company's main point of contact called me and said, "To get the business, we need you to lower your fee by 15 percent." Thanks to all the scripting, role playing, and strategizing, I responded immediately and with confidence, "What happens if we cannot get there?" The contact told me all I needed to know. I knew we were the top choice and knew the contact was asking to get the best deal possible.

In the end, we were able to move forward with the project with a larger scope than expected with only minor concessions and without coming off as aggressive. By the time we were done negotiating the agreement with its procurement executives, we had a better relationship with the client than when we started. The funny thing is the contract was to train their procurement organization across the country to negotiate in a way to achieve better results but not fracture the relationship in the process. These were the people we were going to teach to negotiate. By the end of the process, they could see that our methods worked. Not only was I proud of what we had accomplished, but I also was thankful that Ron had written a book on scripting a few years earlier and I knew firsthand the process worked.

Three Steps to Scripting

At SNI, we simplify the process of scripting your story, speech, or argument down further. Following the model in Ron Shapiro's book *Perfecting Your Pitch*, we teach the three-step process of Draft, Devil's Advocate, and Deliver.

Step 1: Draft As you can guess, Draft refers to writing all of it. Seriously. Write everything you want to say. Getting your stories on paper helps you clarify and explore your key points and arguments. Additionally, there is evidence to support the act of writing something down helps you to learn and remember.

Start by deciding on the goal of your script and writing the key events, points, and arguments you would like to make. Then craft your script. Work through your logic. The opening and closing. Consider questions that might be raised, and script your responses to likely questions.

Writing helps you assess your entire strategy. It also allows you to step away and come back with a fresh mind to assess your arguments and work through the strategy. That is what we will be doing next when playing Devil's Advocate.

Step 2: Devil's Advocate Playing Devil's Advocate is looking at your pitch from multiple or opposing perspectives. Before starting this, take some time away so you can come back and examine your rhetoric with a fresh mind.

When you are ready, play Devil's Advocate with yourself. Read through it in your mind or say it out loud. Hearing your pitch out loud makes you more aware of what you are reading and the arguments behind it. It helps you see holes in your story and how you can better relate the message you want to communicate.

Playing Devil's Advocate helps you to think through the expected and/or possible objections and how you might counter them. By understanding possible objections, you can address your arguments for how you will reduce or surmount them in your story before they even come up.

For a more impactful analysis, get people to review your script or pitch. Ask them to beat it up and identify any objections you might be missing. We are often blind to the holes in our logic, searching for information that confirms our beliefs and disregards information that disconfirms them. Thus, getting an outside opinion can help craft our stories.

Step 3: Deliver Finally, you need to deliver. Deliver refers to all the factors surrounding the presentation of your argument. It includes the context of the situation, the time and place, style and tone, and how you will deliver it (in person, via video chat, through email).

Deliver also includes following up to make sure your message was received and understood. To do this, it may help to script some questions to ask (1) before you deliver your script to make sure you are on the same page and to ask (2) after you deliver to reiterate your message and to make sure it was understood.

Importantly, practice several times before you deliver the real thing for the first time. Practicing your pitch helps you remember it, as well as refine your pitch and increases your confidence because you feel as if you have had parts of the conversation.

Never Sent, Never Signed

Scripting, writing what you want to say, can serve several means. It helps you think through what you want to say and can dispel your own negative emotions through the lost practice of the unsent angry letter.

One proponent of the unsent angry letter was Abraham Lincoln. Whenever he would get angry, Lincoln would sit down and write a "hot letter" expressing his frustration with whomever he was upset. He would put it aside until he had calmed down and wrote "Never Sent, Never Signed" on the envelope.

Lincoln wrote one such letter to General George Meade, who led the fight against Robert E. Lee at the Battle of Gettysburg. Frustrated that General Meade allowed Lee to escape, Lincoln wrote:

> "Again my dear general, I do not believe you appreciate the magnitude of the misfortune involved in Lee's escape– He was within your easy grasp, and to have closed upon him would, in connection with our other late successes, have ended the war– As it is, the war will be prolonged indefinitely. If you could not safely attack Lee last Monday, how can you possibly do so South of the river, when you can take with you very few more than two thirds of the force you then had in hand? It would be unreasonable to expect, and I do not expect you can now affect much. Your golden opportunity is gone, and I am distressed immeasurably because of it–. . . ."

Though the letter was not scathing, it would have certainly embarrassed General Meade, who had, after all, defeated Lee and the Confederate Army at Gettysburg. Lincoln decided not to send this letter, and it remained unknown until after his death.

Anaphora

Anaphora is repeating of the same few words at the beginning of a statement or sentence. This is often used to emphasize and reinforce words and ideas. The use of anaphora gives rhythm to a script. This rhythm makes the words and ideas memorable, and it makes what comes after them more important, for example, "We came. We saw. We conquered."

In public speaking, repeating key phrases can give an especially great rhythm to a speech. Consider Dr. Martin Luther King Jr.'s

"I have a dream" speech. Dr. King understood the power of repetition. He uses anaphora in two different instances in his speech; he uses "I have a dream" in the speech eight times and "Let freedom ring" 11 times.

> "My country 'tis of thee, sweet land of liberty, of thee I sing. Land where my fathers died, land of the Pilgrim's pride, from every mountainside, let freedom ring!
>
> And if America is to be a great nation, this must become true.
>
> And so let freedom ring from the prodigious hilltops of New Hampshire.
>
> Let freedom ring from the mighty mountains of New York.
>
> Let freedom ring from the heightening Alleghenies of Pennsylvania.
>
> Let freedom ring from the snow-capped Rockies of Colorado.
>
> Let freedom ring from the curvaceous slopes of California.
>
> But not only that:
>
> Let freedom ring from Stone Mountain of Georgia.
>
> Let freedom ring from Lookout Mountain of Tennessee.
>
> Let freedom ring from every hill and molehill of Mississippi.
>
> From every mountainside, let freedom ring."[22]

Try It for Yourself

In this exercise, craft a script yourself. Imagine the following scenario:

You are a director at a professional services firm. You have been providing one of your clients, a smaller business of $20m in revenues, support through your advisory and tax lines of business. Your client has been loyal for over seven years, and you have built a great relationship. The pandemic has hit it hard, its revenues are down 35%, and it cannot cut its expenses by that much. Your contact, Tim, has asked you for deferring payments and reducing the overall cost of the work. However, the projects you are working on will have as much if not more value than originally expected. You told him you were unsure you could do either, but you would certainly investigate it for him. You are now about to hop on the video call to deliver the update, which is less than ideal because your partner has said you cannot lower your price because the work has mostly been done and the client can defer the payments a maximum of 30 days, which is not much.

Now, see if you can put together a short script on how you would manage this conversation. Determine the goal of your script and write the key points you want to address. For this exercise, the goal of your script is to maintain your relationship with this client.

After you have written the key points you want to address, write your script.

____

____

____

____

____

____

Yes, do it before continuing forward.

Once you have crafted your script, after ideally taking some time away, come back and assess the script you have written. Does your script accomplish its objectives? Is it too long-winded? How is the tone? How can you make sure you are on the same page and your client understood your message?

When you have written your script, compare it to ours. Here is what our sample script for this scenario might look like:

Preliminary Questions (before delivering the script):

1. How do you feel our two current projects have gone so far? And do others at your firm feel the same way?

2. Can you tell me more about the price reduction you are asking for?
3. Can we talk more about your cash flow situation and why it would be important to push back payments? Maybe there are some other solutions we can come up with?

Tim, I promised I would investigate reducing the price and extending payment. I have pushed hard internally. I can tell you that, as a firm and personally, we can relate as our revenues are also down and our expenses, mainly made up of top-notch consultants, is not something we can afford to cut to keep up our high level of service. I pushed hard internally and could push back all payments an additional 30 days. Though I was unable to get you a price break because of our own pressures and the fact that we have mainly done all the work, I would be willing to roll up my sleeves personally and help you prepare your presentation to the board on our two projects. I have always said that my goal is to deliver value to your firm and make you look good, and I will continue to make sure that happens, especially during these troubled times.

Follow-Up Questions (after delivering the script):

1. What are your main challenges moving forward?
2. Is there any other way I can help you or the firm?
3. How will you communicate this internally? Any way I can help you do that?

Mirroring

Mirroring is the act of imitating the body language, gestures, pattern of speech, or vocabulary of another. We cover this with Engaging Emotions because mirroring generally invokes positive (or negative, if not done well) emotions.

The goal of mirroring is to build likeability and credibility, and to be able to shift conversations toward more desired emotions. However, mirroring cannot be forced. It needs to feel natural. According to

David Hoffeld, the author of *The Science of Selling*, mirroring is "...not something you do to someone. It's something you do with someone."

When mirroring is subtle and done correctly, it can build a greater connection with the other party, which in turn develops relationships and allows you to have more influence. On the other hand, when done incorrectly mirroring can feel awkward for both parties and can possibly put people off.

Body Language and Non-vocal Mirroring

The first place to begin noticing and practicing mirroring is body language and non-vocal mirroring. In fact, when engaging emotions, our words typically say much less than we think. Research indicates that body language and non-vocal communication make up more than 55 percent of the communication of emotions.[23]

What makes mirroring so powerful? You can use it to shift someone's mood. Our body language and cues show and express our emotions, and they have the power to shape emotions as well.

To subtly apply mirroring, you can begin by imitating the other person's body language and cues and shift them toward more productive emotions by shifting their body language.

Aside from body language and posture, several other non-vocal cues express emotion and can be mirrored. These include facial expressions, gestures, eye contact, and breathing.

Body Language and Posture Body language and posture are ripe with emotions. Positive body language like an open and relaxed position, turned toward each other, upright posture, etc., can be mirrored to increase likability and build credibility. However, if your conversational partner displays negative body language, your goal is to increase the use of mirroring until you can draw the other person toward a more positive body language. For example, if your conversational partners have their arms crossed, cross your arms to match. After a minute or two, uncross your arms and smile. Often, people with whom you are speaking will uncross their arms as well. They may even return your smile, putting them in a better mood.

Positive Body Language Signals	Negative Body Language Signals

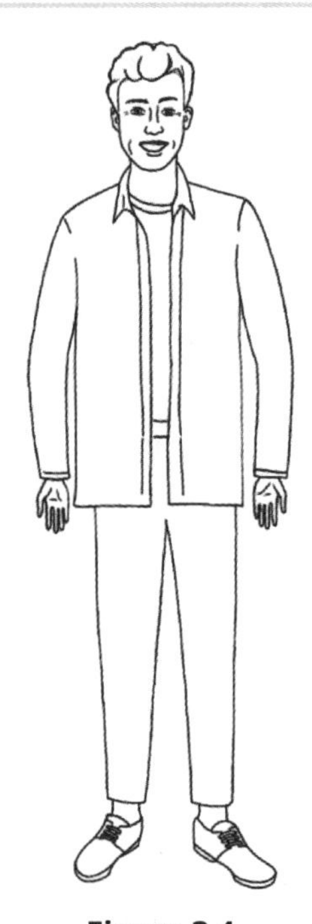

Figure 3.4

Figure 3.5

Open position—arms unfolded	Closed position—arms crossed
✔ Body turned toward you	✘ Body turned away from you
✔ Upright posture	✘ Slouching posture
✔ Leaning forward/toward you	✘ Leaning back/away from you
✔ Arms relaxed, hanging at sides	✘ Wringing/tightening of hands
✔ Makes appropriate eye contact	✘ Avoids eye contact
✔ Genuine smile	✘ Frowning or furrowed brow

Facial Expressions Facial expressions can tell us a lot. Fear, disgust, anger, contempt, and surprise are easily recognizable facial expressions. Mirroring facial expressions is an easy way to direct conversations toward more positive emotions. One example of this is smiling. Seeing someone else smile triggers a reaction in your brain that makes you want to smile. When you consciously smile more often, the person you are communicating with is more likely to smile.

Gestures Gestures, typically movements of the arms, hands, and head, hold great power in understanding and mirroring emotion. Gestures are often used as punctuation, or conversation symbols, often without our knowledge. In the game of poker, this is called a tell. The next time you are in a conversation, pay attention to whether you and/or the people with whom you are conversing have a punctuator. If the people with whom you are conversing have a "tell," nod in conjunction with their gesture or imitate a gesture at the appropriate punctuations as a subtle way to show you are paying attention and understand what they are saying.

Eye Contact Eye contact is a curious thing. Too little eye contact and you risk people seeing you as nervous, uncomfortable, or disinterested. Too much eye contact and you might be viewed as off-putting or a little crazy. How much eye contact is normal? The general opinion is to follow the 50/70 rule. When you are speaking you should maintain a gaze 50% of the time, making eye contact for four to five seconds at a time before glancing away. When you are listening, the amount of time you should maintain a gaze increases to 70%.

Breathing Breathing can be another powerful cue to mirror. By adjusting the pace and depth of your breath, breathing in sync with your conversational partner is a great way to build rapport. Though it can be difficult to mirror breathing while speaking, this task is easier while listening. In instances where mirroring another person's breath is unfeasible, use crossover mirroring. Crossover mirroring is mirroring someone's body language (such as matching the pace of breath) with a completely different type of movement while matching the pace, cadence, etc. In this case, you could match the pace of someone's breath with the blinking of your eyes or tapping your finger or pencil.

Vocal Mirroring: Vocabulary, Sound, and Style

Often, when people think about mirroring, they imagine the forms of nonverbal mirroring discussed in the previous section: mimicking body language and gestures, eye contact, and distance and physical space. However, verbal mirroring is an effective method of increasing likeability, building credibility, and engaging emotions.

Several aspects of an individual's speech can be mirrored. These include a person's rate and volume of speech, vocabulary and jargon, language and vernacular, and vocal pitch and tone.

Rate and Volume of Speech One of the easiest things to mirror is the rate and volume of the other party's speech. If the people you are attempting to mimic speak quickly and are loud, mirror them by increasing the rate and volume of your speech as well. If they speak slowly and softly, bring the rate and volume of your speech closer to theirs.

Vocabulary and Jargon Several benefits exist for repeating the words a person just said to you in your response. First, repeating back what a person said to you shows you are listening. In doing so, it clarifies that you understand. Second, mirroring the same vocabulary and showing you understand suggests you can communicate more effectively. The optimal way to do this is to repeat one to three words from the last sentence(s) the other person said in the first portion of your response. For example, if your colleague says, "I am frustrated that *Michelle isn't listening* to any of my suggestions for this project," you might respond with, "*Michelle isn't listening* to any of your suggestions? Tell me more about that."

Language and Vernacular Language and vernacular can be mirrored to facilitate liking, build credibility, and engage emotion. For instance, if you know the people with whom you are conversing speak a language other than your own as a native language, take the time to at least learn to say hello in their language. In doing so, you demonstrate you at least care enough to learn the proper greeting.

Vocal Pitch and Tone Vocal pitch and tone are two additional characteristics of a person's speech to which mirroring can be applied. According to a study by Yale University School of Management scholar Dr. Michael Kraus, we are more accurate at reading people's emotions in their voice than from facial expressions. Kraus found that people read emotions best when voice is the only cue. He opined that we focus on the subtleties in people's voice more when we do not have to decipher visual and vocal cues; thus, we can read their emotions better.[24]

What Is Your Voice Saying?	
Upward Inflection	Surprise, questioning, insincerity, or suspense
Downward Inflection	Confidence, certainty, finality, or power
Level Inflection	Disinterest, indecision, or boredom
Quickening Pace	Excitement, urgency, passion, or insincerity
Slowing Pace	Importance, seriousness, confusion, or sadness
Loud Volume	Excitement, urgency, or anger
Soft Volume	Calming, importance, seriousness, or shyness

Name Repetition Another subtle form of mirroring is using a person's name in your conversations with them. People love hearing their own name. According to Dale Carnegie, in his book *How to Win Friends and Influence People,* a person's name is the sweetest and most important sound in the whole world to them. Carnegie says, "The average person is more interested in their own name than in all the other names in the world put together." Scientific evidence exists to back this up. One study published in the journal *Brain Research* found that when people hear their own first name, compared to hearing other first names, unique brain activation occurs in regions of the brain associated with social behavior, memory, and information processing.[25]

What Is Wrong with Him?

One of our clients, a large manufacturing company that serviced commercial and residential construction companies, asked us years ago to help figure out why one of its best salespeople was performing poorly. He had performed well in four different roles over the course of eight years, but now it appeared he could not make a sale. We looked at his record of accomplishment, spoke with him and peers, and we could not figure it out either until we joined him on three sales meetings one day. His success had all occurred in the southeast.

Though he changed territories and moved to bigger accounts and regions, his easygoing and casual style was disarming in Georgia, the Carolinas, Louisiana, and Mississippi. However, his new role covered the DC to Philadelphia corridor, and the construction companies he was talking to there were quickly getting the impression he was not prepared or professional, and at times, not bright. He and our client were concerned, thinking it would need to relocate him again, which he was adamantly against, having two kids in primary school. Our client was thrilled when we gave him a crash course on adjusting his style. Wearing a suit, getting to the point faster, having clean visuals to support him on an iPad, and emailing a summary of the meeting to the client the next day was all he changed, and his results were top five in the company again.

Next time you are going to meet with someone, think about your attire, speech pace, vocabulary, and all the other variables that are MORE likely to build a bond than what you say.

Try It for Yourself

Practice mirroring to get more comfortable. The next time you are having a conversation with friends or family members, subtly mirror one of the aspects of communication to shift the conversation.

To do this, first match their body language and nonverbal communication. When it feels more comfortable, try directing them to what you want them to do by shifting your own body to a more favorable position.

How did it feel? Did it seem natural? Did you get more comfortable doing it? Which aspects of nonverbal communication do you find easiest to mirror?

Verbal Mirroring	Nonverbal Mirroring
Vocabulary and jargon	Body language and posture
Language and vernacular	Gestures
Vocal pitch and tone	Facial expressions
Rate and volume of speech	Eye contact
Repetition of their name	Distance and physical space
	Breathing
	Dress

A MIRRORING MISSTEP

Emotions are a funny thing. We know that rightly engaged, they can be a powerful persuader. But we also know that clumsily employed, engaging emotions can feel very manipulative and do some serious damage to a relationship. Here's Jeff's story on how a mirroring blunder complicated one of the most important relationships in his life.

As most anyone who knows me is aware, my first career out of university was as a U.S. Peace Corps volunteer working in the Himalayan Kingdom of Nepal on a project for micro-lending, loosely based on the successful work of Nobel Prize economist Dr. Muhammad Yunus at the Grameen Bank.

Most anyone I know is aware of my Peace Corps service because it is probably one of the most formative experiences of my life. It is ". . . the toughest job you'll ever love." I mention Nepal and assume that many of you are familiar with the country or at least its position as the home to at least one-half of Mt. Everest, the tallest mountain in the world as well as home to the world-famous Sherpas who trek back and forth on its slopes ferrying mostly Westerners from point to point as they attempt to "conquer the summit" of the great landmark.

Unfortunately, at that time of my life, fresh out of college, I was not as well informed, nor nearly as worldly as you may be. When the Peace Corps office called me to tell me that I was being offered an assignment in Nepal, I went around for three days telling everyone I knew that I was going to spend the next two years in the Peace Corps. In Italy! I was woefully misinformed. Fortunately, I found my way to a map before I reported for duty and ended up in Nepal, the landlocked country in South Asia rather than the seaside town of Naples on the coast of Italy.

I am happy to say that by my second year of service I was feeling comfortable in my assigned village, where I worked as a loan officer at the Nepal Bank Limited. I was well on my way toward fluency in Nepalese, a cousin to the language of Hindi. And I was grasping some of the subtle nuances of the culture and was becoming a true citizen of the world wise in the ways of the gamut of international emotions. Or so I thought.

In the middle of my second year of service, I met a young, unmarried woman who saw me making a well-attended presentation at a local farmer's home and approached me about getting a loan from the bank to improve her small cottage industry of making pounded rice. For me, it was love at first sight. She was strikingly beautiful, and she was unique among her country women as she looked me in the eye and told me about her plans to improve her business with the help of a loan from the bank. I asked her, "Most women here in the village will not speak to me directly, much less look me in the eye as they do so. Why do you?" She replied, "You're the man who gives the loans right? How else am I going to explain what I need?" I knew I had found my match.

So, I proceeded to do everything I could to make sure that she received a loan. For me, it was an excuse to see her on a regular basis. It was my plan to woo her. Meanwhile, her family was arranging a suitable marriage for her as well. As a result, her mother was not happy that she was spending time with me.

But I knew the secret to winning her mother over. I could have made a logical argument my intentions were pure, but that would probably have generated more skepticism than comfort. I decided I would have to appeal to her emotionally. Now, did I think this through and devise a plan? Yes and no. I knew my wooing would have to shift from the daughter to the mother, but I did not utilize the teachings of Aristotle. However, my instincts were honed, and I had read Dale Carnegie's *How to Win Friends and Influence People*. I knew from that timeless classic that the sweetest sound to people's ear is the sound of their own name. So, I went to work.

I started visiting my girlfriend's family every chance I got whether she was there or not. In fact, it went even better when she was not there, and I had direct access to the mother. I was careful to use her full name: Netra Kumari Chaudhari every time I address her. I was sure my American accent and charming broken Nepalese was playing a symphony in her ears every time I spoke the melody that was her name. I said it quickly, I said it slowly, I said it with dramatic pauses. However, the most important thing was to make sure she heard the "sweetest sound to anyone's ear" every time I had a chance.

Though I did not know it at the time, I was appealing to her sense of achievement. I noticed I never heard someone's name proclaimed as often as I spoke Netra Kumari Chaudhari's musical moniker. By allowing her to hear me address her by her name, I was making sure her name rang throughout the village. Oftentimes, after I said her name, I would hear the elders who occasionally gathered to drink tea on her veranda murmur her name after each time I said it.

Unfortunately, instead of liking me more, she seemed to like me less after each visit. Finally, I stopped making the effort. I gave up and figured I would be one of those individuals who did not get along with his in-laws. Eventually, however, my boyish charm won out. That Nepali girl has been my wife and partner ever since we were married in 1991. I am even happy to report that I became a tolerated if not loved part of the family.

So, how is that for using clear tried and true skills for winning someone over emotionally? Well, I have my doubts. In fact, years later I was explaining to some friends about how I won over my mother-in-law using, "the oldest trick in Dale's Carnegie's book" when my wife over-heard me. She said, "Is that what you were doing? I thought that you were trying to antagonize my mother. Everyone in Nepal knows you never call a person who is older than you by her name." I guess this stuff does not work the same all over the world.

Though we focus on influencing principles that are fairly universal in this book and provide cultural notes throughout, keep this story in mind the next time you are attempting to persuade someone from another culture.

The Science Behind Mirroring

Although the concept of mirroring has been alluded to by philosophers for hundreds of years, the science behind this phenomenon was discovered recently and by accident.

The discovery can be attributed to neuroscientist Giacomo Rizzolatti and his team of researchers at the University of Parma, Italy. Dr. Rizzolatti and his colleagues were studying the electrical activity of neurons in the brains of macaque monkeys. The researchers knew the neurons they were studying fired when the monkeys performed various actions, such as reaching for an object, and they were hoping to learn more about how these neurons worked in the brain.

The monkeys had razor-thin wires implanted in their brains. When the monkey moved, neurons would fire, and researchers recorded and analyzed which neurons were firing in which regions of the brain.

One summer day in 1991, one of the researchers returned from lunch with an ice cream cone, which he decided to eat in full view of the monkey. Surprisingly, when the researcher went to take a bite from the cone, neurons in the monkey's brain fired.

After some experimentation, the researchers found the neurons that were firing in the monkey's brain corresponded to the same neurons that would fire when the monkey made similar movements. The neurons in the monkey's brain were mirroring what the monkey observed. Thus, the initial discovery of "mirror neurons," the unfolding science behind mirroring, occurred.[26]

Mirroring Do's and Don'ts

When you engage in mirroring, keep the following do's and don'ts in mind:

DO

- Base your use of mirroring on the person and the situation
- Build a connection first
- Prioritize listening and practicing empathy
- Mirror both verbal and nonverbal signals
- Nod, make eye contact, and smile

DON'T

- Overdo it (subtlety is key)
- Mimic the other person's signals exactly
- Imitate verbal or nonverbal signals that are negative
- Devote more energy to mirroring than listening and participating in the conversation

Putting It All Together

Step 2: Engaging Emotions

You are now armed with the knowledge and tools to engage (the right) emotions to help you influence decisions and people more effectively. Let us review the primary emotions associated with influencing along with some of the ways you can harness the power of emotions to influence others.

Emotions

The primary emotions associated with influencing are:

Achievement: The need to win or to obtain something you do not have is a strong motivator. To draw on the need for achievement, focus on eliciting emotions associated with satisfaction, interest, and joy.

Fear: The need to avoid negative consequences, or emotions associated with fear, is one of the strongest drivers of decision making. Make attempts to assuage fears or focus on eliciting emotions associated with relief and the elimination of fear.

Obligation: Humans also have an innate need for fairness; thus, obligation and the need for reciprocity drive many decisions. To harness the power of obligation, draw on the feelings of admiration and satisfaction.

The Influencer's Toolbox

Manage Your Emotions: Enhance your emotional intelligence by learning to assess yourself, manage your emotions, practice empathy, and manage the influence of emotions on decisions. Remember to label your emotions, take a break if you need to, be aware of other people's emotions, and consider keeping a journal of the emotions you feel.

Tell Relevant Stories: Incorporate storytelling into conversation to engage emotion throughout the influencing process. Though facts and figures are easily forgotten, you are more likely to remember a good story. Remember, for a story to be powerful, it must be relevant to your listeners and capture their attention.

Script: Write everything you want to say. Take some time away to review it with a fresh mind. Then practice, practice, practice. Go through it in your mind reading it or, better yet, saying it out loud. And solicit feedback. Consider asking someone else to review your script or listen to your pitch.

Mirror Others: Learn to get comfortable mirroring body language and other forms of nonverbal communication to build rapport, increase liking, and engage emotions. You can even use mirroring to change the body language of others. Copy subtle physical or verbal cues from the other party. Then redirect the other party using your own cues. But remember, mirroring that feels forced or unnatural may do more harm than good.

4 Demonstrating Logic

"Most of us, in our civilized society, rely too heavily on reasoning capacity to make things happen. We've been raised to believe that logic will prevail. Logic, in and of itself, will rarely influence people. Most often logic doesn't work."
– *Herb Cohen,* You Can Negotiate Anything

When influencing or persuading, most people lead with logic when, unfortunately, decades of research indicate they should not. This may be the reason that famed American author Herb Cohen suggests in the quote above that "*most* often logic doesn't work," because decisions are rarely made without emotion. However, there is a time and place for logic because it is an important step in the influence process. Thus, understanding when and how to convey your logic to be the most persuasive is crucial.

Why is demonstrating logic important if most people rely on their emotions to make decisions? Because demonstrating the logic behind the decision helps people *feel* confident in the decision. It allows them to *justify* it.

Let us think about this for a moment. You are pitching your spouse on seeing a specific movie you want to see instead of the movie your spouse suggested. After you have engaged his/her emotions by comparing it to a movie that he/she enjoyed, you might want to share the reviews on IMDB or Rotten Tomatoes. The reviews will not be the reason he/she accepts, but it will be what helps him/her justify the choice. But if you always do this and your spouse never ends up liking your movie choices, you will eventually lose your credibility.

Once people feel confident in the decision, you are one step closer to yes. In this chapter, you will learn how to convincingly demonstrate logic, but remember, you must first take the time to build credibility and engage emotion.

Logic and Rational Decisions

Once you have built rapport and engaged the proper emotions, it is time to demonstrate the logic of why the decision or solution you propose is the right choice. To do this, you need to demonstrate your decision or solution is logical (makes sense) and rational (agreeable with reason and all available knowledge).

Although the difference between logic and rationality may be easy to miss, this distinction is important. Something can be logical yet still be irrational. Take a moment to think about the following example:

> **Premises:** If someone is at the door, the dog will bark.
> The dog barks.
>
> **Conclusion:** There is someone at the door.
> Provided the given premises, the above statement is logical. It makes sense, but it may not be rational. We would need several additional pieces of information before we could determine the rationality, such as does the dog only bark when someone is at the door? Maybe the dog barks when he needs to go out. Maybe the dog barks when he sees another dog, a stray cat, or a squirrel. Can you see where the logic above fails?

So, what exactly constitutes logical and rational decisions? Logical and rational decisions are decisions that make sense and are agreeable with reason using all available evidence and knowledge.

Thus, we highlight three key steps to demonstrate the logic and rationality necessary to influence and persuade: (1) communicate natural and logical consequences, (2) offer social proof, and (3) offer documented proof. However, before we get into these, understanding the rational decision-making model is important, along with a few tools, concerns, and issues involved with making rational decisions.

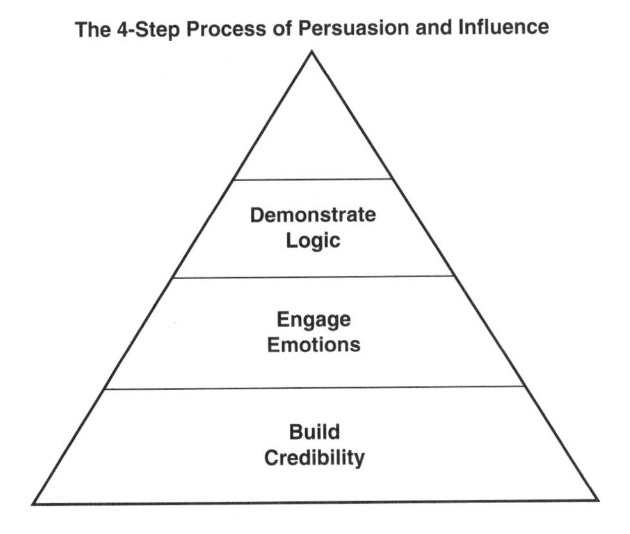

Figure 4.1

The Rational Decision-Making Model

Given the role that logic and decision-making play in influencing, you must arm yourself with a model to better understand how you, and the people you are influencing, make decisions.

The rational decision-making model highlights seven steps to making a decision. Learning about the rational decision-making model will help you understand how your logic will be processed by others to make a decision.

These steps are the following:

1. Define the Decision
2. Determine the Important Criteria
3. Weigh the Criteria
4. Identify Alternatives
5. Evaluate Alternatives
6. Select the Best Alternative
7. Implement the Decision

Once you have implemented a decision, you're ready to move on to the next decision.

Figure 4.2

The Weighted Criteria Matrix

The weighted criteria matrix, or the weighted decision matrix, is a helpful decision-making tool to evaluate alternatives against your specific, weighted criteria. Hence, the weighted criteria matrix will help you make decisions more rationally.

As the name implies, the weighted criteria matrix takes the form of a matrix (or table). To construct a weighted criteria matrix, list three to five of the most important criteria to your decision down the left-hand column.

In the next column, assign weights to each criterion, reflecting how important that criterion is in proportion to the decision.

Third, list and evaluate your alternatives. Evaluate and rate each alternative on its ability to satisfy each specific criterion. Assign lower scores to alternatives that only minimally meet the criterion and higher scores to options that satisfy that criterion. This is the raw score. To determine the criteria scores, multiply the weight by the raw score.

Finally, add up the criteria scores for each alternative. This is the total score, reflecting each alternative's estimated potential to optimize the value of your decision.

Criteria	Weight	Alternative 1 ABC Company		Alternative 2 First Choice Svc		Alternative 3 Service First Co.		Alternative 4 XYZ Company	
		Raw Scores	Criteria Scores	Raw Scores	Criteria Scores	Raw Scores	Criteria Scores	Raw Scores	Criteria Scores
Performance	4	2	8	5	20	4	16	3	12
Reliability	4	2	8	3	12	2	8	3	12
Customer Service	3	2	6	4	12	4	12	3	9
Cost	2	5	10	1	2	2	4	4	8
Contract Length	2	5	10	1	2	2	4	3	6
Total Score		42		48		44		47	

Performance- 1: Acceptable Performance → 5: Excellent Performance
Reliability- 1: Acceptable Reliability → 5: Excellent Reliability
Customer Service- 1: Acceptable Service → 5: Excellent Service
Cost: 1: High Cost → 5: Low Cost
Contract- 1: Long Contract → 5: Short Contract

Figure 4.3

The Ben Franklin Method of Decision Making

Benjamin Franklin was a big proponent of using weighted pros and cons to make decisions. According to Franklin, his way of making decisions was "to divide half a sheet of paper by a line into two columns; writing over the one Pro and over the other Con. Then during three or four days' consideration, I put down under the different heads short hints of the different motives, that at different times occur to me, for or against the measure. When I have thus got them altogether in one view, I endeavor to estimate their respective weights; and where I find two, one on each side, that seem equal, I strike them both out. If I judge some two reasons con equal to some three reasons pro, I strike out five; and thus proceeding, I find where the balance lies; and if after a day or two of further consideration, nothing new that is of importance occurs on either side, I come to a determination accordingly."[27]

A STORY IN DECISION MAKING

When the pandemic hit, like many of you, my wife and I had some tough decisions to make concerning our children's education. We had researched extensively for the right school for our children. For us, we wanted our children to be exposed to and learn several languages. I exclusively speak Spanish to them at home, and of course, they are exposed to English everywhere else. So, we were thrilled to find and have our boys be accepted to an outstanding Montessori school with Mandarin immersion.

However, as the pandemic escalated and schools closed in the spring, we had a terrible experience having to homeschool our two young boys. And when we had to decide for the new school year, we were concerned, like it or not, that was going to happen again. In their Montessori school, COVID for one other student or one teacher shutters the class. And what if flu season symptoms look like COVID and impact closures as well? It seemed unpredictable for two working parents.

My wife and I began by compiling alternatives. We could return our children to Montessori school in person and take the chances with the pandemic spreading the disease, closing classes, and disrupting their education. We could also enroll our children in several other options like homeschooling them entirely ourselves from the beginning of the semester, enrolling them in online school through our local public school, or several other online options.

I called my friend, Robert, a PhD economist, and he said, "I want you to assemble your criteria and the weight you put on each and then score each option." What he was asking us to do was to use the rational decision-making model.

First, we had to create our criteria: the quality of the education; the socialization, consistency and predictability; minimizing the COVID exposure, etc. Then we created an Excel spreadsheet with the various options, our criteria, and assigned weights to each. Though I had done this before professionally, I honestly did not think to use it in a situation like this.

When it was all said and done, this process helped us not only reach the best outcome but actually come up with a hybrid. We did a pod with another family, hired a teacher who spoke Spanish, and used online Mandarin lessons. We got the consistency and predictability we wanted, some of the socialization, and plenty of Spanish, along with some Mandarin so our boys could continue learning that as well. The process helped. Taking a step back and being as objective as you can helps. Sitting down with my wife and talking about it this way allowed us to figure out what we cared about and to make the decision that best suited everyone's needs.

The above explains the value of a formal decision-making process. But how does knowing this help you influence others? Although I am generally the risk taker in our relationship, the situation above shows I was more conservative than my wife. She was leaning toward sending our kids to the school that would be open while I was leaning toward one that would at least start online. We had the same criteria and reservations, but our prioritization was different. So, as we went through the process, I made sure to spend a lot of time improving the option I preferred. It was not a coincidence that I came up with the concept of podding with another family; it addressed her major socialization concerns, and fit in with my more conservative preference. As you can see from this story and the book in general, knowing how others make decisions is a critical aspect of influencing them.

Although the rational decision-making model is designed to reach optimal decisions, several reasons exist that the rational decision model often breaks down. First, the rational decision model assumes decision makers are rational, that they are reasonable and open to new information. The rational decision-making model also assumes all alternatives can be known. However, gathering information and generating and evaluating alternatives may cost money, time, or both.

For these reasons, the rational decision-making model has come under criticism for its oversimplified assumptions and inability to be carried out in the real world. When making a decision concerning an uncertain future, emotions come into play and gathering every piece of relevant information is impossible. However, an understanding of the model and how logical and rational decision making should ideally be carried out provides you with additional insight on how to approach your decision making and how to shape your arguments to influence and persuade.

The Role of Prior Belief in Reasoning

What do you think it would take to convert a Democrat into a Republican? Or vice versa? If your first reaction is to think it is highly unlikely, you are right. The question is, why? Because once they have made up their minds about something, everything that comes after is filtered in a way to support their prior beliefs rather than to continuously consider whether those beliefs are true and optimal.

One factor that holds many people back in their ability to make decisions using logic and reason is their prior beliefs. This is especially true when presented with complex information or making complex decisions.

Understanding Belief Biases

Previously held beliefs and expectations influence decision making through two well-known heuristics that go hand-in-hand: the belief biases.

The first of the belief biases is the tendency to believe something is true because it aligns with what you already believe even though it may not follow logic or reasoning. Our brain's need to be "right" causes us to accept and even seek out information that confirms what we believe. In psychology, this is referred to as confirmation bias.

When we are presented with complex information or are making complex decisions, we tend to give additional weight to information that favors our previously held beliefs.

Research on the confirmation bias suggests that when we are presented with an illogical argument, we are more likely to accept the argument as valid if the conclusion matches what we believe.

One study, conducted at the University of Toronto by Drs. Walter C. Sá, Richard C. West, and Keith E. Stanovich, used syllogistic reasoning problems to examine the influence of our beliefs on reasoning.[28]

Consider the following statements and decide for yourself if the reasoning holds true:

All living things need water.

Roses need water.

Therefore, roses are living things.

Do you believe that the above statements offer a valid argument? If you do, you fall into the 70% of participants in the study who believed the same way. However, the argument itself is not logical. Just because all living things need water does not entail that all things that need water are living. Your prior knowledge that roses are living things led you to believe that the argument itself was valid.

Let us look at another example. This one is a little more obvious. Consider the follow set of statements:

All cell phones need electricity to charge their batteries.

Laptops need electricity to charge their batteries.

Therefore, laptops are cell phones.

Although this argument is essentially the same as the one above, seeing the flaws in the logic of the argument is easier when the conclusion contrasts with what you believe.

That brings us to the second way that prior beliefs influence decision making: belief perseverance. Belief perseverance is the predisposition to reject information that disproves our beliefs or to not pay attention to it at all.

There may not be a better example of the blinders we humans have than the invisible gorilla study by Daniel Simons at Harvard University. He asked participants in a study to count how many times a basketball was being passed around in a video and participants were so focused on the ball that approximately half of them did not notice that a gorilla walked right through the whole screen, even stopping to pound his chest right in the center for a few seconds.[29] Though the participants who had not seen the gorilla were shocked to find out they missed it, we are not because it is another example of our selective attention. What we believe and focus on has such an impact on us it affects what we see.

Another recent study by researchers at Harvard University exemplifies how much information our brains can ignore. Harvard psychologists Trafton Drew, Melissa L.-H. Võ, and Jeremy M. Wolfe recruited radiologists to examine five single slice medical images to look for cancerous nodes in the lungs. However, in the final image all the radiologists examined, it included a matchbook-sized gorilla in the center of the image. But the radiologists were looking for cancerous nodes, not a gorilla.[30] What we focus on matters not only to what we see, but also what we do not.

The same concept applies to our efforts to influence and persuade. You can be so focused on your own perspective that you fail to see the perspectives of anyone else.

Overcoming Belief Biases

The good news is, there are several things we can do to overcome belief biases. The first is to slow down the decision-making process. When rushed to a quick decision, we are much more likely to use our biases and heuristics to make the decision than we are to take the time to think through the decision logically and rationally.

In one classic study on biases and heuristics, Princeton scholars Charles G. Lord, Mark R. Lepper, and Elizabeth Preston unveiled another strategy for overcoming belief biases. In their study, they asked participants to read and evaluate the methods and conclusion of two studies related to a controversial topic: the efficacy of the death penalty—one of which argued for the death penalty, and one of which argued against the death penalty. Participants were split into two groups. One group was asked to "weigh all of the evidence in a fair and impartial manner." The other group was asked to consider the opposite perspective: "Ask yourself at each step whether you would have made the same high or low evaluations had exactly the same study produced results on the other side of the issue." The group that was asked to be fair and impartial exhibited the same biases in alignment with their prior beliefs. However, in this study, the group asked to consider the opposite viewpoint overcame their biases.[31]

So, next time you want to change people's mind, ask them to consider the opposite belief. We often hear people talk about being impartial or objective, but you are better off asking them to think about the other side of the argument. This is more effective because it allows people to do what you want them to do: consider other viewpoints or alternatives without the judgement that comes with asking them to be fair or impartial, insinuating they naturally are not.

One final way to overcome belief biases is by practicing "active open-minded thinking." Actively open-minded thinking is putting in the effort to be open minded, weigh new information, and consider multiple perspectives. But it is also being willing to update your beliefs, as necessary. That seems to give us the most trouble. Take a minute to think about when the last time was you changed a strongly held belief?

You can do several things to practice being more open minded. The first is to ask yourself more questions. How much do you know?

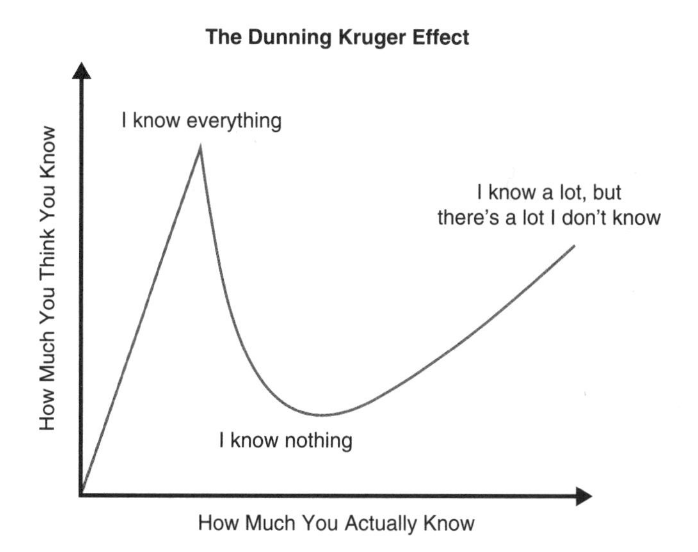

Figure 4.4

While asking yourself questions, keep in mind you might be wrong. People often overestimate what they know. In psychology, this is known as the Dunning Kruger effect. The Dunning Kruger effect suggests that the more you learn, the more you realize you do not know. Thus, we are more likely to believe we are experts in areas where we have limited knowledge and experience. However, as our knowledge and experience grow, we realize the limits of our knowledge and that there is still a lot we do not know.

When facing a big decision, it also may help to discuss the decision with a neutral party. Preferably find an expert or a trusted advisor to discuss major decisions, but in many cases, any neutral party will do. Sometimes, talking through a difficult decision helps us consider multiple perspectives.

It may take intentional resolution and action to approach decision making with a more open mind, but it is possible when you let go of the need to be right and focus on a desire to learn and to find the truth.

To sum these points up more briefly, follow these tips for overcoming belief biases:

- Slow down your decision-making process.
- Take a moment to consider what if the opposite of what you believe is true.

- Practice active open-minded thinking in the following ways:
  - Ask yourself questions
  - Recognize you might be wrong
  - Confer with an expert, a trusted advisor, or a neutral party

The Three Steps in Demonstrating Logic to Persuade Others

If you want to influence and persuade people, use three key steps for demonstrating logic and rationality: (1) communicate natural and logical consequences, (2) offer social proof, and (3) offer documented proof, as shown in Figure 4.5.

Communicate Natural and Logical Consequences

The first step in demonstrating logic is communicating the natural and logical consequences of your proposed decision.

One effective way to do this is by using the if/when-then-because formula. The if/when-then statement originated from the psychology and science behind planning and goal theory. The if/when-then formula goes something like this: **If** and **when** something happens- **then** something is expected. Or, to state it another way—**If X, then Y.**

This is an exceptionally useful formula in planning and implementing goals, as if/when-then statements have proven to be successful in instituting change. In psychology, these are known as implementation intentions. It helps you set specific goals, and it specifies when to do them. For example, let us say you have a goal to get more exercise. Your if/when-then plan might be like this: "When my alarm goes off in the morning, then I will go for a run."

But to make the logic formula even more convincing, you should add a "because" statement. So, the formula becomes more like this: **If** and **when** something happens- **then** something is expected- **because** of some set of natural or logical consequences.

Figure 4.5

If/When ➡ Then ➡ Because

Figure 4.6

The because statement is powerful. Many of us know this intuitively but are unsure why it works and unsure as to how to optimally use this practically. The addition of because is effective because it provides a reason and the other party assumes, upon hearing it, the reason is valid. Essentially, it is signaling the brain there is justification for whatever was said before the because statement, making the entire statement more powerful.

In one classic experiment, Harvard researcher Dr. Ellen Langer conducted research on the power of the because statement. In her research study, Langer had Harvard students ask to cut in line to use a copy machine. The students were given one of three cues to ask, requesting to print either 5 or 20 pages:

1. "Excuse me, I have 5 (or 20) pages. May I use the Xerox machine?"
2. "Excuse me, I have 5 (or 20) pages. May I use the Xerox machine, because I have to make copies?" and
3. "Excuse me, I have 5 (or 20) pages. May I use the Xerox machine, because I am in a rush?"

Among individuals asked for the smaller of the requests, she found people are naturally helpful. Without being provided a reason, 60% of students who were asked, "Excuse me, I have five copies. May I use the Xerox machine" were willing to let another student cut in line. However, when the because statement was used, compliance with the request jumped from 60 percent to 93 percent and 94 percent, respectively, even when the reason provided was not persuasive (i.e., ". . .because I have to make copies").

If you take a step back for a moment and think about this finding, it is surprising and useful. One may be able to increase compliance with a request by 50% or more by simply following the request with a "because" statement and about any semi-valid reason. Be that as it may, based on our extensive experience in the field (and backed by findings from our own research), we would recommend using the strongest justification possible. However, this study and many others demonstrate that having any reason can be more impactful than how strong the reason is.

The larger the request, the more important the reason becomes. In other words, if you are asking your spouse to pick up the dry cleaning on the way home from work, the reason you provide may not have to be as compelling as asking a friend to loan you $100,000 dollars.

IF-THEN-BECAUSE . . . ZOOM

A client reached out to us to help its sales team transition to virtual selling early in the pandemic. We provided different tools but the most impactful one was if-then-because. We worked with the client to determine how much more effective it was when using Zoom at least one-third of the time with its potential and current clients. Expected revenues were higher. So, the first step was convincing the sales team to get on more Zoom calls. Some knew this, some needed a little reminder, and others needed to be persuaded. We put together an effective session on this thanks to concepts, such as the media richness theory and return on investment (ROI) calculators based on the research we had done on the sales team and Zoom usage. Once we were done convincing everyone to use it more, we needed to show how to maximize the probability a client would accept a Zoom call rather than a phone call or email. We supplied the team a sample script: "If we can hop on Zoom, then I can introduce you to a subject matter expert who can provide some great resources because we have found that to be most effective for clients of your size and industry." Four weeks later, our client called and confirmed that Zoom calls were up dramatically, and 12 weeks later, the first set of results were in and revenue was up significantly.

Use if-then-because and you will be surprised by the results. It is a direct way to communicate the logical consequences of whatever you are recommending and accounts for the value of a pre-emptive but short explanation for why you are doing something.

Evidence from Decision Makers: Providing Rationale

We tested this question through our study of decision makers and found additional proof that providing a valid rationale does, in fact, increase the likelihood of compliance. Those who were presented with valid rationale along with a request were more likely to comply than participants who were not presented with a rationale. However, contrary to some prior findings, we find that what follows the because statement may have to be valid. In this example, decision makers who were presented with an unconvincing reason were less likely to comply than those who were presented with no reason at all.

Next time you make any kind of request, incorporate a because statement using the if/when-then-because formula.

Tips for Using the If/When-Then-Because Formula To get the best results when using the if/when-then-because formula, keep the following points in mind:

- Always provide a reason for your proposed solution or your request. Providing a reason tells other parties why they should comply with your request.
- Use as compelling of a reason as possible. For small requests, the reason seems not to matter too much. However, the larger the request, the more compelling the reason needs to be.
- Make the reason personal. If possible, include the word "you." Making the reason personal engages emotions and helps others see how your proposed solution benefits them.

Social Proof

One of the strongest ways to back up or strengthen your because statements is to offer social proof. Social proof is just what it sounds like: offering evidence that others (society) act and believe the same way you do.

Why does offering social proof help demonstrate your logic? Well, when facing a decision where we do not know what to do, we often look to others to determine the most appropriate response. We are inclined to follow the wisdom of the crowd. In addition to that, most people have a desire to conform. We want to fit in.

The higher the uncertainty, the less likely we are to know what to do and the more we rely on social proof.

In what has become known as one of the classic experiments on social proof, in 1951, psychologist Solomon Asch conducted an experiment on conformity within groups. Asch wanted to investigate whether people would conform to a group even when the answer was clearly wrong.

To conduct his experiment, Asch gathered participants for a "perceptual test." For this perceptual test, participants were placed in rooms with seven other people and shown a series of 18 images (like the one in Figure 4.7) in a line judgement task.

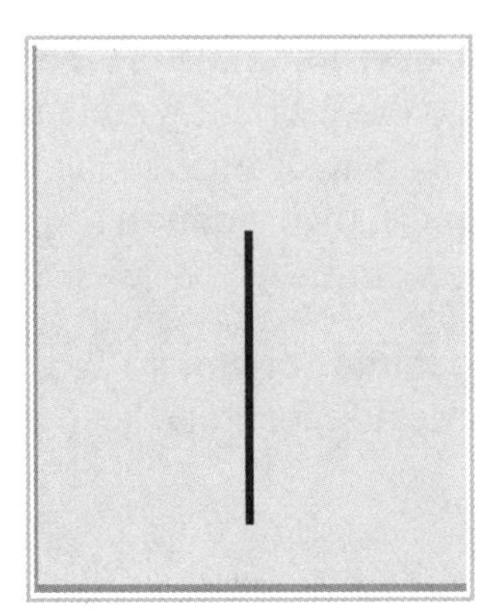

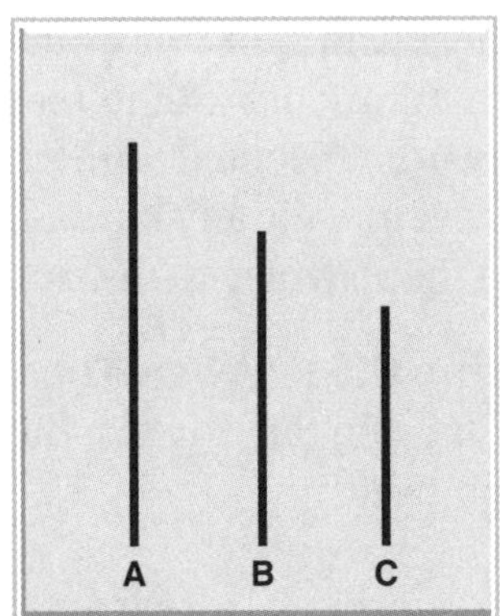

Figure 4.7

Participants in the study were then asked to say out loud which line on the right matched the line on the left. What the participants did not know was that the other people in the room were not actual participants but were in on the experiment. So, for most images shown, Asch's conspirators unanimously chose the wrong line, with the actual participant always going last.

Through the series of 18 tasks, 75% of participants conformed with the group and provided the wrong answer in at least one of the 12 tasks where the bogus participants provided the wrong answer. For the six trials where the bogus participants gave the correct answer, the actual participants in the trial picked the wrong line less than 1% of the time.[32]

Examples and evidence of the use and importance of social proof abound. Look at most businesses, websites, and marketing messages. You will find ratings, reviews, hit counters, testimonials, "also boughts": all types of social proof.

Take Amazon, for instance. When you shop on Amazon, it provides you with a star rating and the number of reviews the product has received, providing you with social proof. When you click on the reviews, you can see who reviewed it and whether it is a confirmed purchase (i.e., was purchased on Amazon) by that customer: more social proof.

We will introduce you to three general types of social proof: collective proof, peer proof, and thought leader proof. Then we will provide some examples of how you can use each type of proof to increase your persuasive capabilities.

Collective Proof Collective proof refers to evidence from the masses. This evidence may come from reviews, testimonials, number of likes, comments, social media followers, or the sheer number of customers served. Think McDonald's: Billions and billions served.

The more people we see behaving in a similar manner, the more likely we are to rely on collective proof to determine our own ideas, beliefs, and actions. In one study, social psychologists Drs. Stanley Milgram, Leonard Bickman, and Lawrence Berkowitz conducted an experiment on the streets of New York City. In their experiment, they began by having a man stop and look up, staring into the sky for one minute. When one man looked up, only about 4% of passersby stopped and looked up. However, when they repeated the experiment with five men looking up, this increased to 18% of passersby stopping and looking up. And when 15 stopped and looked up, 40% of passersby jumped on the bandwagon.[33]

Collective proof is powerful. As you may be aware, user reviews, ratings, and testimonials are a heavily relied upon factor in purchase decisions. In fact, according to the 2019 Bizrate Insights Consumer Shopping Survey,[34] over 92% of Internet shoppers read product reviews before deciding whether and what to purchase. When was the last time you purchased an unfamiliar product without considering the rating or reading the reviews?

And most companies know this. If you make any kind of online purchase, you are more than likely to get an email, notification, or text message asking you to submit a review of your purchase. This is because the more reviews a product or service has, the higher the likelihood that potential customers will purchase it. According to the 2019 Consumer Shopping Survey, 65% of online shoppers prefer products to have more than 10 reviews before purchasing an item, and more than 15% of online shoppers prefer at least 100 reviews.

One way you can share collective social proof in business is by sharing your milestones. Milestones may include things, such as the number of customers (McDonald's: billions and billions served or Instagram: 1 billion+ users), the number of years in business (Lee Jeans: Since 1889), the number of countries you do business in (Nielsen: collaborating across 100 countries), years of experience (e.g., more than 100 years of combined experience), or even the number of shares, likes, saves, or downloads. When you reach major milestones, you can incorporate these into your messaging, script them into your stories, and use them as evidence to strengthen the logic and reasoning in your argument.

Collective proof can also be leveraged in a peer-to-peer sort of way. For example, Peloton, the fast-growing online bike and workout company, has its users ride live with other users to motivate them. Knowing other riders are going through the same session helps to push its users and serves as collective proof.

MY 10 MINUTES AS A FAMOUS ARTIST

Many years ago, I studied abroad in the United Kingdom for a semester. The trip was an incredible experience. I met friends with whom I remain close. However, the two most memorable portions of the trip were securing front row seats for Wimbledon Men's Finals, which sadly was the year before my favorite player, Roger Federer, started his run and the accidental sociology and psychology study I executed at the Tate Modern museum in London.

I was with a few friends admiring the work at Tate Modern and we got to a section where I felt the art was something a young child could do and was not impressed. I said I could do better, and challenged by my friends and classmates, I put down my McDonald's paper bag on the floor in an empty corner of a room and moved the ropes around. I confidently said that people would be amazed and they were not.

I, however, was not going to give up. I asked my friends to do me a favor and appear interested for three minutes as I would sit down and sketch the McDonald's bag. Within 60 seconds, several other visitors stopped to look at my "art" as well, and within three minutes, a small crowd had formed.

I gave it 10 minutes before being concerned by the cameras and the trouble I would get into, so I took it down, but within those 10 minutes, we observed multiple people whisper how brilliant or ironic the piece was. Comments around how one person's garbage is another's treasure and how it was calling attention to societal issues.

No one stopped to look when the bag was there, but when the ropes were there and others were looking, it gained credibility in the eyes of others. How powerful is that? Sorry to any Tate Modern artists or employees who find this offensive; it was nothing more than an experiment from a young person finding his way through the arts.

Five-Star Reviews for Sale Reviews have become so important to a product's success that some third-party sellers have cooked up some elaborate schemes to get those reviews. From paying people to leave a review to offering free products in exchange for a five-star review, they have tried it all.

Albeit many companies, including Amazon, have prohibited the use of paid reviews, many sellers find a way around it. For example, invitations to receive cash and free products in exchange for a five-star review are common on freelancing platforms, websites, and in social media groups dedicated to the topic.

Although Amazon claims that less than 1% of its reviews are fictitious, some data suggest this is an understatement. For instance, according to one outside source, ReviewMeta, of the 2 million unverified reviews in March of 2019 (reviews in which Amazon could not verify a purchase), more than 99% were five-star reviews.

Negative Social Proof Which do you think is a more compelling message?

"Don't be among the millions of people in the United States who will miss out on reading this book this year."

or

"Be among the millions of people in the United States who will read this book this year."

If you thought the second message was more compelling, you are right. The first message is an example of negative social proof. Although you want to create an argument creating a fear of missing out (FOMO), the first message has the opposite effect. Here you are offering social proof that many, many people will not this book, so it is also all right if you do not read the book either.

One classic example of the power of social proof is an experiment conducted by Robert B. Cialdini and his colleagues at Arizona's Petrified Forest National Park. The park was having a serious issue with visitors stealing the petrified wood that makes the park famous. Although no visitors took large amounts, the sheer number of visitors who stole petrified wood from the forest made this a major problem.

Cialdini and his team were called upon to study and solve this problem. One of the first things they noticed when entering the park was a sign stating, "Your heritage is being vandalized every day by theft losses of petrified wood of 14 tons a year, mostly a small piece at a time." Can you see the negative social proof there? Cialdini and his team certainly did, and they hypothesized this sign might be part of the problem.

To test the effects the negative social proof may be having on the theft of the petrified wood, the researchers created several new signs. These included signs that read "Many past visitors have removed the petrified wood from the park, changing the state of the Petrified Forest" and "Please leave petrified wood in the park." They divided the park into sections, placed the signs at the entrances, and examined the effects of the signs on the theft of the park's petrified wood.

They found that in the areas of the park with the sign that provided negative social proof ("Many past visitors have removed the petrified wood from the park, . . ."), the petrified wood was nearly five times as likely to be stolen than the sections of the park that asked visitors to leave the petrified wood in the park (7.92% compared to 1.67%).[35]

When offering social proof, make sure you are providing positive social proof and hurting your cause instead of helping it.

Peer Proof Perhaps a stronger offering of proof than proof from the masses is proof from your peers. You are more likely to take the word of someone you know or someone who is like you as opposed to strangers. This is because we place more weight on advice and actions of people most like us. Thus, a key factor in the strength and attraction of social proof is how much similarity we see between ourselves and the source of the social proof.

In psychology, this is known as implicit egotism. Implicit egotism suggests that humans tend to prefer people, places, and things we associate with ourselves. According to one study conducted by Drs. Brett W. Pelham, Matthew C. Mirenberg, and John T. Jones, implicit egotism permeates the public and private aspects of our lives, even where we choose to live. In their research, they found that our unconscious preference for things resembling ourselves extends as far as preferences toward living in cities that resemble our own name (i.e., people named Louise in St. Louis) or begin with our birthday numbers (i.e., Two Harbors, MN) and the career we choose (i.e., there are a disproportionate number of dentists named Dennis and Denise).[36]

So, how much more of an influence does peer proof offer than other forms of social proof? It appears quite a lot. According to a 2012 study by Nielsen, though 70% of people trust consumer reviews posted online, that number jumps to 92% when recommendations come from your peers or someone you know.

DO I KNOW YOU?

At SNI, we have been fortunate to work with clients from some of the most respected companies in the world. We are fortunate to have been provided testimonials, written or video, by our clients. We post these on our website and elsewhere proudly. Though we have found they do have a positive impact on a prospective client, we found a better way to convince that on-the-fence prospect choosing between us and another firm. We have asked one of our clients with something in common with the prospect (e.g., shared business challenge, CRM, industry, location), to proactively call the prospect. We share that the priority is to make a mutually beneficial relationship. We feel this brings value to both parties, which is in line with our objectives and how we wish to be perceived in the marketplace. Of course, if our client decides to share their positive experience working with us and the impact we have had on their organization, we would be thrilled, but we feel all parties are better off even without that aspect and leave it entirely up to our client. Amazingly, this has resulted in a high conversion rate. Why? When we asked these converted prospects after they surprised us, we thought it would be because someone else proactively calling another company would be unique and catch their attention, but it was because they generally hit it off, based on their similarities, and then if/when they received a glowing review about us from the client, it meant more to them than a testimonial online or a note from someone they did not know.

Keep this in mind the next time you want to land a big account. Consider inviting them to a round table with current clients rather than sharing a testimonial. Consider setting up a conference call with the prospect and the client, and following up with the relevant case study that now has more impact. If going with the testimonial route, make sure to give the client the opportunity to take a personal approach that will feel relevant and connect with a prospective client so that the positive feedback means something to viewers.

Thought Leader Proof The third type of social proof is the proof we associate with authorities. Thought leader proof is provided by people we look up to and respect. For some people, these may be experts in their field or on a given topic. For others, it could be athletes, celebrities, or other people they admire, such as social media influencers.

While following the lead of experts makes sense, you may be wondering why the endorsements of athletes, celebrities, or influencers matter. This is because we tend to let positive impressions of people in one area of their lives to positively influence our assessments of other areas of their lives as well. In other words, we tend to believe that because these people are good at what they do, they must be good at everything. In psychology, this is known as the halo effect.

Dr. Edward Thorndike was the first to coin the term halo effect in his 1920 study "The Constant Error in Psychological Ratings."[37] In his experiment, Thorndike asked army officers to rate their subordinates along several dimensions, which included physical qualities, intelligence, leadership, and character. As suspected, he found that high ratings in one aspect of a person's qualities were closely correlated with high ratings in other aspects, and the reverse was also true. Low ratings in one aspect of a person's qualities were correlated with low ratings in other aspects of their lives.

Research suggests that physical attractiveness can play a major role in the halo effect. Thorndike's study found that physical qualities correlated highly and evenly with intelligence, leadership, and character.

Recent research backs this finding up. In one 2016 study published in *PLOS One*, Dr. Sean Talamas and colleagues examined the influence of the halo of attractiveness. In their study, Talamas asked participants to rate the physical attractiveness, intelligence, conscientiousness, and perceived academic performance of 100 photos of the faces of university students. They compared that information to the actual academic performance of the students. Even though no relationship between attractiveness and actual academic performance existed, attractiveness was highly correlated with intelligence, conscientiousness, and perceived academic performance.[38]

What this means to you is being perceived positively in one area impacts how you are perceived in many others. So, dressing appropriately, having an impressive online profile, the quality of your slide deck, and many other aspects that feel like insignificant details will have more impact than you think.

Documented Proof

Another way to strengthen your because statements is to offer documented proof. Documented proof is not necessarily a document. Rather, it is the body of evidence outside of your own beliefs, opinions, and words.

Documented proof may include market research, white papers, case studies, or statistical analysis. It could include certifications, memberships, awards, or other signals of expertise or affiliation.

One of the most trusted forms of documented proof are research reports and white papers. As with other forms of proof, the source matters, but most important is the relevance and value of its content. Finding a website that does offers white papers is easy these days and rightfully so because they are one of the most valued and trusted type of content. They serve to build credibility for the author, borrow credibility from others sourced in the document, and educate and persuade readers.

Case studies are another powerful form of documented proof. How powerful? Second only to in-person events in the business-to-business (B2B) marketing landscape, where 65% of people feel it is an effective marketing tool. Case studies allow you to tell the story of the value you offer. They allow you to highlight your success through a real story, with a real client, in an impressive but not boastful way. Most commonly, they use the same structure of a compelling story: They start with the challenge or reason a client hired you, move to the solution you provided, and share the results. Again, the key here is to make the case study relatable. Pick a challenge that prospective clients will share to maximize its impact.

A shorter version of case studies are client testimonials. Testimonials are compelling, especially when they are from recognizable and relevant companies and situations. For example, sharing a testimonial from a small local business with a Fortune 500 client is not very impactful and potentially even raises concerns about your experience with organizations their size. At SNI, we are proud to have many written testimonials from our clients, but we have found the most powerful testimonials comes from more specific video testimonials. We use written testimonials for volume because a potential client can scan through and see many on our website, but we use video testimonials to share in more depth how unique we are and the impact we have on our clients. The richness of the video testimonial makes the message stronger than the written testimonial.

DOCUMENTED PROOF IN YOUR STORIES

A few years ago, SNI had been working with the Cleveland Indians. For many years, we had trained and advised their organization on selling and negotiating large ticket items, mainly sponsorships and suites. At the time, they had a particularly important sponsorship renewal coming up. Early in the process, the client came to them with a strong request to cut their spend by 30%. The Indians' sponsorship team was savvy and experienced but felt enough was at stake to warrant getting some assistance. We got in the trenches with them, reviewing client history, all communication leading up to the request, relevant precedents in the industry, etc. Then we worked closely with them as they communicated with the client for the remaining six months in their agreement. By using many of the SNI negotiation tools (e.g., preparation checklists, probing framework, and scripting), providing them with an objective and experienced outside opinion, and working together to develop and execute a successful negotiation strategy, the Indians changed their fate, In the end, the Indians' sponsorship team was able to persuade this client to increase their spend by 26% and ultimately worked out a deal that both parties where thrilled to sign – and remain happy about years into it.

The above story utilizes many of the recommendations in this book, in this case and most importantly, documented proof. In the form of a short story, it shared with you, the reader, the types of results a client could expect when working with SNI. It started out with a common situation many organizations find relevant: a challenging negotiation coming up that was important to them. It shares that the client was experienced and savvy but willing to retain help and to avoid a prospect that being experienced and asking for help are mutually exclusive. The data were used as a piece of the story, to make it more credible and specific. William Koetsenruijter, a professor at Leiden University in Netherlands, has done extensive research on this topic and has found that using numbers increases the perceived accuracy, precision, or credibility because it tells readers the impact was measured and tracked. To take it a step further, notice how specific the key number was: 26%. A wide range of research supports that using precise rather than round numbers makes the use of numbers a more compelling persuasion tool. Most notably, Malia Mason, a professor at Columbia Business School, has found that using specific numbers in negotiation signals to the other party that you have knowledge and expertise on the subject matter and, as a result, are more powerful.

So, next time you want to influence someone, think of the story above. Documented proof is persuasive and is best used as part of a specific and relatable story, borrows credibility from sources, uses specific numbers, and demonstrates expertise in a way that is unlikely to be perceived as arrogant.

The Influencer's Toolbox

Framing

What you focus on and devote your attention to helps to shape your attitudes and emotions. When approaching an issue, the context and how information is presented (what each side chooses to focus on and draw attention to) are known as framing.

A framing bias occurs when people make a different decision based on how the information is presented, rather than the facts.

There are countless examples all around us of how the way we communicate a concept impacts its persuasiveness. For example, notice that the choices for abortion are "pro": You choose between pro-life or pro-choice. The frame has been set up in such a way where you support a baby's right to live or the mother's right to choose. The same occurs with gun control: You choose between supporting our rights or supporting our safety.

This topic is not addressed as much as it should, yet it is a powerful persuasion concept. However, *Thank you for Arguing*, a book by Jay Heinrichs, addresses it succinctly and says that if facts work, use them. If not, question them, their quality, and their relevance to the topic.

There is more to come, but, to test this concept, the next time you are writing an email, think about the different ways you could present the same idea. Positively, negatively, stated as fact, etc. This is framing. Testing this with an email is easiest because you have time to think and tinker. As you practice and get comfortable, you may find yourself able to do it in a conversation, which requires you to be quick on your feet.

The Muller-Lyer Illusion

Context matters. Framing does not happen in your stories or perceptions. Look at the Muller-Lyer Illusion shown in Figure 4.8. Which of these lines do you think is longer?

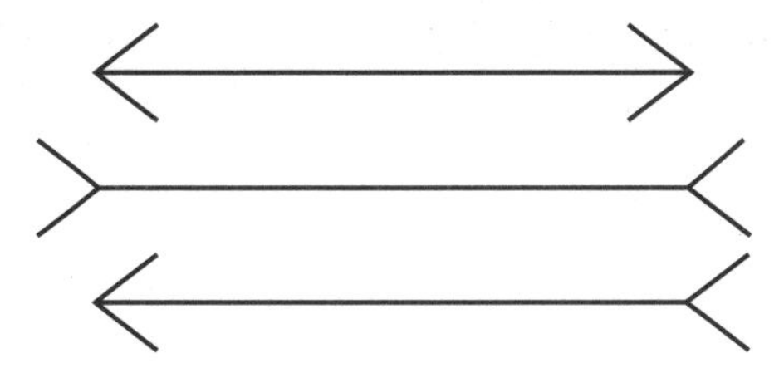

Figure 4.8

Most people believe the middle line, with the reverse facing arrows is longer than the other two lines. However, all three lines are the same length. This optical illusion is an example of visual framing and shows how easy it is to trick the breain.

In another example, researchers at the University of Massachusetts at Amherst conducted an experiment where participants were tasked with picking a red jellybean either from a jar that contained 1 red jellybean and 9 white jellybeans or from a jar that contained 7 red jellybeans and 93 white jellybeans. Even though the jar with 1 red jellybean had a greater probability of picking it (10% compared to 7% for the jar with 7 red jellybeans), participants in this study consistently and repeatedly trusted their gut and picked from the jar that contained 7 red jellybeans. According to one participant in study, "I picked the ones with more red jellybeans because it looked like there were more ways to get a winner even though I knew there were also more whites and that the percents were against me."[39]

Real-life examples of framing abound. I am sure you have noticed how meat is marketed as "90% fat free" instead of "10% fat." When the numbers are low, such as 1% or 2% milk, the percentage of fat is used.

Study after study has found framing to have significant effects on judgment and decision making. In another study, Drs. Irwin P. Levin and Gary J. Gaeth asked participants to taste-test beef and rate it along several dimensions. They found that when the beef was described as "75% lean," it was rated tastier than when the beef was described as "25% fat."[40]

The next time you are providing data to people you are looking to influence, work through the various ways you could express the same piece of information. Think about how they are going to digest it, and make it easy and relevant for them.

How do you take advantage of this phenomenon? Make your data as vivid as possible. For example, if you are running a contest and want people to feel the highest likelihood to win, rather than listing a 20% chance, or 2/10 participants, consider 20/100 participants so your audience feels the 20 chances to win rather than 2.

The Framing Effect

Perhaps one of the strongest and most well documented instances of framing is the framing effect. The framing effect is a cognitive heuristic (i.e., a mental shortcut) that influences our perceptions of the value of our options when these options are presented as gains (or potential gains) versus losses (or potential losses).

The notion of the framing effect draws upon the play between the emotions surrounding the need for achievement and those surrounding fear.

Psychologists have consistently found most individuals are risk averse, that is, we like to avoid risk, and we are willing to do more to avoid losses than we are willing to do to seek equivalent gains.

Let's look at an empirical example to help you understand how this might play out in real-life decision making.

Evidence from Decision Makers: Framing

To test the framing effect, we asked participants in our study one of the two versions of the following survey questions:

> *"You are a business owner. You come across a management consultant that would be able to help you grow your revenues by 5% at a time when you project your revenues to be flat. You believe this will equate to a change of roughly $1,500,000 in your projected profits. How much would you be willing to pay her/him?"*

OR

> *"You are a business owner. You come across a management consultant that would be able to help you maintain your current revenues at a time when you project a 5% decrease. You believe this will equate to a change of roughly $1,500,000 in your projected profits. How much would you be willing to pay her/him?"*

As you can see, the profit increase in both questions is the same. Therefore, logically, we should not expect any significant differences in the value attributed to either framing of the question.

However, we found that participants in our study assigned a higher value to the consultant's services who could help them avoid losses (avg.=$176,284) than to the consultant's services that could help them achieve growth and gains (avg.=$94,472). In this scenario, loss framing leads to more than a 50% higher valuation on identical results depending on whether those results are framed as a gain versus a loss.

As the previous examples show, framing can have significant implications on our perceptions of value even among expert decision makers. In this case, practice does not make perfect. Research has shown that framing effects do not seem to decrease with age or experience. In fact, there is some evidence that framing effects may increase with age, as more experience is typically associated with more reliance on heuristics.

So, what can you do?

As an influencer, you can use the powerful effects of framing to draw attention to the areas where you want to draw the focus. To do this, first use some of the following tips:

- Use common words. They are more persuasive than complex words.
- Define the terms in the broadest context that will be appealing to the broadest audience.
- Then deal with a specific problem/choice that needs to be made and use future tense. We use past tense to blame and future tense to inspire, motivate, etc.

Second, take control of the framing. With your newfound knowledge of the framing effect, you can shape your pitches and arguments to be more persuasive, ultimately leading to more logical decisions that everyone feels is a win-win.

To avoid the negative effects of framing, use these suggestions the next time you are faced with a decision:

- Avoid rushed or quick decisions.
- Give yourself time to explore and understand your alternatives.
- Examine the problem from different perspectives.
- Seek outside guidance and advice.
- Take control of the framing.

Anchoring

As individuals, we rely on the first piece of information we receive. This information acts as a reference point and greatly influences future arguments, estimates, negotiations, and final decisions, no matter whether you are negotiating a business proposal, the purchase price of a used car, or a raise.

In psychology, this is known as anchoring. First described by psychologists Amos Tversky and Daniel Kahneman in 1974, the anchoring effect is another cognitive bias, a well-known yet difficult to overcome hindrance to our decision making. In their study, Tyversky and Kahneman asked participants to watch a roulette wheel that was labeled with numbers 0 to 100 but was rigged to stop at 10 or 65. Participants observed one spin of the wheel and were asked to guess the number of countries in Africa that belong to the United Nations. Participants for whom the wheel stopped on the low anchor guessed, on average, 25 Africa countries belonged to the United Nations. For participants who received the high anchor, the average guess was nearly double, with 45 as an average answer.[41]

Anchoring is a well-known tactic in influence and persuasion. The anchoring effect causes a person to center on the first number presented, which acts as a starting point in any negotiations. In negotiations, this makes any concession seem more reasonable even if it is outside the bargaining range where both parties can walk away satisfied. In fact, anchoring holds true even if the first number is unreasonable or makes no sense.

Even unrealistic and exorbitant anchors have the potential to greatly affect outcomes. In one study, Dr. Robert B. Cialdini asked one group of college students whether they would be willing to chaperone troubled teens on a trip to the zoo. He asked another group of students a more involved request: whether they would be willing to counsel troubled teens for two hours a week for the next two years. When the second group all said "No," he asked them to chaperone the troubled teens at the zoo. In the first group, 17% of the college students agreed to chaperone the troubled teens. In the second group, the number of students who complied with the chaperoning request jumped to 50%, nearly three times the number of students willing to comply in the first group.[42]

THE POWER OF ANCHORING

Here is another real-life example of anchoring and its effects on decision making. We were working with a team that had an upcoming unrestricted free agent in the NBA. The player and his agent had their eyes on a big payday, and they were asking for a certain amount of money throughout the entire year. However, the amount they were asking for was higher than our client had originally expected and higher than what we objectively felt was market value.

However, the player and his agent would not budge. They kept echoing and returning to their anchor, but the team had heard it so much from them that Stockholm syndrome kicked in. If you are wondering what Stockholm syndrome is, it occurs when hostages bond with their captors. While the agent and player did not actually hold them captive, a similar psychological effect was occurring. The team was being anchored by the agent's number and began to justify it internally rather than working through their alternatives or objectively evaluating the player's value to the team, market value, and his alternatives.

As outside advisors we saw what was happening, so each time our client interacted with the agent and anchored with this high number, we reminded them of much lower comps to battle the anchoring that was occurring. A deal was done for a number higher than market but lower than the anchor. When the client looked back a few years later, they realized what happened and became aware and better prepared for similar situations in the future.

I train our sales team to be cognizant of anchors all the time. We have a set pricing structure, but often potential clients will share what they typically pay or have paid in the past. Though this important information should be heard and considered, we have 25 years of experience and a fantastic track record of providing a high ROI with our training. As a result, I push our sales team not to be anchored by what clients have paid in the past or their budget. Most companies would pay more if they were certain that investment would more than pay for itself quickly. And, if their budget is not flexible, we need to adjust our offerings to their budget. Taking things away is one of the fastest ways to test if the budget is fixed and if the other party values it.

MORE ANCHORING IN THE BIG LEAGUES

In the story above, the agent did a great job anchoring our client; however, anchoring can be so powerful, it changes your own reality. An example of this from public information occurred in 2017 between the Cleveland Browns and one of their star players.

At the time, EVP, Sashi Brown, was in charge and had created a strategy of rebuilding the roster by aggressively acquiring draft picks and developing young players while remaining conservative in signing veterans whose prime years were likely to be past by the time the roster would be ready to compete. One of those veteran re-signing decisions was Terrelle Pryor, who was coming off a great year but was an unproven wide receiver after having transitioned from quarterback fewer than two seasons prior.

In free agency, Pryor wanted big money. From his and his agent's perspective, he was worth number one receiver money because of his performance in a handful of games. If he could perform at that level after changing positions, how much better could he get with more experience? He and his agent thought there was a chance that the Browns might use its Franchise Tag on him, which was worth north of $15 million.

From teams' perspectives, they were unsure how his skills as a wide receiver would continue to develop or that he could sustain the recent level of performance. He had played well that season, but he had a short résumé as an NFL wide receiver.

The market was uncertain a year before, but as early March got closer, it was fairly clear that the market for Pryor would be below $10 million per year with teams willing to bet on only a couple of years contract at the most. In 2017, only the 15 top paid wide receivers in the league were on contracts for $10 million or more per year.

The Browns, hopeful to bring Terrelle back, decided to lead the way with what it considered a strong offer: four years at $32 million. However, Terrelle and his agent were disappointed, believing he was worth more. So, they decided to shop it around.

Fast-forward a few weeks later, and the Browns had to shore up its roster and move on with other options; mainly, it signed Kenny Britt to a similar deal it had offered to Terrelle. Unfortunately, for Terrelle, he had to accept a one-year $6 million deal from the Washington Redskins. After an injury sidelined him halfway through the 2017 season, Pryor went on to sign a $4.5 million deal with the New York Jets in 2018 but was released after six games. After the Jets, he had brief stints with the Buffalo Bills and Jacksonville Jaguars but has not seen the same success athletically or financially.

Was he crazy or irrational? No. He believed in himself, and many times this works out for the player, but in this case, believing that he was a number one wide receiver for months anchored himself and his agent at a value that was too high. For them, their anchor to a value the market could not support made it difficult for them psychologically to go from their value to a lower number in a matter of weeks.

In hindsight, it is easy to look back and say that Pryor should have taken the deal. But there is a reason this happens; more often than not we focus on what we want to focus on, what is most convenient, and what is beneficial for us, and then, for better or for worse, we anchor ourselves to this reality.

Evidence from Decision Makers: Anchoring

In our study, we also tested the effect of anchoring. To do this, we asked participants to answer one of the following two sets of questions:

> *"Do you believe the Mississippi River is longer or shorter than 587 miles?"*
>
> *THEN*
>
> *"How long do you believe the Mississippi River is?"*
>
> *OR*
>
> *"Do you believe the Mississippi River is longer or shorter than 1,761 miles?"*
>
> *THEN*
>
> *"How long do you believe the Mississippi River is?"*

The numbers in the first questions were anchored at 25 and 75% of the length of the Mississippi River: 2,348 miles. Participants who received the lower anchor (587 miles) estimated, on average, the Mississippi River was 1,321 miles; participants, who received the higher anchor, estimated an average of 1,949 miles, a whopping 47.5% difference based solely on an arbitrary anchor.

So, if anchoring has such an impact, when do you make the first offer? Here are the two rules of thumb:

> *Make the first offer* when you want to anchor the other party. This is best to use when you and the other party understand the market.

Whoever goes first gets the anchoring advantage within what is reasonable.

In general, the three situations in which it is best to go first include the following:

1. When you both know the market
2. When you are not the default choice, hoping to get a less-biased other party
3. If few competitors exist

Do not make the first offer when one or both parties lack a good understanding of the market. If you are unsure, going first could be a mistake because the other party may know something you do not, and as a result, your first offer will not be optimal. If the other party is not as knowledgeable, your going first eliminates the opportunity for you to get information from the other party's first offer and possibly be pleasantly surprised.

In general, the three situations in which its best to not go first are the following:

1. If the other party is unsure of the market or its criteria
2. When you are the default, in which case, try to go last
3. If many competitors exist

If the other party sets the anchor first, you have three strategies to reset the anchor.

Strategy 1: Diffuse the Anchor

One mistake inexperienced negotiators often make is jumping right to their counteroffer. However, without diffusing unrealistic offers, you are implying the initial offer may be within or close to your bargaining range.

e.g., *"It is clear that we are not on the same page. That is outside the range I had in mind."*

Strategy 2: Gather More Information

Take the time to research and understand the relevant criteria rather than solely relying on your prior knowledge or the information the other party provided.

e.g., "*That is outside the range that I had in mind. I'll need time to gather more information and maybe we can sit down and start again.*"

Strategy 3: Respond with a Well-Informed Counteroffer

If you have come prepared, you should have the social and documented proofs to support your position. When it is time to respond with a well-informed counteroffer, present the information and proof you have gathered.

e.g., *Counter in a way that essentially ignores the anchor and repositions the negotiation in the most favorable place you can reasonably support.*

The Cost of Free

"Free" normally does not mean free, but it is an excellent example of how anchoring is used in our everyday lives.

Think of all the examples of the use of free in marketing and advertising, sales, and user acquisition. These are popular tactics because they work. If you look, you will see them every day. Free Warranty. Free Guarantee. Free Download. Free Trial. Free Continental Breakfast. Buy One, Get One Free.

According to Dan Ariely, author of *Predictably Rationality: The Hidden Forces That Shape Our Decisions*, free is "an emotional hot button, a source of irrational excitement."

But nearly free does not have the same effect. In one of his experiments, Ariely offered participants the choice of Lindt Truffles priced at 15 cents or Hershey Kisses for 1 cent. He offered another group of participants Lindt Truffles priced at 14 cents and Hershey Kisses free. In the first group, even with the nearly free price of 1 cent, 73% of participants chose the truffles, yet 27% chose the kisses. However, when the price went from 1 cent to free, 69% chose the kisses, and 31% chose the truffles. Free excites us and nudges us toward a decision even when free may not mean free.

Features, Advantages, and Benefits

Another tool to help you demonstrate logic is to focus on the advantages and benefits of the decision rather than the features. In business, customers rarely care about the features of your product, service, business, or idea. They care about what it does for them. How does it solve a problem they are experiencing? How does it meet their needs or fulfill their desires? How does it make their lives (or their business) better? The bottom line is, how does this benefit them?

Often, we are drawn to list the features of a decision because they are the most salient components of a solution. However, although others may be looking for particular features in their criteria, the features are important because of what they do (i.e., the benefits they deliver). How does this solution solve their particular problem or meet their particular needs?

So, what are features, advantages, and benefits?

Features: Features are the distinctive characteristic or attributes of the solution you are proposing: your product, service, business, or idea. They are a means of providing advantages and benefits. Features are objective. They define what something is. For example, a cell phone's features might include screen size, battery life, camera resolution, or storage capacity (i.e., a 6.4-inch, 522-pixels-per-inch screen, 12-hour battery life, 12-megapixel camera, and 128 GB of storage).

Advantages: Advantages are what a feature does. They describe how your proposed solution will deliver benefits to the other party. Advantages tend to be factual and objective.

Advantages are useful for describing what differentiates your solution from the other alternatives.

Going back to the cell phone, advantages might include a larger, higher resolution screen for easier reading and streaming video, a longer battery life, a better camera resolution, and an increased storage capacity.

Benefits: Benefits are the outcomes or results the other party will receive by accepting your solution. Benefits tell the other party "What's in it for them." Benefits tell the other party why the advantages are valuable to them. In this way, benefits establish an emotional connection with the other party's needs and desires. Benefits focus on why your solution matters. Why does your solution improve the lives of the party/parties you want to influence and persuade?

> Returning to the cell phone example, benefits of a larger screen may include reduced eye strain, less scrolling, or easier reading. Benefits of a longer battery life include staying connected longer and not having to stop to charge your device. Benefits of a higher-resolution camera may include capturing life's precious moments in stunning clarity. Benefits of more storage may include having your music at your fingertips and/or never running out of space.

Think of features, advantages, and benefits as answering three simple questions: What, How, and Why. Features are what something is. Advantages describe how something gets done. And benefits detail why that is, or should be, important to you.

Accurately describing the advantages and benefits helps show you understand the other parties' wants and needs, and it helps them understand the value that your proposed solution brings to them.

The Features-Advantages-Benefits Matrix

If you have spent any time in marketing or sales, you may know about the features-benefits or the features-advantages-benefits (FAB) matrix, a commonly used tool with marketers and salespeople.

The FAB matrix helps you think about and plot which aspects of your pitch, whether it be a business pitch, a marketing message, or a sales pitch, that you should be focusing on in order to effectively sell your ideas.

To create your FAB matrix, list what you believe to be the most important feature of your proposed solution. Next to that feature, list the advantages. What does this feature do? And finally, list the benefits. Why is this important to the other party?

Then, go deeper. The first benefit statement you arrive at is unlikely to be the underlying problem your advantage is solving. To get to the underlying problem, ask, "Why?" Then repeat and repeat again. By the time you get to your fourth or fifth "Why," you may have found the heart of the problem and what the other party cares about most.

Repeat this process for the next most important feature until you have focused on the benefits of the top three to five features of your proposed solution.

FEATURES	ADVANTAGES	BENEFITS
6.5-inch, 522 pixels/ inch screen	Larger screen for easier reading and streaming	Reduces eye strain, you will not have to squint at tiny letters anymore
12-hour battery life	Longer battery life, made to last the whole day	Stay connected longer
12-megapixel front & rear cameras	Clearer photos and HD video	Capture life's precious moments in stunning clarity
128 GB storage	Stores more pictures and videos	Never run out of space for your memories
	Stores 1000s of songs	Always have your music at your fingertips

PRO TIP To make your message more persuasive, evoke emotion first, by reversing your FAB to address the risks associated with not using your product or service. In the cell phone example, this might be "Never run out of space for your music."

What's in It for You?

Though nearly all sales executives and salespeople know or have been told that they must focus on benefits rather than features, it is easier said than done. As a result, as part of many of our training engagements working with sales teams, we spend some time discussing this.

One of the exercises we like to run is having our trainees list all the aspects their organization offers and their client's value. Then we go through each one and ask them how much more does a client pay for that?

For each aspect the salespeople name, we use a whiteboard to list warranty to customer service to unique technology, whatever they list. Oddly, it always seems to add up to more than 100%. Then we go down the list and ask them three questions: "Of these, which is typically most important and valuable to a client?," "Why?," and "What does it do for them?" This process helps them understand that the warranty does not provide value; it is the risk mitigation in case their product fails, and the ROI tied to a longer-lasting product.

As simple as this exercise is, it always has a big impact. For example, we had a large filter manufacturing client that changed its emphasis on "better quality" to include an ROI calculator in their proposals that could determine, based on the potential clients' filter usage, how much money they would save by buying filters less often. This was a significant additional indirect cost savings from the labor of changing them and made the client rethink how it marketed and sold its products.

For one of the largest paint manufacturers and retailers in the world, we adjusted its sales team's focus toward benefits, such as how it is saving money, making money, or reducing hassle/risk for its clients. We started doing this 10 years ago and, to this day, it is still the way its sales organization pitches clients.

Both clients were global leaders run by experienced and high-performing sales management teams. They knew the importance of focusing on benefits; we just offered it in a way that was easy for their entire sales organizations to execute on a day-to-day basis and that made the difference.

Putting It All Together

Step 3: Demonstrating Logic

You have now learned how to demonstrate logic. Let us review the key aspects of demonstrating your logic and the tools you can use to do this more effectively.

Logical and Rational Decisions

The key components of demonstrating logic include the following:

Communicating Natural and Logical Consequences: The first step in demonstrating logic is communicating the natural and logical consequences of your proposed decision. Remember to use the If/When-Then-Because formula: ***If*** and ***when*** something happens- ***then*** something is expected- ***because*** of some set of natural or logical consequences.

Offering Social Proof: You can use social proof to strengthen the logic of your proposed solution. Whether the evidence is from the masses, from your peers, or from thought leaders and people you look up to, offering social proof offers credence to your "because" statement.

Offering Documented Proof: Another way you can strengthen the logic of your proposal is by offering documented proof. Documented proof could include affiliations, certifications, and awards. It could include market research, test results, statistical analysis, white papers, or case studies.

The Influencer's Toolbox

Frame: Context matters. Approach decision making with the framing effect in mind. Remember, when framing your arguments, people are risk averse and will give up a lot more to avoid losses than they will to seek potential gains. Also, the more vivid something is, the easier people will understand it, which is why metaphors are so powerful when used correctly.

Anchor: Whenever possible, take the initiative to set the first anchor. However, make sure to do your research and set the anchor within (or close to) each party's bargaining range. If the other party does set the anchor first, especially if the anchor is outside of the bargaining range, you may need to diffuse the anchor, provide more information, and offer a well-informed counter anchor.

Benefits Not Features: Avoid describing your solution by its features. Rather, focus on the advantages and benefits, the things the other party cares about.

5 Facilitating Action

"If you are not moving closer to what you want in sales (or in life), you probably aren't doing enough asking."
– *Jack Canfield,* Chicken Soup for the Soul

Now that you have laid the groundwork, you are ready to move on to the final step of the Four-Step Process of Influence and Persuasion: Facilitating Action. No matter how much groundwork you have laid, getting the other party to act, to do what you want, is often the hardest and scariest part. Without this last part, our efforts are not rewarded, not to mention no one likes to hear no. As a result, in this chapter, you will learn various tactics and tips to increase the likelihood that people follow through.

Facilitating Action

As we have noted throughout the book, influence and persuasion are involved in nearly every interaction we have with another person, such as when you are deciding which movie to see with a spouse, convincing your kids to go to bed, asking a colleague for help on a project, seeking additional budget from a boss, or making a presentation to a large audience. If you take a step back and review these examples, along with any others you can think of, you will see they are similar to sales. Yes, we said the dirty word: sales. We feel, as does Daniel Pink, in his book *To Sell Is Human*, that all of these influencing situations are you selling your ideas.[43] You are convincing the other party to buy your concept. Though many of you reading this book are not "in sales," you are, in fact, salespeople. Merely approaching these influencing situations as a sale will improve your performance. It will make you more aware of your objectives, empathic to the other party's needs, and strategic in the way you communicate. As such, in this chapter, we will approach the last step in this process not only as Facilitating Action or moving from conversation to commitment, but also as closing the deal, finishing the transaction, getting the yes, or other phrases we associate with sales.

Despite the thousands of books on sales and closing the deal, no secret exists to closing. The closest concept to a golden rule around this phase is that most of the work is done prior to the close. Think about how much ground we have covered before getting to this chapter. No magic words or special formulas work in every situation. The appropriate way to close is completely dependent on the context and the person you are pitching to.

Instead, closing takes an awareness of the context, asking the right questions, listening to the other parties, and understanding the desired outcomes and possible objections stopping them from deciding.

At some point, you will need to close, as uncomfortable as that may feel. Closing is consistently rated as one of the most difficult and avoided aspects of a sales process for a reason. Our hope is this book has armed you with enough tools and skills to make you more confident and effective when you close. If you have done most of the work prior to asking for approval or acceptance, it is that much easier to ask and more likely to be successful.

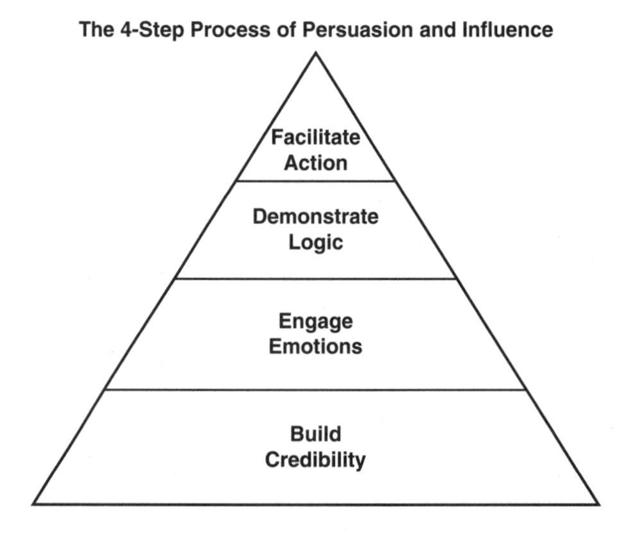

Figure 5.1

Keep in mind that while getting what you want is the desired outcome, you should have other objectives. One critical objective in almost every case is the satisfaction of the other party. A high-pressure, aggressive, or disingenuous approach might work once, but in a situation where you need to work with that person again, at what cost is this "win"?

GETTING UP . . . AND DOWN SUCCESSFULLY

In our training sessions, we frequently refer to what unfortunately often happens to Mt. Everest climbers. Climbers are often so focused on getting what they want, reaching the summit, that they do not pay enough attention to anything else. This "get to the top at all costs" mentality is understandable and natural because of how much work goes into the feat, the limited oxygen supply that negatively impacts cognitive abilities, and the "summit fever" that occurs; the closer the climbers get to the top, the more they want it and the more blinded they become to other areas.

In negotiation, we call this "deal fever." We often see where people are less likely to back out of a deal even if it is clearly a bad one, if they have invested a lot of time and effort into the negotiation. We also see it in poker where decisions should be made based on the probability to win and the amount in the pot, but people are often influenced by how much they have put into the pot themselves. Not folding a hand because one has invested a lot, in poker, is called being pot committed. The best decision makers evaluate a deal based on the future, not the past. Like a climber on Everest, it takes tremendous discipline to walk away from a deal when you have invested so much.

These examples show the dangers of focusing only on what you want and not thinking about anything else. From an influencing standpoint, this serves as a reminder to set the goal not only as getting what you want but also coming away with an improved relationship with the other people involved, which is a result of the outcome and process.

Types of Closes

Closes can be classified into two major categories: soft closes and hard closes. Soft closes are used to elicit information and gather the other party's opinion during the closing process. Hard closes are more direct and ask for a decision in one manner or another.

Choosing the right type of close, at the right time, can make all the difference. The type of deal, the person(s) with whom you are negotiating, and where you are in the process can determine which methods to employ. We will discuss the most popular types of asks/closes, in order of where you are in the negotiating process and your level of assurance you are both on the same page.

Soft Closes: Asking Questions to Yes

So, what is a soft close? In a soft close, you are not asking for any type of commitment; rather, you are asking low-impact (preferably open-ended) questions that will lead you to a close as in these examples:

"How do you feel about what we have discussed so far?"

"Does this sound like something that could work for your organization?"

"Where would you like to go from here?"

Using the soft close has many benefits. Soft closes help you to gather information, understand and overcome objections, and let you know where you are in the closing process and when to ask for the close.

Soft closes should feel natural and be more conversational. At this point, there is no pressure to make a decision, but asking questions about how the other party thinks or feels allows you to identify the objectives and uncover any objections early on and begin to overcome them.

Depending on the answers you receive during the soft close, you may have some more persuading to do or you may lead them directly into a trial close or hard close.

The 70/30 Rule

Practicing the art of persuasion involves asking the right questions and listening as much as it does speaking and wanting to influence and persuade. When you listen, you learn what you need to do to make your argument and overcome objections. In the wise words of the ancient Greek philosopher Epictetus, "We have two ears and one mouth so that we can listen twice as much as we speak."

The 70/30 rule suggests that effective communication requires active listening, and that good communicators tend to spend 70%

of the time listening while they are spend 30% of the time speaking. Asking the right questions and listening shows you want to understand the wants and needs of the other parties, and you care about their best interests.

The lesson here is simple: To be more effective at influence and persuasion, be a more effective communicator. To be a more effective communicator, learn to listen more than you speak.

Benefits and Opportunities of the Soft Close

Another benefit of the soft closes is they open the other parties' minds to your proposed request or solution. A great way to do this is by asking "if" questions, as in this example:

> *"If I can show you how we can help you save at least 10 percent of what you are paying now, would you be interested in learning more?"*

When you ask if questions, you are asking other parties to imagine your request or solution, and this helps them to begin to feel like they have agreed to (or own) your solution.

You have many opportunities where you can employ soft closes during the persuasion process. Think of soft closes not as what you do at the end but what continues to advance the sale of your idea, product, or service. These types of closes are most appropriate when you have highlighted something valuable within your solution (think advantages and benefits) or have overcome an objection.

Soft closes, which often include questions that fall in the spectrum from very soft (e.g., "Would you be interested in learning more?") to more direct (e.g., "Is there anything holding you back from moving forward with us?"). These questions will lead us in the continuum to hard closes.

Though we use soft close to describe these types of closes, you can differentiate between those at the softer end of the spectrum, the question close, and those closer to hard closes, the trial close, as each are useful at differing points in the closing process.

The Question Close

One type of close that may be used to gauge the interest of other parties and probe for more information is the question close. The question close is a soft close that asks the other parties' thoughts, opinions, and feelings. This type of close allows you to gather information, learning more about the other person's wants and needs, as in these examples:

"What do you think about what we have discussed so far?"

"In your opinion, does what I have described sound like it would solve your biggest problem(s) in that area?"

"Do you have any concerns or questions about what we have talked about today?"

The question close provides an opportunity for other parties to state their objectives and what is holding them back from saying yes. Uncovering the other parties' objectives and objections allows you to tailor the rest of your pitch to highlight their most important objectives and overcome any objections

The great thing about the question close is you do not have to wait until the end of your pitch to use it. You can use it at nearly any point in the closing process, and it is a great way to test the waters.

The Trial Close

Another type of soft close is the trial close. Similar to the question close, the trial close is also meant to solicit information to get you to the close. However, unlike the question close, the trial close asks for a decision and may present an opportunity to close, as in these examples:

"What direction would you like to go from here?"

"Is there anything holding you back from getting started today?"

"Is there anything stopping you from X today?"

The best time for a trial close is when you have come to the end of your pitch but may be unsure about how other parties are leaning. This allows you to ask a low-impact question to gauge whether other parties are ready to close or not.

These questions ask for a route to close or for a better understanding of why other parties are not ready to make a decision, highlighting any remaining objections. The other parties' responses to these questions let you know if they are ready to close or if you have more work to do to convince them.

PRO TIP You can soften the close even more by soliciting opinions. Asking for an opinion conveys you care about the other parties' best interests and have a desire to understand them.

By adding the phrase "*In your opinion*" to the beginning of your question, you encourage people to speak more freely and provide more honest answers. Why? Because asking a question seeking an objective answer infers a right or a wrong answer, whereas opinions are more subjective, eliciting what the other parties believe.

The Virtual Soft Close

In 2020, thanks to COVID, we have more than ever worked with clients as they transitioned their sales teams to sell remotely. We have armed organizations of all shapes and sizes with tools, resources, and skills to improve how they built relationships, executed deeper discoveries of the other side, positioned and differentiated, and ultimately closed the deal.

We have found two soft closing questions to be most effective when virtual selling:

1. How will you describe this internally? It is not a true closing question but asking this in the last presentation and having other parties sell you is highly impactful. If they pitch it back to you in a persuasive manner, then you will know they got the most important points and will position you well internally. If not, it gives you a chance to make a few adjustments and focus on the areas they may have missed. In addition to making sure clients are clear on your value proposition, you can coach them on how to sell this to their boss, committee, or peers. Often, the people you are selling to are advocates and they, in turn, need to sell someone else to sign off on your proposal.
2. What are the reasons you would not move forward with us? If asked sensitively, this can be impactful. It needs to be done in a way that potential clients feel comfortable answering honestly. If you can achieve this, they will tell you the biggest barrier(s) to the sale. This gives you the opportunity to address the barriers so they clients do not leave with doubts. Hard to beat the opportunity, especially in a virtual world!

Hard Closes: Making the Ask

Hard closes are direct. They are closing questions that ask for a commitment to your proposed solution. They require a decision, typically yes or no, or they present a question that, if answered, implies an agreement has been reached.

Hard closes may be viewed as assertive or even aggressive.

Various types of hard closes exist. Here is an overview of the most common along with pros and cons of using each.

The Summary Close

The summary close is a type of close that reiterates the value of your proposed solution. The summary close combines a summary of the advantages and benefits discussed with a direct ask for the business at the end as in these examples:

> *"To recap, you had mentioned that saving cost and time to implementation were important. With this proposal, we have managed to save you five percent and have it implemented more quickly than anybody else. Did I miss anything or based on this and should I send over a copy of the agreement for you to review?"*

> *"As we discussed, if you make a decision this week you will receive free delivery, and we can include free setup and training. Would you like to go ahead and get this set up?"*

The summary close can be useful in situations when the persuasion process has been long because it reiterates the value, when there are a lot of competing priorities – to bring focus to key areas, or when it is a complex decision to make it easier to say yes.

The Direct Close

The direct close is the most straightforward way of asking for a commitment to your proposed solution. A direct close asks other parties to comply with your request or proposal, as in these examples:

> *"Can I ask you to commit to hiring a new member to my team?"*

> *"Can I go ahead and place your order?"*

As you can see, when you use the direct close, you ask for a yes or no. Therefore, only use the direct close when you are confident the answer will be yes and/or if you are looking to convey a high level of confidence. It can come off as aggressive so must be used carefully.

The Urgency Close

The urgency close is a higher-pressure closing technique that presents your solution with a sense of urgency.

Urgency is typically associated with a limited time to act or a limited supply. The urgency close often draws on fear, specifically the fear of missing out (FOMO).

The urgency close works especially well when coupled with a limited-time offer, freebie, or discount, as in this example:

> *"We even have a 25 percent discount for customers who sign up this week."*

Urgency closes work best in situations where you believe the other parties are close to deciding but need a little nudge or when you think that if some action is not taken soon, momentum will be lost. Though most people feel this is an aggressive type of close, it can be adjusted to not feel this way, as in this example:

> *"I understand this is a large budget increase I am requesting. If we do not complete this proposed project this year we will be okay; however, if we complete it prior to the end of next month we have a chance of. . . ."*

Note how the example takes a lot of the pressure off but still leaves the value of moving quickly, which makes the urgency close effective.

The Assumed Close

An assumed close involves acting as if the other party has decided to agree to your request or proposal. Talking about the deal as if it *is* going to close. In doing so, when you use the assumed close, you ask a question that, when answered without questions or objections, acts as a commitment to action.

The assumed close is best to use in situations where you are confident you have won the other parties over. However, even if the assumed close leads to questions or objections, all is not lost. Remember, objections are likely to be raised throughout the closing process. Your goal is to assuage and overcome any objections, instilling the other parties' confidence in the decision, and getting back to a close, as in these examples:

> *"We are really looking forward to doing business with you. When would you like to get started?"*
>
> *"Can you have this project done by next Friday?"*
>
> *"Would you like to move forward with the basic, standard, or professional plan?"*

The third example is a deviation of the assumed close whereby you assume other parties are moving forward but you provide them with options. This is a common style because it leverages the assumptive aspect of the close with the feeling of control for other parties. We will cover the value of providing options extensively later in this chapter.

Creating a Sense of Urgency

What is urgency? At its core, urgency is a feeling that something is important and demands your immediate attention or action, whether it be a dangerous situation, limited time to make a decision, or limited availability.

Urgency draws on fear, which we know is an emotion that acts as a strong motivator.

You can create a sense of urgency in many ways. As you learned when we discussed the urgency close, limiting the amount of time to make a decision makes a decision more urgent. We know that limiting the time to make a decision or the number of available products, services, and solutions that are available creates a sense of scarcity. When something is scarce, it is perceived to be valuable and triggers that human need to avoid losses: FOMO.

Another way you can create a sense of urgency is to offer an incentive attached to making a decision sooner rather than later. In other words, urgency can come in the form of needing to move quickly to avoid risk, hassle, and loss or to achieve additional benefit.

However, the urgency you create must be real. When others perceive you are creating a false sense of urgency, they will see you as manipulative, and you risk losing credibility and trust. The most common example of this is when someone provides a deadline, the other person does not act within that time frame, followed by the person using the same approach with a new deadline. How has this impacted your credibility? Though this situation can occur and be genuine, avoid the credibility loss by walking the other party through what will happen if the deadline is not met rather than offering an ultimatum you need to go back on.

Tips for creating urgency are the following:

- Urgency is most powerful when it is consistent and perceived to be real.
- Keep the focus on the problem(s) that your solution solves.
- Offer a reason or enticement for acting quickly.

The best way to improve performance in this area is to experience it and see it from both sides. So, try this mental exercise. Think about a high-dollar purchase you have made and your sales experience. What was the closing process like? Consider the following questions:

- What type or types of closes did the salesperson use?
- What questions did they ask you?
- Did they lead you through a trial close or question close to drive you toward the sale?
- Did they create a sense of urgency?
- At what point in the process did you know that you were going to make a purchase?

After the Close

After people agree to move forward, your job is not done. Follow up and confirm the key elements of the solution you have agreed to, including time lines for any required action steps.

Once you do move forward, do not celebrate and move on. Make sure that you hold up your end of the agreement and keep the other parties accountable. Remember the Everest story. Your objective is to have people do what you want them to do AND feel good about it.

Finally, review the situation, give yourself feedback, and ask for feedback. The most persuasive people are constantly fine-tuning the way they communicate. This means reviewing what went well as well as what you could have improved in situations where you succeeded and failed.

Test Your Knowledge

Match the type of close on the left with the best example from closes on the right.

1. Question Close ________	a. "Are you ready to make this purchase today?"
2. Trial Close ________	b. "If we move forward with my suggested method, we should see 15% increases in efficiency within our supply chain almost immediately and a sustained 40% reduction in human errors due to automation. Can I go ahead and assign a project manager?"
3. Summary Close ________	c. "How quickly would you like us to get started?"
4. Urgency Close ________	d. "In your opinion, is there any reason that our solution isn't a fit for your company?"
5. Question Close ________	e. "If we sign the contract by the end of the week, we can get started on Monday. Should I get the paperwork started?"
6. Assumed Close ________	f. "What are your thoughts on what we have discussed so far?"

The Influencer's Toolbox

Getting the Small Yes

People prefer to be consistent with their previous decisions. You can turn this fact into a quick and effective tactic to leverage to influence people.

In psychology, this is recognized as the commitment and consistency bias. According to the commitment and consistency bias, once we make a commitment, we are compelled to act in consistency with this commitment. In other words, we have a strong desire to remain consistent with what we have said and done.

One way to use this knowledge is by priming people with agreement, (i.e., getting them to say yes).

Small yesses build goodwill.

Small yesses trigger feelings of reciprocity.

Thus, once you begin eliciting small yesses, people are more likely to continue saying yes.

The process begins by asking questions designed to elicit yes responses. The best questions are those that are not completely trivial but for which the answer is highly likely to be yes.

Then, you can begin reinforcing yesses, ideally bringing them closer to the decision context, such as "If I could show you how I can save your company 10 percent on these services, is that something you'd be interested in learning more about?" A yes to this question makes it more likely to get a yes to "Could we schedule another call with your team to show them the platform?" Which then ultimately leads you closer to the final yes.

Use this knowledge of priming for yes to come up with some yes questions for the following scenario.

You are charged with standing on the street and getting people to answer a brief poll. You and a group of 20 other people go out for several days to collect responses. However, only about 29% of people agree to help when you ask, "Would you like to participate in a marketing study?"

Your boss is disappointed by the low number of responses and tasks you with increasing your team's response rate. He asks you for ideas. Drawing on what you have just learned about getting the small yes, what would you suggest?

Go ahead and fill in at least two ideas for yes questions or lines of yes questions before continuing on to read about how one researcher developed and tested a solution.

____

____

____

To test his theories on eliciting small yesses, famed researcher and author Robert B. Cialdini conducted a set of experiments involving these same conditions. In Cialdini's experiment, when asking passersby "Would you like to participate in a marketing study?," he and his team received a rather low response rate of 29%.

Cialdini and his team then primed for agreement (and helpfulness) by asking "Do you consider yourself a helpful person?" prior to asking "Would you like to participate in a marketing study?"

After all, what kind of person would be helpful but not participate in a marketing study?

Priming did have a huge impact because the question above increased the responses to 77.3%.[44]

How can you use this in everyday influencing situations?

Have you ever asked people "Can I interrupt you?" before jumping in and interrupting them? Have people asked you this? Who could say "no," especially when you already have?

Leaders use higher-level and more subtle versions of this tactic all the time. Think of the executive who asks her direct report if he is ready to lead a project. Few people would say no, and the mere answering yes makes it more likely that they will follow through and do a great job on the project.

Tips to get to the Big Yes:

- Start with questions that are likely to elicit a yes.
- Lead your yes questions closer to the decision context.
- Look for meaningful yesses.
- Do not act pushy or force yesses.

Evidence from Decision Makers: Small Yesses

To test Cialdini's theory and differentiate between the priming of a character trait (helpfulness) as opposed to the priming of agreement, in our research we asked participants to answer one of two sets of questions meant to prime them with small yes or no responses. We asked participants in the first group a series of questions meant to elicit a small yes: "*Do you consider yourself to be a helpful person?*"

Participants in the second group were asked a series of questions meant to elicit a no: "*Do you consider yourself to be an unhelpful person?*"

Participants in both groups were then asked, "*Would you be willing to provide additional feedback after the survey?*"

Not surprisingly, we found that, among participants in our study, people primed with a yes were 23% more likely to agree to provide additional feedback compared to those primed with a no. Priming for agreeableness helps. However, a new finding showed those that said they were unhelpful were 15% more likely to provide feedback.

Now it gets interesting. Though the majority of decision makers in our study told us they were helpful (or told us they were not unhelpful), 72% of those who told us they were helpful agreed to provide additional feedback and 85% of those who told us they were unhelpful. In other words, those who told us they were helpful were less inclined to provide additional help than those who told us they were not.

What does this mean? Priming and/or getting small yesses does increase your chances of additional yesses; however, getting people to admit something they are not proud of may have a more powerful impact on getting those people to take that same action.

IF YOU BUILD IT, THEY WILL SAY YES

I was working with our late partner, Charles "Chip" Tames, a few years ago in Canada, with one of the big four accounting firms. We were training a group of advisory partners in an advanced negotiation training session.

We created a few custom roleplays, videotaped each one of the groups roleplaying with us, and coached them on what they did and said.

One of the roleplays had a semi-confrontational edge to it where I played an upset client. I showed some signals of wanting to move forward but showed clear frustration. I was surprised by the price and needed to make some changes to the scope, and I was evidently under some personal pressure.

As we ran through all nine partners, only one of them started with what we agreed on. She asked if I thought the team would do a good job, if I liked the team we had been working with, if I could trust it would do the job on time, etc. Before I knew it, I was saying quite a few yesses and telling her why I thought it was a good fit for the project, rather than having her convincing me. Soon, it led us, with a positive and collaborative energy, to the issues at hand. All of the other partners started with the issues at hand, price and scope, and as one would expect, the tone of the conversations differed.

At the end of the day, we reconvened as a group. With permission, I showed a few samples to the groups, and they were floored by how many different ways the same conversation could go and how much control they had over it.

Starting with points of agreement gets you small yesses, builds wins, and generates momentum. Otherwise, you start with points of disagreement and the feeling of the conversation is divisive rather than collaborative.

That day, all the groups learned that lesson. It worked out well for us because one of the partners shared the impact with the rest of his/her office, and Chip and I went to Canada five more times that summer to train a host of other partners of the firm.

Providing Options

As we discussed in the various close styles, a great tool for facilitating action is to provide options. People value the ability to make choices. They want to feel as if they are making their own decisions. Thus, providing options allows others to feel independent and in control yet forces them to choose from options you find acceptable.

What happens when you provide only one option? Research suggests that when people are presented with one option, it triggers the desire to search for additional options, which makes them less likely to make any decision at all. This has become known as single option aversion.

In one study, Tulane University researcher Dr. Daniel Mochon examined the effects of providing only one alternative. In his study, Mochon divided participants up into three groups and asked them to make purchasing decisions regarding DVD players. One group was provided with a single option: to purchase or not purchase a Sony DVD player. The second group was provided with a sole option: to purchase or not purchase a Philips DVD player. The third group was presented with three options: to purchase a Sony DVD player, purchase a Philips DVD player, or not to make a purchase.

Though 9% of the first group and 10% of the second group chose to purchase the DVD player, 66% of participants in the third group chose to purchase one of the two DVD players, an increase of more than 600%.[45]

What is more, research has found that even the illusion of an option compels people to make a decision. That is right. The second option may not even have to be real.

However, there is a paradox associated with choice. Even though too few options are likely to leave us feeling dissatisfied, we are likely to become overwhelmed with too many options.

We need time and energy to evaluate and compare alternatives. When we are faced with too many options, our brains cannot calculate and compare all the alternatives.

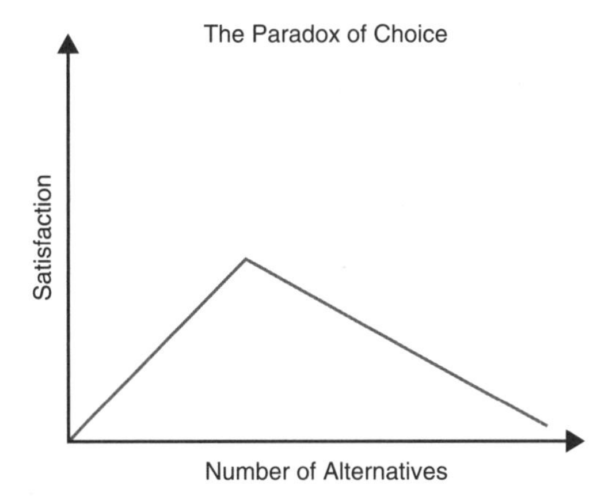

Figure 5.2

So, how many options are too many options? It depends on the complexity of the decision and how the options are narrowed and presented.

Costco Offers More Than Delicious Free Samples

I think I speak on behalf of all three authors when I say I love Costco.

What you did not know is that it usually carries approximately 4,000 different products in its stores; a typical grocery store will carry 50,000 (12 times more) and a Walmart as many as 100,000 (24 times more). Costco does this for two main reasons:

1. Costco does not want to overwhelm you, the consumer, with choice. Fewer options make deciding easier, which has proven to translate into higher sales.
2. Costco wants to focus and ensure its stock is consistent so customers will be more likely to have what they want and come to the store for availability.

In one classic study by Columbia Business School professor Dr. Sheena Iyengar, author of the best-selling book *The Art of Choosing*, she showed the effects of providing too many options. To test the influence of many options on decision making, Dr. Iyengar set up a tasting booth of Wilkin & Sons jams in a California supermarket where, every couple of hours, they swapped between offering 6 varieties of jam to offering 24 varieties.

She found that the larger variety of jams attracted more interest (i.e., 60% of customers entering the store visited the tasting booth when the larger assortment was on display compared with 40% for the smaller assortment). Still, it did not make the decision process easier. Though 30% of people who taste-tested from the smaller assortment purchased a jar of jam, 3% of those who were presented with the larger assortment made a purchase.[46]

This occurred because of a psychological factor called information overload or "analysis paralysis." When people face so many choices or options, decision making becomes difficult, and they are often unable or unwilling to decide.

Research indicates that three to five choices is optimal; fewer choices is not enough, and more than this many choices quickly overwhelms the decision maker.

Evidence from Decision Makers: Choices

We again turn to decision makers to examine how they view choices. We asked decision makers in our study to tell us their ideal number of choices to choose from when making a number of different decisions. We then asked them how many choices they believed would overwhelm them when faced with the same decisions.

According to the decision makers in our study, for most decisions, 5 to 6 choices are ideal. However, they also reported that more than 8 to 10 choices would overwhelm them. The complexity of the decision seems to matter. For more complex decisions such as choosing among job offers, decision makers prefer fewer choices (with an average ideal number of choices of 5.11) and are overwhelmed more easily (at 8.52 choices); for somewhat simpler decisions, such as purchasing a cell phone, these same decision makers prefer slightly more choices (5.95) and can handle a higher number of choices before becoming overwhelmed (10.73).

It is also important to remember that the appeal of more choices may not equate to more decisions being made. As we saw in the jam experiment, the larger assortment of jams drew more customers to the tasting booth, yet fewer purchased a bottle of jam.

From a practical perspective, if you offer more options, you give yourself a better chance of matching the wants and needs of the other parties; if you provide too many, the burden is on the other parties, which can create friction for a decision and make the decision difficult. So, how do you decide how many choices? As our research and study finds, we suggest between three and five, based on the other parties' willingness to participate in the decision and the impact of the decision on them.

The Architecture of Choices

Another important element in providing options is the architecture of how choices are presented. The architecture of choices involves the number of choices presented, how choices are framed, and the default choice presented.

The term "choice architecture" was coined by Richard Thaler and Cass Sunstein in their book *Nudge: Improving Decisions About Health, Wealth, and Happiness*. The idea behind choice architecture is that one can organize the context in which others make decisions. It allows you to present choices in a way that makes it more likely decision makers will make a choice and their choice will be the one you believe they should make.

One important aspect of choice architecture is how choices are framed. In Thaler and Sunstein's book, one of the ways they suggest to nudge people toward a decision is to focus on incentives. We take this a step further and encourage you to focus on the most compelling benefits that create the most value for the other party.

Another important aspect of choice architecture is setting the default choice. The default choice indicates to others what is the expected thing to do (i.e., what is normal).[47]

One popular example of the power of the default is how different countries manage organ donation. In the United States, more than 100,000 people are on the organ donation list, and an average of 20 people die per day waiting for an organ. About 15% of the population are organ donors; however, some countries do not have this shortage of donated organs.

How do they do it? They change the default option. In the United States, organ donation is managed by an opt-in system. With opt-in systems, people must choose to sign up to allow their organs to be donated upon their death. However, many countries, including Australia and most of Europe, have changed their default option. In these countries, you are automatically included in your country's organ donation program and must actively opt out if you do not wish to have your organs be eligible for donation upon your death. The results? More than 90% of people remain registered as organ donors. A 600% increase over the United States. The default matters.

How is this used in everyday life? Think about the dramatic growth in the ongoing income model for software giants, such as Salesforce, Netflix, Microsoft, and Adobe. For instance, with Netflix, you sign up once, and the default is that your subscription will automatically renew. Equally, think about how many monthly retail businesses exist, from shaving products with Dollar Shave Club to food with Blue Apron to socks with Foot Cardigan. Why are they so successful? Brilliant choice architecture: one decision equals recurring income for them. The default is for them to keep delivering the product or service and for the customers to continue paying.

PROVIDING OPTIONS?

How do you persuade people to make the choice that you want them to make? It often is the result of the questions you ask and the plan you have. Our partner, Chip Tames, who died in February of 2018, will long be remembered as a thoughtful individual and world-class facilitator. He also will be remembered for having a few tricks up his sleeve, such as his ability to lead folks through a progression to have them arrive where he wanted them. It often would go something like this:

CHIP: May we discuss a deck of cards?
PARTICIPANT: Sure.
CHIP: How many cards are in a standard deck of cards?
PARTICIPANT: With or without jokers?
CHIP: Either is okay, but for simplicity sake, let us say without.
PARTICIPANT: Fifty-two.
CHIP: I think that is right. They are broken into four distinct units. Can you please name them?
PARTICIPANT: Hearts, Diamonds, Spades, and Clubs.
CHIP: That is right. And could you select two of the suits and name them?
PARTICIPANT: Hearts and Diamonds.
CHIP: Perfect. You could have gone either way, but you chose the Reds. Hearts and Diamonds. We have narrowed it down, essentially cutting the deck in half. There are how many remaining cards?
PARTICIPANT: Twenty-six.

CHIP:	That is right. Twenty-six. So, once again, I would like you to name a suit, either Diamonds or Hearts. Tell me your choice, please.
PARTICIPANT:	Hearts.
CHIP:	Perfect and that leaves which suit remaining?
PARTICIPANT:	Diamonds.
CHIP:	That is right. And what color is it?
PARTICIPANT:	Red.
CHIP:	That is right. And how many of the red Diamonds remain?
PARTICIPANT:	Thirteen.
CHIP:	Correct. You are doing great. Thirteen remain. And what color are they?
PARTICIPANT:	Still red.
CHIP:	That is right; they are still red. And if you split them into two groups, number cards and Face cards including the Ace, I would again like you to make a verbal selection: Numbers cards or Face cards?
PARTICIPANT:	Face cards.
CHIP:	Perfect. How many Face cards are there, and can you name them please?
PARTICIPANT:	Four. Ace, King, Queen, and Jack.
CHIP:	All still red?
PARTICIPANT:	Yes.
CHIP:	Perfect. Select any two face cards and tell me which they are?
PARTICIPANT:	Ace and King.
CHIP:	And that leaves which two?
PARTICIPANT:	That leaves the Jack and the Queen.
CHIP:	Of which suit?
PARTICIPANT:	Diamonds.
CHIP:	Right. The Jack of Diamonds and the Queen of Diamonds. Both are still red, right?
PARTICIPANT:	Right.
CHIP:	One last time, I would like for you to make one last selection. Please name the Jack or the Queen.
PARTICIPANT:	Jack.
CHIP:	Jack of Diamonds?
PARTICIPANT:	Right.

Then, with a flourish, Chip would reveal that he had written only one card prior to starting the conversation, and it was the Jack of Diamonds. He would turn the page of the flip chart and sure enough the flip chart had a drawing of a card and "Jack of Diamonds" written across the top.

Now, I can tell you the conversation did not always go like the one above, but 100% of the time, Chip and the participant arrived at the Jack of Diamonds. Many of you saw immediately what was going on, but I can tell you the participant involved never did. What you may have realized or will see if you review the conversation is that Chip had a specific chain of questions and statements and he had practiced it many times.

If they chose Diamonds, he said, "That's right and what color are they?" He asked about the color to distract the respondents. If they said Hearts, he said, "And that leaves what suit?" "Diamonds?" "Exactly and what color are they?" He was an expert at forcing people to focus on the card he wanted. He created the illusion of free choice, but they were always going the direction he wanted.

Creating a Safety Net

In the early 1900s, building bridges was dangerous work. Falling objects or a gust of wind had the potential to send workers falling to their death. During the building of the San Francisco–Oakland Bay Bridge, 24 workers died from accidents working on the bridge. So, Joseph Strauss, the architect in charge of building the Golden Gate Bridge, prioritized safety on his project. Built around the same time as the Bay Bridge, Strauss believed he "had the idea we could cheat death by providing every known safety device for workers" on the Golden Gate Bridge project.

One of these more revolutionary safety devices employed in the project was to install a safety net under the entire bridge. This was one of the most sophisticated safety devices ever installed on a construction site. Many thought it would keep them safe. And it did. Nineteen men fell off the bridge and into the safety net, saving the lives of each. What they did not realize is it would boost employee morale and they would work more effectively because they could focus on their work rather than not falling because that used to mean they would fall to their death. In fact, they worked so effectively that they completed the bridge ahead of schedule and $1.3 million dollars under budget.

You can do the same thing in your influencing. Creating a safety net is a great way to overcome objections. By providing a safety net, you draw on humans' natural tendency toward risk aversion. By reducing their risk, you help other parties feel more confident in their decision.

Safety nets can come in many forms, from trial periods to money-back guarantees and hassle-free returns and from extended warranties to opt-out opportunities.

Offering a safety net signals you are trustworthy and you stand behind your word. Providing a safety net also increases the other parties' satisfaction and reduces the likelihood of buyer's remorse, the feeling of regret after making a decision. Though buyer's remorse is ingrained in many big decisions, reducing this as much as possible is important to preserve credibility and reputation. The next time you want to influence people, provide them a safety net so they feel more confident in their decisions.

Putting It All Together

Step 4: Facilitating Action

You have now learned how to facilitate your intended action and close the deal. Let us review the key components of getting to a yes along with the tips and tricks you can use to get to yes more easily.

Closing the Deal

The key components of facilitating action include the following:

The Closing Process: Closing can be broken down into five key steps:

1. Lay the groundwork.
2. Understand possible outcomes.
3. Overcome any objections.
4. Create a sense of urgency.
5. Ask.

Soft Closes: Although not exactly closes, soft closes ask low-impact (preferably open-ended) questions to gather information, understand and overcome objections, and let you know where you are in the closing process.

Hard Closes: At some point, you have to ask. Hard closes directly or indirectly ask for a decision. Many direct and indirect ways exist to ask for a close, including summary closes, direct closes, and assumptive closes. Just remember, if you can create a sense of urgency with any of these closes, you will be even more likely to get to a yes.

The Influencer's Toolbox

Get the Small Yes: Get the other party into an agreement mindset by eliciting yesses. Start with questions for which you know the answer will be a yes. Then lead the questions closer to the relevance of your pitch and close.

Provide Options: People want to make their own decisions and feel in control. Providing choices, or at least the illusion of choice, is another great facilitator of action. We recommend three to five choices to be ideal, with the middle option the default (i.e., the one you most want them to choose).

Create a Safety Net: Reduce the risk behind a decision by providing a safety net. Consider how you can add safety nets, such as guarantees, warranties, and opt-out clauses to your next pitch. By creating a safety net, you will reduce the chances of buyer's remorse, which may sour the trust in the relationship.

6 Time and Place

"After hard work, the biggest determinant is being in the right place at the right time."

– Michael Bloomberg, businessperson, politician, and philanthropist

In addition to Ethos, Pathos, and Logos, Aristotle discussed one more element overlapping the principles of rhetorical persuasion: Kairos, or the opportune moment. Kairos is the time and place when conditions are right to persuade. The context in which you deliver your argument. The when and the where.

The When and the Where

The concept of kairos underlies each step of the influence process. From the order of the process, to the communication medium, to evoking the right emotions at the right time, to the right time to make the ask, the principles of kairos have been evident throughout.

According to famed rhetorical theorist Dr. James Kinneavy, kairos is "the appropriateness of the discourse to the particular circumstances of the time, place, speaker, and audience involved."[48]

Consider Dr. Martin Luther King Jr.'s famous "I Have a Dream" speech. Did you know he gave nearly identical speeches at least twice before? Prior to delivering his "I Have a Dream" speech in Washington D.C. in August of 1963, Dr. King delivered dream speeches, with large portions nearly identical, at Booker T. Washington High School in Rocky Mount, North Carolina, in November 1962 and at the Great Walk to Freedom march in Detroit in June 1963.

So, why was Dr. King's D.C. speech so powerful? Well, Dr. King had practiced delivering his speech several times, the where (at the foot of the Lincoln Memorial in Washington D.C.), the when (during the March on Washington for Jobs and Freedom, which also corresponded with the 100-year anniversary celebration of the Emancipation Proclamation), and the who (the more than 250,000 supporters of the civil rights movement) were all opportune.

Another great example of the influence of time, place, and audience is late-night comedy programs like *The Late Show* and *Saturday Night Live*. They take that day's and week's news and make fun of it. The timing is perfect, and it is late at night when people are tired. When you are tired, your brain is tired, and its processing is slowed, your inhibitions lifted, and you are apt to find things funnier.

The show's place is great: in front of a live studio audience, who are often cued to laugh. The producers leverage this, often panning the audience to show they are laughing, which makes it more likely you will laugh along at home (remember social proof from earlier). The audience laughter tells you what you are watching is funny and that laughing is okay, even recommended. How important are these social cues? In lieu of live studio audiences during the pandemic, some late-night shows have added a laugh track, a technique used in comedies and sitcoms since the 1950s used to prime the audience to laugh. Late-night comedy takes advantage of the impact of kairos: the time, place, and audience to make their entertainment more appealing.

The Right Time

Timing can be everything. As you have learned, the four fundamental steps in the process build upon each other and need to be employed in a particular order. You must first build credibility and engage emotion because to demonstrate logic and facilitate action, you must be credible and able to connect with individuals to influence and persuade.

One of the first things you need to consider is if your argument is relevant to the time and situation. What are the norms? How are people feeling at that time? What is their mood like?

Take for example, the commercial by Pampers during the 2019 Super Bowl. The Pampers ad featured dads changing diapers, a nod to the changing times. But these were not any dads. These were John Legend and Andy Levine, whose band happened to be playing the

Super Bowl Halftime Show. The ad was relevant for the times and the occasion.

Another consideration of time is urgency. Is there a deadline? Have you created an advantage to or need to act now?

In the previous chapter, we discussed the influence of urgency. Attaching time considerations to proposals creates a sense of urgency. Time considerations instill the need to act now. Think of the timers on infomercials or online sales like the Deal of the Day. Think of "Don't miss out" or "You better act now."

How impactful is timing? Well, in one example, we covered the Linda problem in Chapter 3. Would you be surprised to know that answers changed with the time of day? Research indicates we are sharper in the morning and more creative at night. This is supported by studies on how corporate communication is received by analysts and investors, judges making decisions on cases, students perform in standardized tests, doctors and nurses taking care of patients, and aggregate twitter language. We are more positive, careful, thoughtful, and less likely to make mistakes in the morning. Keep this in mind when you are solving a problem for yourself or are matching this timing to the influencing strategy you are pursuing. If you are persuading someone to complete a creative task, save it for the late afternoon or evening if possible. However, if you are working through something complex and/or analytical, consider communicating the message during the mid-morning. Perhaps the only time that should be avoided is lunch time. Just ask the prisoners who had nearly 0% chance of getting parole shortly before lunch, only to see their early morning and after lunch peers have a probability of approximately 65%.[49]

If you absolutely cannot avoid optimal timing, then consider implementing a time-out. For long situations, multiple pauses are helpful, especially a pause before key information is provided or a critical decision is made. Other forms of leveraging this concept include taking a lunch break outside or at least not at your desk, going for a walk, or as we wrote previously, listening to your favorite music before a big presentation or test, rather than cramming until the last minute.

These are all examples of timing in a micro context. On a more macro scale, humans tend to be more motivated at the beginning of a pursuit by our progress, but as we near the end, we transition to become more motivated by reaching the end. So, for example, if you were motivating your team to complete a three-month project, during the first two months you might focus on what you have been able to accomplish; however, in the final month, you could spend more time focusing instead on how close the project is to completion and how much of an impact it will have.

The Forgetting Curve

Another consideration related to time is memory. According to what we know about memory and the theory of the forgetting curve, memory, meaning retention, reduces with time. The longer it has been since you have been presented with information, the less you will remember it.

Of course, the complexity and amount of information matter to how long it will be retained. However, for complex, long, and drawn-out instances of rhetoric, information is likely to be lost before recall or decisions.

We have provided you with several tools to overcome the forgetting curve. One way to do this is to employ the summary close. In the summary close, you review the key benefits of your request or proposal.

To make what you say more memorable, you can also make it emotional. We are more likely to remember things we connect with emotionally. Better yet, you can use stories. Stories connect with emotion and are far more memorable than facts and figures. You should also

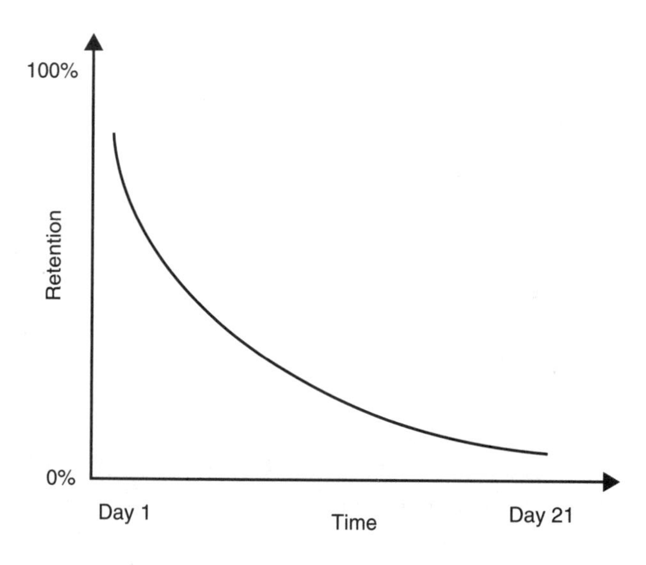

Figure 6.1

focus on advantages and benefits of whatever you are pitching, to address what your audience cares about.

The Right Place

Choose the location in which you are attempting to influence wisely. To seize the opportune moment, you must choose the right place, or environment, which can have a big effect on your ability to influence or persuade.

The environment refers to the entirety of the location: the setting, the lighting, the noise, the ambiance.

There is no doubt the environment can set the mood.

Are you looking to create an informal environment? If so, meeting for coffee or lunch creates a more informal atmosphere.

Would a more formal environment suit the situation better? Meet in an office or conference room. Meeting at your own office is a power move. Meeting at the other party's office allows you the ability to come and go as you please.

Are you looking for an intimate setting, perhaps to build and nurture the relationship? Try dinner at a small restaurant.

The environment can be used to build credibility. Think about doctors who meet patients at their office where you see their degrees or a courthouse meeting where judges are elevated and behind a big desk, presiding over their courtroom.

A TUNA SANDWICH NEVER TASTED SO GOOD

In 1981, Cal Ripken, Jr., who would go on to become baseball's Ironman, a Hall of Famer, and one of the most recognizable players to ever play the game, was looking to select his agent. He was wined and dined all across the country by agents. Then, Ron Shapiro, our (SNI's) founder, who was a successful sports agent before SNI, entered the discussion. Ron had represented several players on the Orioles and did not believe in this recruiting strategy. Instead, he invited Cal to his office where they shared a meal, a tuna sandwich and a can of Coke to be precise, and before lunch was done, Cal had signed with Ron.

In this example, Ron chose the right environment for this meeting, a down to earth, get to know each other style that Cal appreciated. It successfully differentiated him from the other agents because, otherwise, it would have been an arms race for who provided a fancier meal and experience rather than what they offered him as his representative and as an extension of him off the field.

Next time, think about whether a coffee shop, white tablecloth dinner, or office meeting is best and decide based on your objectives. A fancy meal can impress but feel stuffy. A coffee shop is casual but less private. A visit to your office feels more personal and offers the other party a window into your environment. Maybe you should go to their turf, home or office for example, which can be personal and change the perceived power dynamic.

Media Richness

Another aspect of "location" is the medium with which you choose to communicate. According to media richness theory, or information richness theory, different communication mediums (i.e. person-to-person, video call, phone call, text message, email) have varying levels of effectiveness conveying information.

For instance, richer communication channels allow you to communicate more information. Where person-to-person communication or a video call might allow body language, facial expressions, and tone of voice to provide richness to your communication, reports, texts, and emails do not afford the same opportunity.

Take sarcasm, for example. Detecting sarcasm in person is easier than when by written communication. Sarcasm relies on a number of cues, including facial expressions (rolling the eyes), tone of voice, and body language, but these cues cannot easily be conveyed in written communication.

On the other hand, if the information you want to convey is complex or highly technical, written communication may be a better option. Even if you are planning on communicating your message in person, you may need to be prepared with a written report, proposal sheet, or contract to convey complex information. Better yet, send an email ahead of time so the other party has time to review the information beforehand.

As you can see in Figure 6.2, it is all about picking the right medium for your message.

If you are wondering how much of a difference the medium makes, Daniel Balliet, Professor of Human Cooperation at Vrije Universiteit (VU) Amsterdam found that face-to-face meetings are 2.63 times more effective

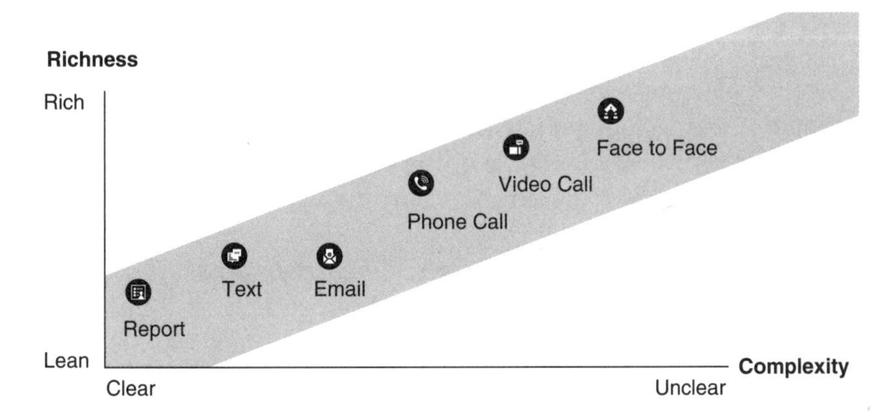

Figure 6.2

as a means of communication than written communication.[50] So, how can you use your knowledge of media richness to improve your ability to influence? One thing you can do is to build relationships through more personal communication channels, such as in person or via video chat when face to face is not possible. Richer communication channels allow you to take in more verbal and nonverbal cues, get to know and understand the other party better, and form a deeper connection.

That said, there are times when other less rich communication can be more effective. For example, you send texts to signal responsiveness and have more frequent and informal dialogue with people. You email people if you want them to read and digest information prior to a meeting. This can be particularly useful when the subject matter is sensitive or there is too much information to absorb in one meeting. Email also works well to follow up and document what was discussed during a meeting and lay out the agreed upon action steps.

So, what is the rule of thumb? Generally, richer is better, but richer means more time consumption and less efficiency, so advantages exist to using other media in specific situations, the most common example being written forms to document or increase precision.

The Right Audience

Just as important as the right time and the right place is the right audience. You must understand and be aware of whom you are trying to influence and persuade. What is important to them? What messages will resonate with them?

PERUKE, YOU SAY?

Time and place take into account the entire decision-making environment. In Australia, people are even willing to go as far as having the entire court wear wigs so everyone looks the same. Why? To eliminate biases. Here is Jeff's story on learning why Australian lawyers wear those silly wigs:

On one occasion, my daughter brought her roommate from school home for Thanksgiving. She was a lovely Australian girl who obviously was not going to make the trip back to Australia for a long weekend and who did not want to stay at school. She mentioned her family was coming from America in a few weeks to retrieve her and look around a bit while they were visiting. So, we invited the parents to our home for a family dinner.

It turns out that the girl's father was Peter Dunning, who between 2014 and 2019 held a commission as the Solicitor-General for Queensland. Now this was a particular stroke of luck for me because I had finished watching the first five episodes of, "Crownies," an Australian Courtroom Drama, and I had a lot of questions. Number one of which was, "Why do lawyers in Australia wear those ridiculous wigs?"

Peter and his wife could not have been more delightful, and he was happy to answer all my questions, idiotic (many) and inane (more). Regarding the wig, he had a wealth of insight. And his answers are below:

It is not a wig but a peruke, which is what they call their wigs.
Yes, I suppose peruke is an even sillier name than wig.
They wear them as a "symbolic distancing effort."
Symbolic distancing is an effort to keep everyone on the same level. One guy in a wig and robes looks much like another. It prevents bias due to appearance and status.
Yes, they are itchy, but if you buy an expensive one, it is rather comfortable.
Yes, I can tell the difference between an expensive wig and a cheap one.
Okay, then I suppose the bias due to wealth sort of goes out the window, but the intent is great.

Yes, I suppose people who can afford nicer wigs buy them, and those who cannot wear cheaper wigs.
No, no one gets teased for having a cheaper peruke, but we can tell. Younger folks tend to have cheaper wigs.
Yes, I suppose everyone looks ridiculous

So, we see an inherent bias is associated with how people look and Australians and many other former countries from the British Commonwealth wear wigs as a means of eliminating bias. Unfortunately, it leads to a new bias.

To do this, you need to focus on the individuals. What are their wants and needs? What objections might they have? What is their body language conveying? What is their personality? What is your audience's mindset?

In the next two chapters, we will address more of the who. But, if you have been following the process thus far, you should have a good idea of your audience.

The Influencer's Toolbox

The Empathy Gap

Dr. George Loewenstein, professor of psychology and economics at Carnegie Mellon University, coined the terms hot-cold and cold-hot empathy gap in the early 2000s. It referred to the concept that humans are state dependent and, as a result, struggle to empathize with themselves and others in different states. He found that if we are upset, we tend to overestimate how long we will be upset and as a result make suboptimal decisions; for instance, say, we are angry our car has required repairs and we sell it, remembering shortly after we need a car to get to work. The same occurs in reverse; when we are in a good mood, we have a hard time understanding what it is like to be in a bad mood. An example of this would be smokers who, when not craving cigarettes, decide to quit but underestimate the difficulty to control the urge to smoke when their state changes.

This empathy gap is one of the many reasons the right time is so important for influencing, and this impacts both parties. The most powerful communication occurs when all parties are in sync and in the same state.

This is why attending a rally, march, or sports home game is so powerful and even creates that goose-bump feeling. Almost all people there are sharing the same state and objective, and that creates a unique environment, which makes people particularly impressionable and persuadable.

I HATE MY SPOUSE

I have a friend with whom I often play squash, and almost equally as often, he complains about his wife. He is frustrated and even angry with her. Enough of that comes up throughout our squash games: before and after the game and during breaks. Intuitively, most people would side with him and allow him to vent, yet I generally do the opposite: I side with his wife, based on what he has told me. Where he overreacted, I find she was well intentioned, or generally there was simply a misunderstanding around the issue(s) at hand. The first time I took this approach, I expected him to be upset with me and that I would take the brunt of his anger. But the opposite occurred. Almost every time, he came away from our games feeling more positive about the situation with this wife. At first, I was thrown off, but I believe this was because he, like all of us, innately did not want to remain upset, which is a powerful enough pull to be equalized by our conversations.

I have credibility with my squash partner, so I have an easier time accidentally helping him shift from a hot to a cold state. But this is evidence that this shift is possible. However, unless you have a long-standing relationship with someone, taking on this challenge may not be a good idea.

The state of the person you want to influence and, therefore, timing is critical. Influencing is as much about what you do as when you do it. If I was playing with my squash partner on a monthly basis rather than weekly I would not likely take the same approach. If my partner's issues have incubated, I likely would take the brunt of his anger and have a lower chance of changing his mind. I happen to play against him often enough where he is upset and not so raw that he will not listen but not so incubated that his anger is baked and hard to divert. Knowing what to do and when always is impossible, but being aware of your own state and the state of whomever you want to influence are critical to making better decisions and more successfully persuading others.

Happy Endings

How you end an activity has a large bearing on how people remember it. Countless studies have shown how gifting a chocolate or mint at the end of a meal results in a larger tip. Elizabeth Dunn from the University of British Columbia found the same occurs with vacations. Make the last day of vacation great and you are more likely to have better memories. How something ends has a disproportionate and lasting impact on memory of the entire event. So, how do we use this when influencing others? Ensure to have a strong positive ending to your presentations and people will remember the entire meeting better. Or if you manage people, suggest they write down a few things they accomplished at the end of each day.

Putting It All Together

The Opportune Moment

Kairos is the idea of the opportune moment to influence and persuade, underlying the entire process.

The Right Place and the Right Time

The opportune moment all boils down to being in the right place at the right time.

The Right Time: The right time refers to the relevance of your message to the time at hand and to the situation. To get the timing right, work through the Four-Step Process of Influence and Persuasion, building on the previous steps. You also need to consider how the individuals are feeling at that time. What is your state and the state of the party you are trying to influence? Keep in mind that the ending of a situation has a disproportionate impact on how it is remembered.

The Right Place: Another important element of finding the opportune moment is the location and environment in which you will be influencing and persuading. The environment sets the mood. Pay attention to your communication mediums. The complexity of the information determines the richness of the communication medium through which you should converse.

The Right Audience: Keep your audience in mind. Better yet, take the time to get to know your audience. The other people's state, their mood, whether they are a morning person or a night person, could all determine the opportune moment to persuade.

The Influencer's Toolbox

The Empathy Gap: Understand that people are state dependent, and it can be a challenge to empathize with them and others in different states. Recognize the hot-cold state disparity and use it in deciding the time and place of communication.

Awareness of State: Being aware of your own state and the state of others to help you determine when and how to best reach them. Your frequency of interaction with other people can also affect your ability to gauge your communication with them as well.

Happy Endings: Know that how an activity ends has a huge impact on how it is remembered. If you end a conversation, meeting, or day with something positive, everyone will walk away with more enthusiasm about it.

7 Body Language

> *"What you do speaks so loud that I cannot hear what you say."*
>
> *– Ralph Waldo Emerson, philosopher and poet*

People often do not say what they mean or mean what they say. As influencing relies on understanding and communicating with people, body language plays a key role in the influencing process. In fact, body language is one of the most important aspects in communication. As alluded to by Emerson in the quote above, body language does speak louder than words.

Body language acts as a window into people's true intentions: how they think and feel. In this chapter, we will provide a practical guide to harnessing the power of body language to understand others as well as to use your own body language to convey the appropriate information and emotions.

Reading and Understanding Body Language

What is body language? Body language is a form of nonverbal communication where behaviors such as posture, gestures, and facial expressions communicate information – thoughts, feelings, attitudes, and intentions.

In his research, *The Importance of Effective Communication*, Dr. Edward G. Wertheim describes five key roles that nonverbal communication may play:

1. Complimenting your verbal message
2. Accentuating your message

3. Repeating (and strengthening) your verbal message
4. Substituting your message
5. Contradicting your verbal message[51]

In and of themselves, any one behavior signal may not tell us much. The key to reading body language is watching for consistency. Is there consistency among the nonverbal signals that someone is displaying? And, is there consistency between a person's nonverbal communication and what they are saying?

For instance, crossed arms is usually seen as a defensive position; however crossed arms could mean that someone is insecure or even cold. If crossed arms are accompanied by a change in body position. Someone changes their body angles to face away from you also; it is more likely they are not pleased with what you are talking about.

It appears our brains are hardwired to pick up on inconsistencies. Research from neuroscientists and psychologists at Colgate University used electroencephalograph (EEG) machines to study what happens in the brain when we are exposed to inconsistencies between nonverbal communication and the message. They found that when gestures did not match the verbal message, the brain reacts in the same way as when we hear nonsensical language. In other words, when you see one thing and hear another, your brain cannot make sense of it.[52]

Posture

Posture, or body position, is one of the first things people notice. Your posture can tell people whether you are open or defensive, interested or bored, or confident or insecure. Your posture may determine if you appear approachable at all. The good news is that posture is often fairly easy to read in others and is one of the easiest things to control in your own body language.

Open Posture versus Closed Posture

One way to perceive posture is as open posture versus a closed posture. Standing or sitting with your arms at your sides or on the arms of your chair in an open position typically conveys, not surprisingly, openness. An open posture reflects that people are receptive: friendly, interested, and ready to listen.

Signals of openness include uncrossed arms and legs, maintaining appropriate and relaxed eye contact, using many gestures, and directly facing the person with whom you are conversing.

On the other hand, a closed posture typically signals defensiveness, insecurity, uncomfortableness, and/or deceit or hidden motives. Signals of a closed posture might include crossed arms and legs, avoidant eye contact, facing slightly away from the people with whom you are conversing, and keeping your hands close to the body and in front of you.

Open Posture	Closed Posture
Uncrossed Arms	Crossed Arms
Uncrossed Legs	Crossed Legs
Appropriate/Relaxed Eye Contact	Avoidant Eye Contact
Directly Facing	Turned Away Slightly
Many Gestures	Hands in Front of and Close to Body

Stance

The way people stand or sit can reveal a great deal about them. First, always stand up straight. Standing or sitting up straight displays confidence, self-assurance, and poise while slouching conveys anxiety, insecurity, or boredom.

One common body language signal is standing with hands on the hips. Standing with hands on the hips maximizes your size to make you look larger; thus, this pose is often seen as a signal of dominance or aggression.

Because standing with hands on the hips is an open gesture, it alludes to not perceiving any threats; however, because your arms are out, ready to take action, this posture conveys a confident and sometimes subtly threatening signal.

Another common way you may see people stand is with their hands clasped behind their back. Standing with your hands behind your back can take on several meanings. Standing with your hands behind your back can signify a power pose. Standing with your hands behind your back and legs spread apart implies control, with no need to be defensive or worried about any threats. In this pose, the shoulders will often be neutral or slightly elevated, and one hand will be rested in the other.

Figure 7.1

However, standing with your hands behind your back and grasping your wrist or your arm can signify frustration, uncertainty, or deceit. Grasping the wrist or arm is a self-comforting pose, keeping your body pulled close together, like a hug. The grasping of the wrist or arm could signify holding something back, either frustration or maybe even the truth.

Crossed Arms

Crossing your arms across your chest is one of the most common body language signals and one of the easiest nonverbal signals to notice and identify. However, because crossed arms are an easy signal to read, they can be easily misunderstood.

Crossed arms are typically seen as a defensive position. When you cross your arms across your chest, you create a barrier between yourself and the outside world. This posture is often associated with defensiveness and being closed off.

Crossing the arms across the chest can also be a sign of disagreement. When people hear something they disagree with or get "bad news," they will cross their arms to protect themselves from this news.

However, because crossing one's arms is so common, it can be a comfortable position for people, a result of uneasiness, or a natural response to feeling cold.

Another explanation for crossed arms has been described as a self-hug. Crossing your arms brings comfort, relieves stress, assuages fear, and makes you feel secure.

One clue to determining whether crossed arms provide a signal of the other parties' feelings is to pay attention to the hands. If people's hands are balled up into fists, they are likely displaying defensiveness or hostility. On the other hand, if other people's hands are open or gripping their arms, it is not as conclusive and could merely be temperature, minor uneasiness, or a more comfortable position.

Crossed Legs

Crossed legs are another body language signal associated with a defensive position. Although crossed legs are more subtle than crossed arms because we tend to notice the lower half of the body less than the upper half, they are more accurate revealers of emotions or communication we want to hide, such as deceitfulness.

In one body language study by famed body language researchers Dr. Paul Ekman and Wallace Friesen, they suggest that when someone lies they produce more body language cues in the lower part of the body than the upper part. Their research showed videos of people lying and asked participants to determine whether the subject in the video was lying or telling the truth. Participants in their study more accurately detected deceit when they were shown videos that included the lower part of the body than they were when shown videos that only included the upper part.[53]

Steepled Hands

Hand steepling is another common body language signal, often seen in leaders or exhibited in superior-subordinate relationships. Hand steepling is performed by touching the fingertips together with palms apart, resembling the steeple of a church.

According to renowned body language expert Dr. Ray Birdwhistell, many people who consider themselves prominent or elite use minimal gestures aside from the hand steeple, which reflects certainty, confidence, self-assurance, and sometimes arrogance.[54]

Hand steepling is a power move, thus should be used sparingly and only in the proper situations.

Gestures

Gestures, or movements of the hands or head, are some of the most obvious and direct forms of nonverbal communication, and they are effective.

One study by Vanessa Van Edwards, Lead Investigator at the Science of People, found that great speakers use A LOT of gestures. To investigate how gestures were perceived and received, her team watched hundreds of hours of TED Talks. In the most popular TED Talks, which averaged 7,360,000 views, they found speakers used a whopping 465 gestures in an 18-minute talk; in the least popular TED Talks, averaging 120,000 views, the speakers only used 272 gestures. So, though you may want to avoid jazz hands, do not be afraid of using an abundance of gestures.

Gesturing with the Hands

Waving. Wagging your finger. Pointing at something. We use hand gestures every single day. They say hi. They help get your point across. They accentuate. They communicate.

Many gestures tend to be consistently received around the world. Open hands or palms insinuate honesty or openness. A clenched fist symbolizes intensity or anger. Rubbing your hands together proclaims excitement, but wringing your hands shows insecurity, nervousness, or stress.

However, countless gestures, like many of the aspects of our communication, are often not universal. For example, in North America. pointing at something signifies it is important, but in numerous cultures pointing, and especially pointing at a person, can be considered rude. We will discuss the importance of cultural differences, but for now, be aware of and understand cultural differences before your gestures send the wrong message.

Finger Tapping

Finger tapping (or foot tapping or pencil tapping) is another nonverbal signal I am sure we have seen. Finger tapping is typically associated with impatience. The faster the tapping, the more impatient the tapper is becoming. This tapping, also known as a metronomic (regular and repetitive) signal, sends an interrupting signal to people who are speaking. It tells speakers to move on from whatever they are saying.

Metronomic tapping can also be a sign of anxiety, frustration, nervousness, or boredom. Tapping may be a sign that people are thinking. However, even this may be associated with people's impatience or frustration with themselves and that they are unable to come up with an easy solution.

Touching the Face

Touching the face, especially repeatedly, typically signifies nervousness or insecurity. However, touching the ear, eyes, nose, or mouth may each signify different feelings and emotions.

For instance, tugging or pulling at the ear usually signifies indecisiveness, a non-committal attitude, or you haven't made a decision.

Rubbing of the eyes may signify disbelief or doubt whereas rubbing or touching the nose is often a signal of dishonesty.

Again, you must understand the context and pay attention to more than one nonverbal communication signal to decode these unspoken messages.

Gesturing with the Head

In addition to gesturing with the hands, examples exist of gestures made with the head. From a "yes" nod to a vigorous shake of the head "no," how people turn or tilt their head can be revealing.

For example, tilting the head to the side often shows interest and may be done to show you care, are listening, and do not have any hidden motives. However, tilting the head backward exudes arrogance, doubt, or suspicion.

THE GUESSING GAME

My wife and I were at dinner a few years ago. It was the first night out after our second child was born and it was nice to get away even if only for a few hours to have dinner on a patio. For the first bit, all we could think about was whether her mom would be fine watching both kids, but quickly we got into conversation and totally forgot about them.

About halfway through dinner, a neighbor, who was single, walked by us. We said hi briefly and shared a laugh about how far all of us had come: The restaurant was 200 feet from our house. Anyway, he sat down with a young lady we presumed was a date. As we looked around, we realized that we were surrounded by many couples and dates.

I asked my wife, "Who do you think is having a good time here?" We scanned the room and watched their body language (e.g., whether both people were laughing at the table, if they were leaning into each other, if they ever looked at their phones, if they were angling their bodies away). It was interesting to think about it in such a scientific way, wanting to read others solely on what we saw, not what they said or any other context.

My wife and I have had great times doing that. On the rare occasion we get to go out, we play this little game, even a few times daring to go and talk to the couple to get a better sense if our body language reading was accurate.

For those looking to improve your reading of body language, I recommend you try it, even by yourself at a coffee shop. Look around, read people's body language, and watch for consistency or change over time. Look for whether both people appear to be on the same wavelength. You will be surprised how much you pick up and learn, all of the subtleties you might normally miss, and you'll enjoy doing it.

Does it work? Well, the last time my wife and I read body language, we were at a gastropub with five other couples celebrating a friend's birthday. The one other couple we said was most in sync had been together the least amount of time, was married first in the group, and was now having twins, so you be the judge.

Facial Expressions

Facial expressions are an important part of nonverbal communication. Your face is a window of emotion. With 43 muscles and the ability to make over 10,000 facial expressions, it is no wonder that facial expressions have the ability to reveal so much about us.

However, unlike posture, gestures, and the use of space, you have far less control over your facial expressions.

Microexpressions

Microexpressions are quick, involuntary facial expressions appearing on the face for a fraction of a second. Research has identified a number of expressions found in people around the world that appear to be universal.

Charles Darwin was one of the first to suggest that the use of facial expressions to express emotion was universal: persistent across people and cultures. However, much of the modern research into microexpressions began with Dr. Paul Ekman, who has been studying microexpressions for more than 40 years.

Dr. Ekman, originally doubting Darwin's theory that the use of facial expressions was universal, set out to find the truth behind facial expressions. Ekman studied the facial expressions of participants from Argentina, Brazil, Chile, Japan, the United States, and Papua New Guinea. In many of his studies, he showed photographs of people expressing different emotions and asked the participants to guess the emotion being displayed. To his surprise, Ekman found that Darwin was correct and that certain facial expressions were practically universal. They became known as the seven universal facial expressions: anger, disgust, fear, surprise, happiness, sadness, and contempt.[55]

Anger The first universal facial expression is anger, a strong feeling of being upset, annoyed, or displeased.

- Lowered eyebrows drawn into scowl
- Lips tense and drawn firmly together
- Clenched teeth
- Eyes glaring or bulging out
- Wrinkling of the forehead
- Lower jaw may be jutted out

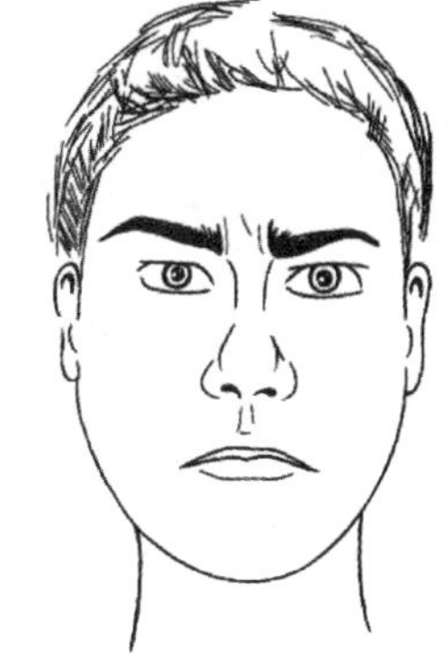

Figure 7.2

Disgust Disgust is the strong feeling of dislike, disapproval, or revulsion.

- Lowered eyebrows
- Narrowed eyes
- Raised upper lip
- Wrinkling of the nose
- Raised cheeks

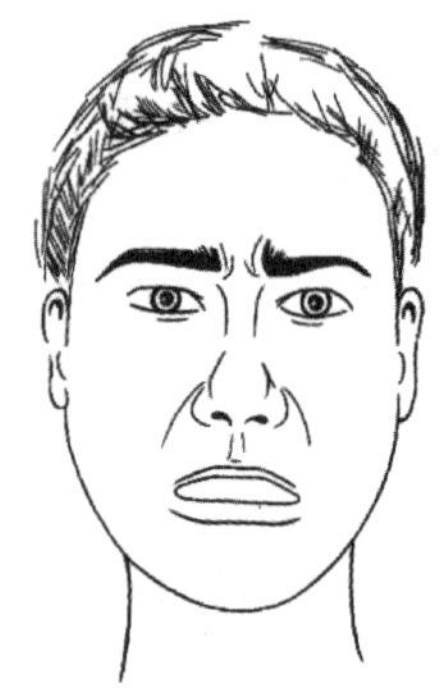

Figure 7.3

Fear Fear is the unpleasant emotion brought about by an awareness or apprehension of danger.

- Raised eyebrows and pulled together
- Raised upper eyelids
- Tensed lower eyelids
- Lips partly open and stretched thin

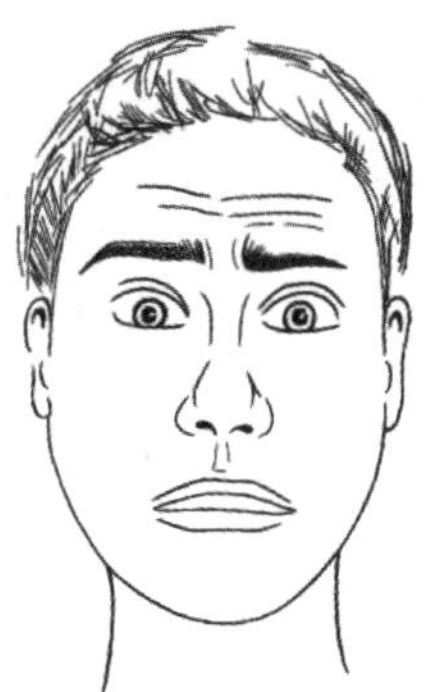

Figure 7.4

Surprise Surprise is a startled response brought about by an unexpected event, appearance, or statement.

- Arching eyebrows
- Upper eyelids raised
- Slightly dropped jaw
- Wrinkling of the forehead
- Dilated pupils

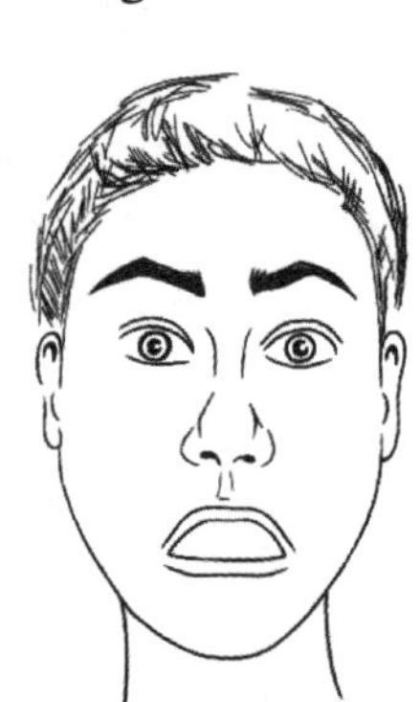

Figure 7.5

Happiness Happiness is a positive emotion ranging from a general state of well-being to a state of contentment to joy.

- Raised corners of the lips
- Raised cheeks
- Slightly narrowed eyes
- Tightening of the eyelids
- Crow's feet appear around eyes

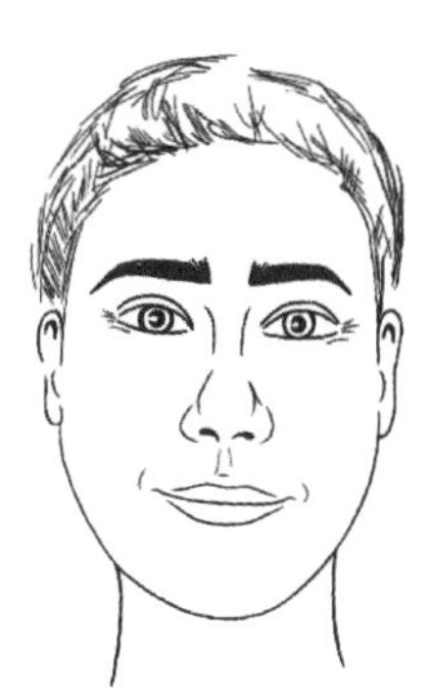

Figure 7.6

Sadness Sadness is a negative emotion associated with unhappiness, loss, grief, disappointment, or sorrow.

- Lowered corners of the lips
- Drooping eyelids
- Eyes pointing down
- Pouting lower lip

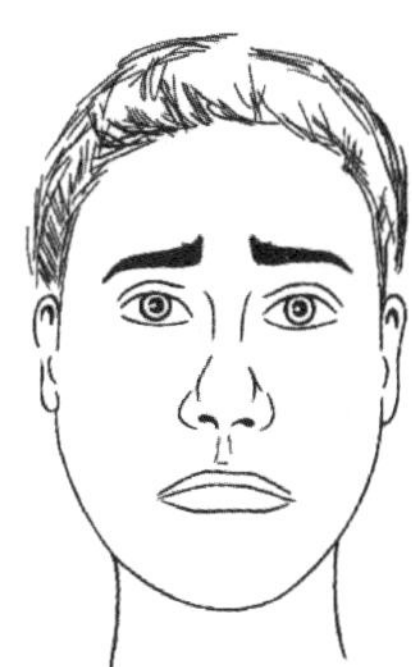

Figure 7.7

Contempt Contempt is an emotion associated with the act of despising, disdaining, or feeling someone or something is beneath you.

- Raised lip on one side
- Lips tightened

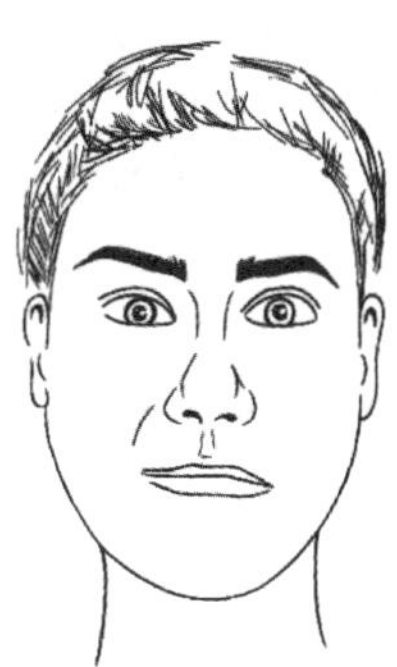

Figure 7.8

Try it for yourself. Stand in front of the mirror and make the face you associate with each of the seven universal microexpressions. Do you notice all of the features associated with each? If not, that is okay. You may not exhibit or notice all of the associated microexpressions when you are practicing unless you are experiencing those emotions. But this gives you an opportunity to notice which ones are missing when you are faking an emotion compared to when you may be experiencing one.

Eye Contact

Though microexpressions may be universal, eye contact is more culturally sensitive. Whether and how much one should make eye contact are dependent on culture. For instance, though a lack of eye contact would be considered rude or insincere in many cultures, in a number of Asian and Caribbean cultures making eye contact can be seen as rude and an act of aggression.

In the many cultures where eye contact is considered appropriate, it is an important element of facial expression and communication. After all, much of the time spent in conversation with people is spent looking at their face. The eyes are the window to the soul.

Making eye contact shows you acknowledge someone. It shows you are listening and paying attention, and you care. When someone avoids making eye contact, they are often perceived as insecure, dishonest, or deceitful. However, be careful not to overdo it. When eye contact goes on too long, when it turns into a glaring gaze or intense stare, it can be perceived as creepy and threatening.

So, what is the appropriate amount of eye contact?

Studies, and our own experience, have led us to believe you should maintain eye contact approximately 50% of the time when speaking and 70% of the time when listening. To do this, you should make eye contact for four to five seconds and then glance away for a few seconds before returning your gaze to make eye contact again. This range appears to be optimal because it balances showing interest in the other party, which requires eye contact, with not appearing aggressive, which is often the feeling perceived when you feel a constant stare with no breaks.

Raised Eyebrows

Being so close to the eyes, the eyebrows draw a great deal of attention. If you are making appropriate eye contact, you are bound to notice your conversational partners' eyebrows.

Raising one's eyebrows can signal a number of things. Raising the eyebrows can be an indication of surprise or fear. Here, raising the eyebrows signals you are concerned and paying attention, almost conveying a look of submission.

They can also be a sign of doubt, disbelief, or skepticism. People often raise their eyebrows when they have a question, want something clarified, or disbelieve what they heard.

On the other hand, a quick flash of the eyebrows might signify interest or attraction. Again, this reminds us that you need to pay attention to context and more than one body language signal. There is a big difference between thinking someone is flirting with you and thinking someone is lying to you, although those two may often be one and the same.

Smiling

Smiling is another universal body language signal most commonly associated with happiness. According to Darwin, smiling is our body's way of expressing positive emotion.

However, not all smiles are created equal. Research suggests that smiles serve three main social functions: reward, affiliation, and dominance. Reward smiles are smiles of true happiness, and they act as a

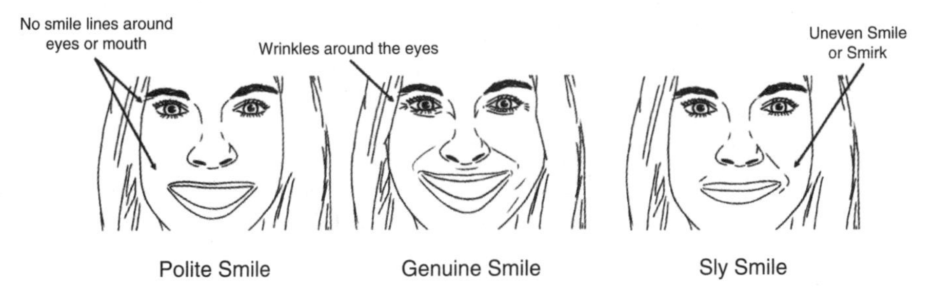

Figure 7.9

reward to motivate ourselves or others. These smiles arise from positive feelings such as approval, fulfillment, and satisfaction, and they are the most genuine type of smile.

The second social function served by smiles is affiliation. Affiliation smiles are smiles that function to build and reinforce social bonds. These smiles are friendly, gentle smiles, and they are often used to comfort or reassure others, be polite, and communicate trustworthiness and good intentions.

The third social function of smiles is dominance. Dominance smiles function to maintain the social order, conveying power and control. Dominance smiles may resemble more of a smirk or a sneer and are often unbalanced, where only one side of the mouth curls up. They are often associated with emotions, such as arrogance, superiority, derision, and contempt.[56]

The Duchenne Smile

The Duchenne Smile, also known as smiling with the eyes, is a smile identified by French anatomist Guillaume Duchenne. The Duchenne Smile signals pure happiness and joy and is one of the most genuine of smiles. Whereas all smiles involve the turning up of the lips (performed by the zygomatic major muscle), the Duchenne Smile involves the raising of the cheeks and narrowing of the eyes (performed by the orbicularis oculi muscle), resulting in the formation of crow's feet around the eyes. This formation of crow's feet around the eyes has become known as the Duchenne marker.[57]

Why is this important? It is often used to determine a polite smile or even a fake smile from a genuine smile. Because the orbicularis oculi muscles cannot be controlled voluntarily, the Duchenne marker and the Duchenne Smile cannot be faked. They are seen as honest and natural smiles.

The Duchenne marker is also associated with other emotions aside from happiness. In one recent research study, researchers at Western University found that the Duchenne marker conveys the sincerity and intensity of several emotions, including expressions of pain and those associated with sadness.[58]

Awareness of Cultural Differences

As you have learned, body language has many aspects, such as microexpressions, which seem to be expressed fairly universally across people and cultures. However, other aspects of body language have different meanings based on where you are in the world or the culture of the other party.

Handshakes

Although most cultures around the world recognize the handshake as a sign of greeting, there are many different ways of shaking hands and cultural differences you should know. For instance, in some countries, such as the United States, Canada, and Brazil, a firm handshake is considered the norm. However, in most of Europe, Asia, and other parts of the world a light, loose handshake is considered appropriate. And, in Turkey, a firm handshake can be considered rude.

There are also cultural differences in who should shake who's hand. For example, in Russia, Morocco, and many Islamic countries, shaking hands with someone of the opposite gender is inappropriate. In Australia and other cultures, women customarily do not shake hands with other women.

Hand Gestures

Hand gestures are also another form of body language that do not communicate the same across cultures. For instance, in many parts of the world, the "okay" sign signals understanding, acceptance, or approval; however, in Brazil, Greece, and Spain, the okay sign is used to call someone a jerk.

In another example, in the United States and parts of Europe, turning the palm up and curling the index finger is generally interpreted as a gesture beckoning someone to come closer. In other parts of the world, such as Asia and Oceania, this is seen as rude and can get you arrested in the Philippines.

Another hand gesture is the "thumbs up." In many cultures, giving a thumbs up is a sign of approval or a job well done. However, in Greece, the Middle East, and parts of Africa, a thumbs up is equivalent to giving someone the middle finger in the United States.

Nodding Your Head

Even nodding your head is a body language signal that can cause confusion across cultures. Though nodding your head up and down means yes in most of the world, in Bulgaria, Greece, Turkey, and other parts of eastern Europe nodding your head up and down means no.

Eye Contact

The appropriate amount of eye contact is another element of body language that differs across cultures. In the United States and many Western cultures, making eye contact conveys acknowledgment, attention, and confidence. However, in many African, Asian, and Latin American countries, eye contact more than a glance may be considered rude, confrontational, and aggressive.

Physical Distance

The appropriate physical distance, or personal space, heavily relies on cultural norms. Some cultures, particularly in North America, Northern Europe, and Asia, have become known as non-contact cultures. People prefer to avoid touching, stand apart, and keep a large amount of personal space. On the other hand, other cultures are contact cultures, as in South America, the Middle East, and Southern Europe. In these cultures, standing close together is more common, and individuals do not feel the need for as much personal space.

Body Language for Virtual Selling Environments

Due to COVID-19, virtual selling has become a critical skill overnight; however, we do not expect the importance of this skill to go away as quickly as it arrived. Most of this book's content is valuable regardless of the medium, but specific tools are impactful when communicating and selling virtually. Here are a few tips specifically related to body language and video calls:

- Focus. When making a key point or sharing something personal, put the focus on you. We often share a screen on a video call, but as we might turn the screen black when in person to tell a story, turn off screen sharing when making an important point so your audience focuses on you and your message.
- Use hand gestures. Body language expert Vanessa Van Edwards found that the most viewed TED Talks were done by speakers who were more active with hand gestures. Hand gestures make a message easier to understand and more memorable. Consider these gestures during your next video call:

    a. Use your fingers to support a number that you share. For example, if you say three reasons exist for something, consider using the gesture of three fingers visible to your audience.
    b. Use two hands to compare. When making a comparison of any kind, use your right and left hands spaced out to provide a visual that supports that concept. Think apples and oranges.
    c. Show togetherness. Just as using two hands apart is a great visual for comparison, putting your hands together is a strong visual for providing an additional visual to go along with your message.
    d. Talking about yourself. When telling a story or something personal about yourself, consider bringing your hands in, in front of you with your fingers touching your chest, to accentuate this message.

- Smile. We talked about this earlier and research indicates that smiling is a powerful communication tool, especially on virtual calls where you do not have many other tools at your disposal. Do it early and often; it impacts your state of mind and your audience's because it is contagious. If you need more convincing on the importance of your facial expressions, know that Alexander Todorov, a Professor of Psychology at Princeton University, could predict with 70% accuracy senate election results in the early 2000s solely by aggregating people's responses to questionnaire where they briefly looked at candidates faces and answered who looked more competent and honest.[59]

- Be engaging and interactive. The best ways to do this is spend time getting to know the person at the start of a video meeting. Do not hurry the personal aspects of a video call. You can always send an email, PowerPoint, or proposal, but you cannot replicate the impact of getting to know someone. Once you get down to business, have a list of questions prior to all meetings to remind you to engage the other side. Finally, if you are presenting to a bigger group, use polling, chat, breakout rooms, collaborative whiteboarding, and other features your platform has to engage.
- Set yourself up for success. This means prepare a script for the meeting so you present with confidence and manage your environment. Also include having an organized background, dressing the same way you would for an in-person meeting, having lights on you, and doing activities you enjoy (e.g., listening to music or going for a brief walk) to get in a positive frame of mind.

The Influencer's Toolbox

Making a First Impression

In the first few seconds of meeting someone, they are forming lasting opinions of you based on your appearance, body language, and behavior. In the United States, you can do five things with your body language to make a good first impression:

1. Be approachable. Maintain an open posture. Open postures are generally perceived as positive, so to make a good first impression,

stand or sit up straight with your hands at your sides or on the arms of your chair. Make sure to face the person you are meeting directly, and keep your arms and legs uncrossed.

2. Focus on the person or people who you are meeting. To do this, look them in the eyes and maintain appropriate eye contact. Proper eye contact conveys respect, attention, and interest in what the other person is saying. Though you do not want to stare, research suggests the appropriate amount of eye contact is to look at someone who is speaking 60–70 percent of the time.
3. Greet them with a firm handshake. A proper handshake is a sign of confidence. You do not want to crush the hand of the person you are shaking, but you do not want to come off as insecure or insincere either.
4. Smile. Smiling shows you enjoy people and are glad to meet someone; people who smile are seen as kinder and warmer as well. Smiling when you meet someone is powerful too. Some research suggests that a person's smile is one of the most memorable things about meeting someone in personal and professional relationships. However, make sure your smile is sincere.
5. Avoid appearing nervous. Things like touching your face, wringing your hands together, finger or foot tapping, can all be interpreted as a sign of nervousness, doubt, disinterest, and dishonestly. If you are nervous, be aware of your tells of nervousness and minimize them, especially during first impressions.

Body Language as a Tool for Managing Your Own Emotions

In addition to reading cues in other people's communication and improving your own communication, did you know your body language has the power to elicit moods in yourself as well. By altering your own body language, you have the power to manage your own emotions.

Take smiling, for instance. Smiling is a rewarding experience. Even the act of smiling induces a pleasant mood and makes us feel good.

When you smile, your brain releases dopamine, endorphins, and serotonin, the feel-good chemicals in your brains, putting you in a better mood. To better manage your own emotions, the next time you are in a bad mood, smile.

Your posture has an effect on your mood. Research has shown your posture has an effect on your stress, anxiety, alertness, and energy. Poor posture has been linked to fatigue, lower levels of alertness, and feelings of stress and anxiety. Sitting up straight or walking in a more upright position has the power to increase your alertness and energy, improve your outlook, and reduce stress and anxiety.

Your posture can influence your confidence because you look more confident when you practice good posture, and your posture has the power to help you feel more confident as well.

How much of a difference can your posture make?

According to Harvard University researcher Dr. Amy Cuddy, quite a lot, especially when it comes to your confidence. According to Cuddy, "When our body language is confident and open, other people respond in kind, unconsciously reinforcing not only their perception of us but also our perception of ourselves."[60]

Cuddy suggests using the power pose to increase one's confidence. Power posing involves altering your body language toward signals of confidence and power. These signals of confidence include posture and gestures, such as standing up straight, holding your head high, puffing your chest out, and opening yourself up to make you seem larger (e.g., putting your hands on your hips or holding both arms up over your head in a V).

Try this quick power posing exercise. Stand up straight. Spread your legs about shoulder width apart. Relax your arms and put them on your hips. Puff up/out your chest a little and leave your chin slightly elevated and aligned with your shoulders. Hold this pose for 30 seconds.

How did it make you feel?

Most people report it helps them feel more confident, powerful, and dominant.

Why is this such a powerful tool? Dr. Cuddy found that people who were in power positions felt more powerful, and holding a power pose affects your body chemistry. The hormones released

Figure 7.10

increase the feeling of power and confidence, which are often associated with improved outcomes in everything from negotiations to job interviews. Though this research has been controversial since it became popular in 2010, we have seen it be successful and recommend trying it. Other versions of this include listening to your favorite music prior to an important meeting to get you comfortable. Your mindset affects the way you communicate, so use that to your advantage.

Body Language as a Tool for Managing the Emotions of Others

Your body language can be a powerful tool for managing the emotions of others. Body language conveys powerful messages. So, by using these messages accordingly, you can influence the emotions of others. Here are some of the ways you can use your body language to manage the emotions of others.

Smile

Although we have discussed smiling and the different types of smiles, a smile has power in managing the emotions of others. Not only can smiling change your own mood to be more positive, smiling also directly affects the emotions of others.

For one, smiling conveys liking. And liking, in turn, increases trust, which is an important part of building credibility.

Smiling is also contagious. As you have learned, people naturally mirror the body language and facial expressions of others. Thus, smiling increases the chance of other people smiling as well. Smiling is also rewarding. When people smile, it makes their own mood more positive. Hence, by smiling more, you prompt others to smile back, increasing their liking and trust and putting them in a more positive mood and influencing them to be more helpful and cooperative.

Show Interest and Active Listening

When people are interested in what is being said, their body language will tell you they are paying attention and listening. In most cases, when people are actively listening, they will face you directly and will lean forward or toward you.

When people are interested and listening, they typically display signals of positive emotion; they are likely to smile more and nod their head. Nodding your head says I am listening and I hear your point, although this does not always mean other people agree with you.

The eyebrows are another signal that convey interest and active listening. As you learned, raised eyebrows are often a sign of interest and curiosity. Drawing the eyebrows together can be a sign of concentrating or thinking. However, be careful with reading this signal because drawing the eyebrows together could indicate distrust or anger.

What your audience is doing with their hands may be another clue. When people have their hands clasped together or they stroke their chin, these are often signs of thinking, processing, and judgment.

On the other hand, there are also clear signals when someone is not listening and you are losing your audience. Watch for signs of impatience. Signals like tapping the hands or feet or tapping with an object are common signs of impatience or boredom. When you see these signals, you may be spending too much time on a topic and your audience is letting you know it is time to move on.

So, how can you use what you know about interest and active listening? To start, when others are speaking, remember to take actions to show you are interested and actively listening. Lean forward, look them in the eye, smile, and nod your head.

When you are speaking, pay attention to your audience. If you are starting to lose them, you can draw your audience back in by interacting with them more. Ask questions. Make them think. If speaking to groups, get them moving by asking them to stand up or raise their hand in agreement. Get them involved.

PRO TIP Practice listening. It takes concentration and conviction to be an active listener, but the rewards pay off. First, listening to someone makes the speaker feel good. People like being listened to, and neuroscientists suggest this is built into our brains. One study using functional magnetic resonance imaging (fMRI) technology revealed that perceiving being listened to activates the reward system in the brain.[61]

Listening shapes how much they share and how they convey this information. Research has shown that whether or not someone appear to be listening determines how speakers choose to share information and whether they choose to share it.[62]

Break the Negative Poses of Others

Now that we know what the various aspects of body language can mean, the most experienced influencers can put it all together to impact other people. So, how do you do this? Combine your knowledge of body language with mirroring.

For example, let us say you are speaking with potential investors for your startup at a happy hour. You notice their arms are crossed, they have turned their body slightly from you, and occasionally scan the room looking for other people. You realize they are not fully engaged and maybe want out of the conversation.

What can you do? First, you can change the subject because what you are discussing is not working. Shift from the market opportunity to the direct need and why you started the business, for example.

Next, mirror subtle things the potential investors do, such as which direction they tilt their head, their smile and facial expressions, and their pace and tone of voice.

Finally, use positive body language, such as open hands, smiling, head slightly tilted, to move both of you into a more positive space. The objective is for you to take the mirroring lead so they will copy you in all of the positive body language you are using.

Will the above work? In this example, you are not guaranteed to succeed. However, using these tactics will give you a higher chance. If you don't receive a large investment from the people in the story above, you will know you did everything you could, which, though still disappointing, is more satisfying than if you do not use every tool at your disposal.

Test Your Knowledge

Now is the time to test what you have learned. Without looking back, see if you can match these facial expressions with the seven universal microexpressions: anger, disgust, fear, surprise, happiness, sadness, and contempt.

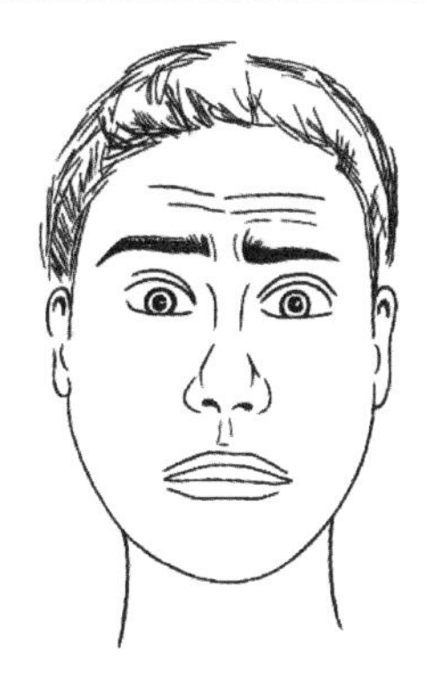

Figure 7.11

a. _______________

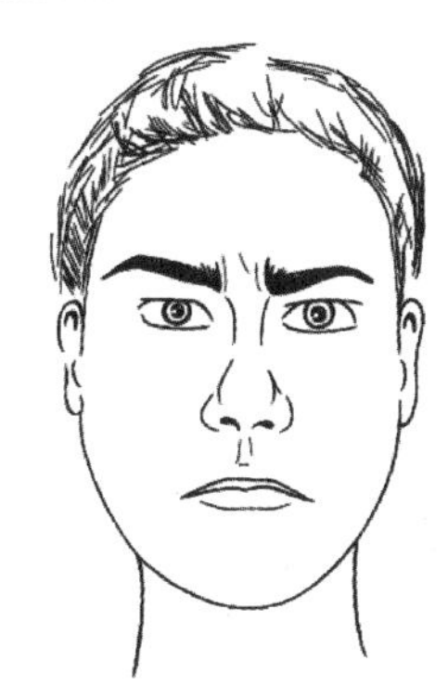

Figure 7.12

b. _______________

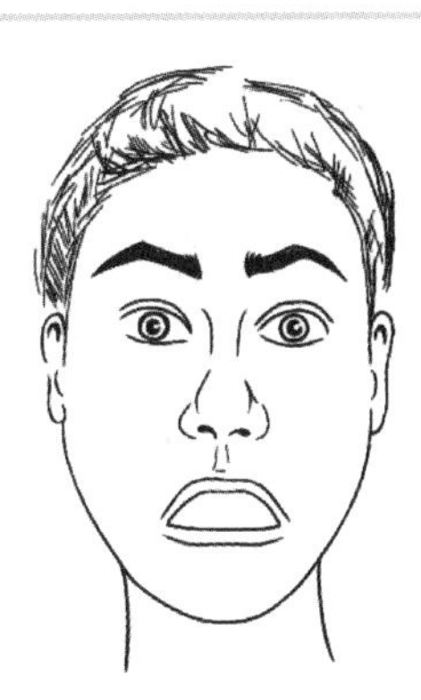

Figure 7.13

c. _______________

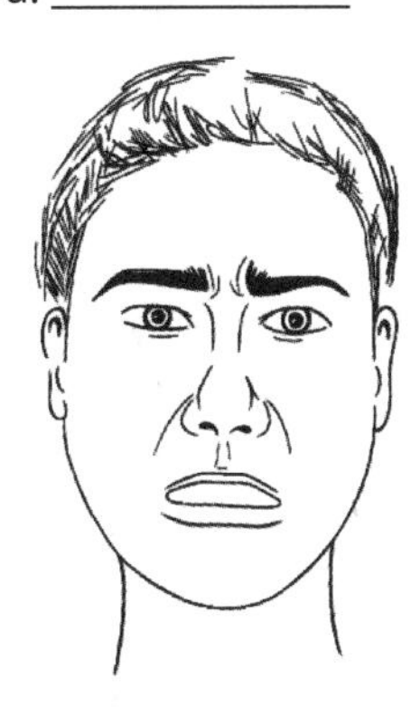

Figure 7.14

d. _______________

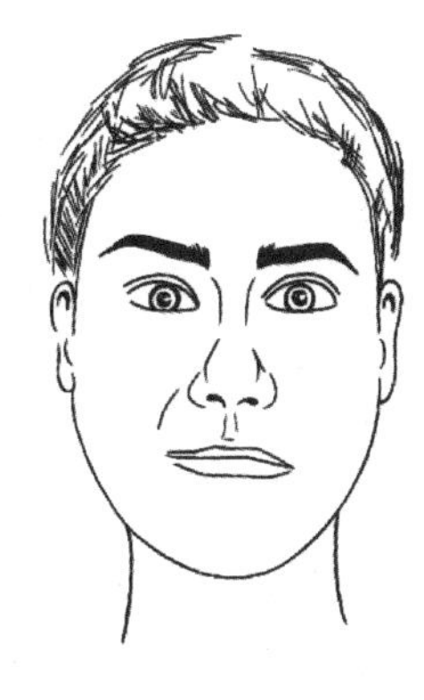

Figure 7.15

e. _______________

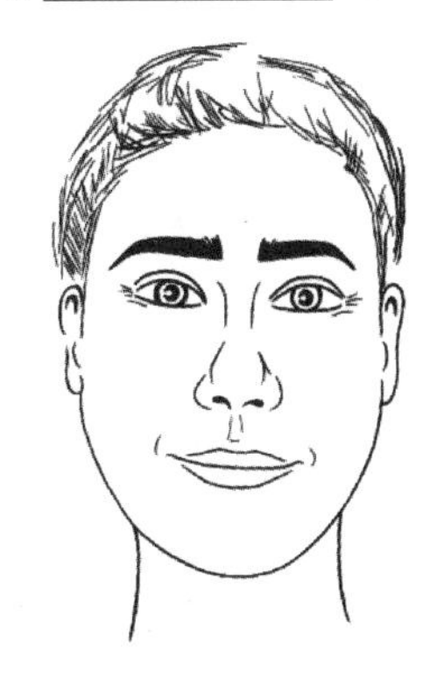

Figure 7.16

f. _______________

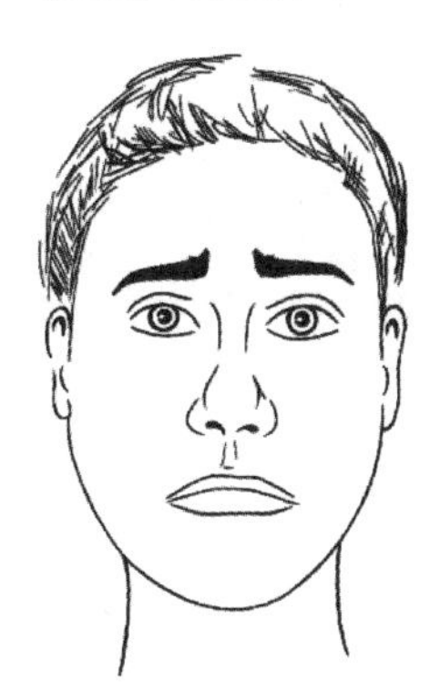

Figure 7.17

g. _______________

Answers: There are a number of minor similarities and differences between some of the facial microexpressions. The answers here are a = Fear, b = Anger, c = Surprise, d = Disgust, e = Contempt, f = Happiness, g = Sadness. If you find some of these confusing, return to the sections that discuss them in the chapter and review some of the details.

Putting It All Together

Body Language

You now have a better understanding of how to use body language to better communicate, influence, and persuade. Let us review the most prominent body language indicators and some ways to use body language to increase your chances of influence.

Reading and Understanding Body Language

You need to be able to interpret several types of body language.

Posture: Pay attention to the messages your posture is communicating. Keep open postures, which communicate you are friendly, receptive, interested, and ready to listen.

Gestures: Be aware of the gestures you and others make with your hands and head. Do not be afraid to use gestures when communicating. They are powerful communicators, and great speakers use A LOT of gestures.

Facial Expressions: The face provides many opportunities to glance into another person's emotions and thoughts. Watch for signs of the seven universal microexpressions to tell if the other party is feeling angry, disgusted, afraid, surprised, happy, sad, or contempt.

The Influencer's Toolbox

Make a First Impression: One of the first things you can do in forming a relationship of any kind is to make a good first impression.

Remember to be approachable, focus on the people you are meeting, make appropriate eye contact, smile, and greet them with a firm handshake.

Use Body Language to Manage Your Own Emotions: Adjust your body language to send a message to others and to adjust your mood. Feeling down? Smile. Feeling stressed, anxious, low on energy? Adjust your posture. Not feeling confident? Try a power pose.

Use Body Language to Manage the Emotions of Others: You can use body language to manage the emotions of others. The first rule is to smile, which is contagious. You can combine what you know about body language and what you have learned about mirroring to break the negative poses of others, bringing them around to a more receptive nature and changing their mood.

8 Personality

"The ability to understand people is one of the greatest assets anyone can ever have."

– *John C. Maxwell,* Becoming a Person of Influence/Talent Is Never Enough

We have talked so much about influencing that it makes sense to step back and ask: Whom are we influencing? Up to this point, this book has provided you with resources for persuading others requiring little adjustment based on your audience. However, whom you want to influence should impact how you approach the situation, perhaps none more than the other people's personalities. So, in this chapter, we will provide a crash course on diagnosing the Big Five Personality Traits and how to adjust your behavior accordingly when influencing each.

Characteristics, Traits, and Types

Personalities can be described by their characteristics, types, or traits. These words are often used interchangeably; however, some distinction exists.

Personality characteristics can be thought of as features. Individual aspects of one's personality that together describe our personality types or traits. Creativity is a personality characteristic. Organized is a personality characteristic. Outgoing is a personality characteristic. Characteristics are the individual features of our personality.

Personality type research emerged in the first half of the 20th century as a new way to study and understand personality. Personality types are classifications of people based on their personality characteristics. You have probably heard of at least one of the personality assessments:

the Myers-Briggs Type Indicator (MBTI), the DiSC assessment, True Colors, or ColorCode (The People Code).

Though personality type assessments may be useful for self-assessment and gaining self-perspective, they have come under some criticism for their methods and their scientific validity. One of the major draw-backs of personality type assessments is they tend to classify people as belonging to one of two dimensions. For example, you are an introvert or an extrovert. However, we know people may fall anywhere along the continuum from introverted to extroverted.

By the second half of the 20th century, personality trait theory began to emerge as a better way to understand personality. Personality traits are patterns of thoughts, feelings, and behavior that are relatively stable within a person throughout their lifetime and across situations. The most popular personality trait framework is the Big Five Personality Traits (Big Five) framework. In the Big Five, traits are measured along five dimensions: openness, conscientiousness, extroversion, agreeableness, and neuroticism.

Prior to discussing the Big Five, you should understand your own personality traits. Try the following short version of the assessment developed by data collected from the Open Source Psychometrics Project using items from the International Personality Item Pool.[63,64]

Measuring Your Personality Traits

Assessments are available to assess your personality traits. You can assess your own personality traits using the following short assessment developed from the 50-item International Personality Item Pool.[65]

1.	I start conversations	1 - 2 - 3 - 4 - 5 - 6 - 7
2.	I get stressed out easily.	1 - 2 - 3 - 4 - 5 - 6 - 7
3.	I have a vivid imagination.	1 - 2 - 3 - 4 - 5 - 6 - 7
4.	I am not interested in other people's problems.	1 - 2 - 3 - 4 - 5 - 6 - 7
5.	I pay attention to details.	1 - 2 - 3 - 4 - 5 - 6 - 7
6.	I feel comfortable around people.	1 - 2 - 3 - 4 - 5 - 6 - 7
7.	I worry about things.	1 - 2 - 3 - 4 - 5 - 6 - 7
8.	I am full of ideas.	1 - 2 - 3 - 4 - 5 - 6 - 7
9.	I am interested in people.	1 - 2 - 3 - 4 - 5 - 6 - 7

10.	I often forget to put things back in their place.	1 - 2 - 3 - 4 - 5 - 6 - 7
11.	I do not talk a lot.	1 - 2 - 3 - 4 - 5 - 6 - 7
12.	I change my mood a lot.	1 - 2 - 3 - 4 - 5 - 6 - 7
13.	I am not interested in abstract ideas.	1 - 2 - 3 - 4 - 5 - 6 - 7
14.	I sympathize with others' feelings.	1 - 2 - 3 - 4 - 5 - 6 - 7
15.	I like order.	1 - 2 - 3 - 4 - 5 - 6 - 7

To score your Big Five, do the following:

For items 4, 10, 11, and 13 you will need to reverse the item's score before entering the score below, that is, if you scored yourself a 1 rescore below as a 7. For a 2 rescore to 6; 3 rescore to 5; 4 does not change; 5 rescore to 3; 6 rescore to 2; and 7 rescore to 1.

Extroversion	Neuroticism	Openness	Agreeableness	Conscientiousness
Item 1: _____	Item 2: _____	Item 3: _____	Item 4: ____*	Item 5: _____
Item 6: _____	Item 7: _____	Item 8: _____	Item 9: _____	Item 10: ____*
Item 11: ____*	Item 12: _____	Item 13: ____*	Item 14: _____	Item 15: _____
Total: _______	Total: _______	Total: _______	Total: _______	Total: _______

The Big Five Personality Traits

The Big Five Personality Traits (Big Five) correspond to Openness, Conscientiousness, Extroversion, Agreeableness, and Neuroticism (OCEAN) model.

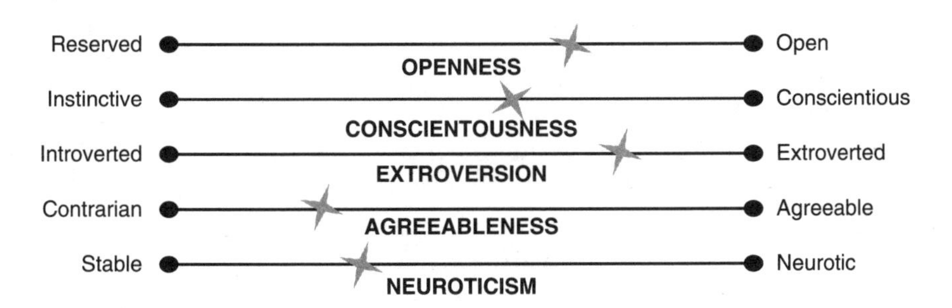

Figure 8.1

Openness

Openness, sometimes called openness to experience, refers to how open-minded you are. It represents your willingness to try and think about new things. It concerns your curiosity and how receptive you are to new experiences and ideas.

Key characteristics associated with openness include adventurousness, artistic interests, emotionality, imagination, intellect, and liberalism.

RESERVED	OPEN
Traditional/Practical Thinker	Thinks Outside the Box
Prefers Routine	Creative
Does Not Favor New Things	Open to New Things/Experiences
Dislikes Change	Curious
Matter-of-Fact Thinker	Imaginative

People who score high on openness are often creative and enjoy "thinking outside the box." Those who score high on openness typically have a broader range of interests. They are adventurous, like to try new things, are characterized as especially curious, and they enjoy learning new things. Of course, with this curiosity comes a downside. Those in this group tend not to be detail oriented and sometimes do not see all of their commitments through because they have moved on to their next new experience, interest, or project.

People who score low on openness are often more traditional and closed-minded thinkers, preferring the routine to something new. They are predictable, and generally dislike change. People who score low on openness may resist new ideas and think analytically and may dislike or struggle with abstract thinking. This lack of desire for change makes this group more consistent and reliable and more likely to appreciate and uphold traditions.

Conscientiousness

Conscientiousness expresses how self-controlled you are. It is your level of self-discipline and how you regulate and control your impulses. Conscientiousness also indicates your inclinations toward goal setting and goal-directed behavior, hard work, organization, and responsibility.

The key characteristics most closely associated with conscientiousness include cautiousness, self-discipline, self-efficacy, responsibility, achievement striving, and orderliness.

INSTINCTIVE	CONSCIENTIOUS
Acts by Instinct and Emotion	Self-Disciplined
More Likely to Feel Incompetent	Exhibits Competence
Trusts Their Gut	Values Preparation/Proactive
Able to Function Without Order	Organized
Burdened by Accountability	Responsible

People who score high on conscientiousness are most often reliable, responsible, self-disciplined, thoughtful, and careful. Highly conscientious people set goals and are not afraid of hard work to achieve them. They pay attention to detail, tend to plan ahead, and are highly organized. Unfortunately, this group does not handle surprises well and finds managing unexpected events or disorganization challenging.

People who score low on conscientiousness often act instinctively and sometimes compulsively. Those in this group follow their gut. They do not often plan ahead and are able to succeed without order, although this may lead them to procrastinate on some tasks. They are more likely to feel burdened by accountability; thus, they are reluctant to set goals and are also more likely to feel inadequate or incompetent.

Extroversion

Extroversion (or extraversion) concerns how a person interacts with others and the environment. It is your level of outgoingness, talkativeness, and energy. It concerns how assertive you are and how comfortable you are starting a conversation or when in social situations.

The key characteristics related to extraversion are friendliness, gregariousness, assertiveness, cheerfulness, activity level, and excitement seeking.

INTROVERTED	EXTROVERTED
Prefers Solitude / Reserved	Outgoing / Sociable
Exhausted by Social Interaction	Energized in Social Situations
Thinks Before Speaking	Speaks Before Thinking
Uncomfortable Starting Conversation	Enjoys Starting Conversations
Dislikes Being Center of Attention	Enjoys Being Center of Attention

People who score high on extraversion are usually outgoing and sociable. They are energized by social interaction; thus, they enjoy starting conversations. Extroverts are often assertive in their opinions and are not afraid to express their emotions. Extroverts enjoy being the center of attention, bring a lot of energy, and are often considered the life of the party.

People who score low on extraversion are known as introverts. They are often seen as reserved, prefer listening over speaking, and become exhausted by social interaction; thus, they usually prefer solitude. They are uncomfortable starting conversations, tend to think through what they are going to say before speaking, and dislike being the center of attention. Following social interactions, they will often need a period of quiet and solitude to recharge. This group does not speak as often, but when they do, listening to them is worthwhile. Unlike extraverts who gain energy from others, this group is more able to motivate themselves.

Although we most often discuss introversion versus extraversion, these traits are measured on a continuum. A significant number of people can fall in the middle of the spectrum. These are known as ambiverts, and their personalities are balanced between introverted and extroverted characteristics.

Agreeableness

Agreeableness deals with how you approach situations and how you treat others. It is your level of cooperation, trust, friendliness, and empathy, and it concerns how much you care about others and the level of altruism you display.

Key characteristics associated with agreeableness include cooperation, morality, trust, sympathy, modesty, and altruism.

CONTRARIAN	AGREEABLE
Aloof	Friendly
Competitive	Cooperative
Demanding	Altruistic
Indifferent	Sympathetic
Skeptical	Trusting
Indirect	Straightforward

People with a high degree of agreeableness are seen as cooperative and helpful and having a great deal of care and concern for others.

Agreeable individuals typically exhibit positive, prosocial behaviors and are typically more trusting and quite straightforward. High agreeableness does come with a desire to avoid confrontation, unlikelihood of stating ideas with conviction, and to going along with situations even if they do feel uncomfortable.

People with a low degree of agreeableness are often seen as aloof and discordant and typically have a difficult time showing empathy. They often come off as competitive, may be seen as uncooperative, and are often characterized as demanding. Contrarian individuals are typically skeptical and distrusting and may approach situations being indirect or manipulative. This group makes for excellent devil's advocates. They question everything as a result, and though painful at times, they often make everyone around them better and/or they present ideas with a tremendous amount of confidence.

Neuroticism

Neuroticism depicts your overall emotional stability. It influences how you see and react to the world and infers your predisposition to experiencing negative emotions. Neuroticism relates to how you approach and handle anxiety and stress.

Characteristics associated with neuroticism include anxiety, anger, depression, vulnerability, self-consciousness, and immoderation.

STABLE	NEUROTIC
Emotionally Stable	Experience Excessive Stress
Relaxed	Anxious
Calm	Contentious
Confident	Self-Conscious
Rarely Sad or Depressed	Dramatic Shifts in Mood

People who score high on neuroticism are more inclined to experience negative emotions, often worry about things, see the world as threatening, and are apt to experience stress and anxiety. They tend to be anxious, depressed, irritable, and experience mood swings. However, this group also tends to have a high IQ and confidence, so they controversially often find themselves in high-level decision-making positions. Additionally, due to their constant worrying, they tend to think several steps ahead and are prepared for surprises.

Conversely, people who score low on neuroticism are more likely to apply a more positive and stable approach to their lives. They often conduct themselves in a calm and relaxed manner. Stable individuals are more emotionally resilient. They rarely have mood swings or experience sadness or depression. Their calm nature makes them less prepared for surprises, and they tend to be equally less passionate about what they enjoy than they are stable when things go wrong.

Altercasting

Altercasting is projecting a personality characteristic or personality trait onto someone else in order to influence and persuade.

Altercasting is a form of priming that changes people's mindset into one that is more likely to comply with your request as in this example:

> *"You are a good mechanic, right? Would you mind looking at my car?"*

You are priming someone with the concept that they are a *mechanic* and *good* at fixing cars. You get them into that mindset and then nudge them toward your preferred answer or direction.

Remember when Cialdini increased the number of people who were willing to help out with a survey by more than 200%? He preceded his request with the simple question: "Are you a helpful person?" That was altercasting. He projected a personality characteristic of helpfulness onto the individuals before asking for them help.

How would you use this when persuading others? Here are a few examples:

- A father may say to his daughter, "You are great at going to bed. Let us head upstairs and start bedtime in five minutes."
- A director might tell one of her direct reports, "You are one of the best on our team at making presentations. Would you mind taking the lead on the meeting on Tuesday?"
- A general manager of a sports team tells an agent who represents one of his player, "One of the things I've most enjoyed about working with you is that you push hard for your client's needs, but you know when to make a deal as well."

IN OUR OWN BACKYARD

Our organization had been in the cloud for years but not exclusively remotely until now. I stressed to the team we needed to communicate. Over-communicate.

Well, despite my own advice, I totally missed the tensions forming between two of our team members, and there was a blow-up. One was a creative and high-level thinker (Instinctive and Competitive); the other was detail oriented (Conscientious and Agreeable). Without a high level of understanding, problems were bound to occur. Although the situation got tense for a brief period, as we started to dig in, we realized the issue was a matter of personality and communication preferences. When in the office, they would get along fine because they could see intention, body language, tell tone, and have more context. Online, that did not come through.

So, what did we do? I asked one of our facilitators who had extensive experience in leadership training, Mike Patterson, to run a virtual session for us on communication and empathy. The result was amazing. We got to the heart of the issue, and we accidentally unanimously realized the entire team missed the social aspect of the office and wanted to do more "out of work" activities as a group. The change in communication did not happen overnight but it got there, and when it did, there was an immediate improvement. Then, my job was to continue to coach and hold our team accountable.

When working with other people, especially virtually, take note of their style. Is their office organized? Are their emails bulleted or do they include typos? Do they like digging into the details? Then communicate in a way that empathizes with their style. You do not have to change who you are, but being mindful will make a huge difference.

Personality Type Assessments

There are many different personality type indicators. Perhaps you have taken the MBTI, DiSC, True Colors, ColorCode, or one of the many other forms of personality type assessments that have become popular in business as well as online. Although personality type research has fallen out of scientific favor, because these assessments are popular and can be useful for self-assessment, self-improvement, and learning and career counseling, we thought we would introduce you to some of the most common personality type assessments you may run across.

The Myers-Briggs Type Indicator (MBTI)

The Myers-Briggs Type Indicator (MBTI) is a personality assessment developed in the 1940s and 1950s by Isabel Briggs Myers and her mother Katharine Cook Briggs and is based on Carl Jung's theory of personality types. The MBTI assesses individuals along four different categorizations: Extroversion vs. Introversion, Sensing vs. Intuition, Thinking vs. Feeling, and Judging vs. Perceiving.

The Myers-Briggs Type Indicator uses a 93-question self-assessment to classify individuals into 1 of 16 personality types. Each personality type is indicated by the first letter of the four categorizations, such as ESTJ or INFP.

The MBTI is one of the most popular personality assessments and can be useful in gaining self-perspective. However, despite its popularity, like other personality typographies, the MBTI has not held up to scientific scrutiny and it has been noted to have poor validity and poor test-retest reliability, meaning people get different results when they retake the test.

The DiSC Assessment

Around the same time that Myers and Briggs were developing the MBTI, others were working on studying and measuring personality types. In 1956, industrial psychologist Dr. William Clark designed the DiSC assessment, another personality trait indicator that helps people gain self-perspective. Clark based the DiSC assessment off the work of psychologist Dr. William M. Marston, who theorized in his 1928 book *Emotions of Normal People* that people exhibited their emotions through four behavior types: Dominance, Influence, Steadiness, and Compliance.

The DiSC assessment is assessed through a series of yes and no questions and assigns individuals up to three styles: a primary style, a secondary style, and a tertiary style.

- Dominance: direct, assertive, and demanding. Those with the Dominance behavior type value competence, action, and results. They are competitive and driven by their need for achievement. They need to win.

- Influence: outgoing, charismatic, and enthusiastic. Those with the Influence behavior type value relationships, collaboration, and social recognition. They are charming, friendly, and trusting and are often optimistic, if not overly optimistic. They also need to be liked.
- Steadiness: easygoing, calm, and patient. Those with the Steadiness behavior type value stability, cooperation, and loyalty. They value compromise and do not like offending others or letting people down. They are supportive and helpful and are good at listening. They need peace in their lives.
- Compliance: analytical and detail-oriented. Those with the Compliance behavior type value accuracy and quality. They like facts and data and are influenced by logic. They are careful, tactful, and systematic. They need to be right and fear being wrong.

Like the MBTI, the DiSC assessment lacks consistent compelling scientific evidence. Although the dimensions of DiSC have been shown to correlate with other personality typography and with some of the Big Five, there is little evidence of validity or test-retest reliability.

True Colors

A third popular personality assessment is the True Colors personality assessment. Don Lowry developed True Colors in the late 1970s to categorize four different learning types. Lowry's goal was to simplify our understanding of the complex results from personality typographies, such as Myers-Briggs, down to four, easy-to-understand, personality types based off of their temperaments: Blue, Green, Gold, and Orange.

- Blue: guided by their ideals. True Color Blues are authentic, caring, and compassionate. They care about others and relationships. Blues are often great communicators; although others may see them as over-emotional, they view themselves as unique and authentic.
- Green: guided by trust. True Color Greens value knowledge. They are logical and analytical. Greens are highly task focused and tough minded, valuing knowledge, perhaps more than people do.

- Gold: guided by order and sensibility. True Color Golds are dependable and loyal. They value duty and tradition. Golds are goal-oriented, but realistic with their goals and approach them organized and well prepared.
- Orange: guided by excitement. True Color Oranges love fun and enjoy variety and spontaneity. They approach life with energy and optimism. Oranges are often witty and charismatic and are generally liked.

True Colors has also come under criticism for a lack of scientific evidence. Though subjects have rated their True Color classifications as accurate, no peer-reviewed research has found support for True Colors.

ColorCode

Another color-based personality assessment is ColorCode (The People Code), which was formally known as the Hartman Personality Profile. The ColorCode was created by Dr. Taylor Hartman in the late 1990s. The 43-question self-assessment classifies individuals into one of four colors: Red, Blue, White, and Yellow.

- Red: driven by the feeling of power. ColorCode Reds are the go-getters. The doers. The action oriented. They are motivated by their goals and the task at hand. Reds are often assertive, even dominant. But this is often in their determined, if not obsessive, effort to reach their goals.
- Blue: driven by intimacy and emotion. ColorCode Blues are the idealists. Those who do what "feels" right. They are motivated by their relationships and emotions. Blues are often consistent and loyal, remaining deeply committed to their relationships and ideals.
- White: driven by harmony. ColorCode Whites are the pacifists. They are agreeable to the core. Those that seek peace and avoid confrontation. They are motivated and feel good when there is peace, harmony, and accord. Whites are respectful, kind, and accepting of others and go out of their way in the name of kinship.
- Yellow: driven by enjoyment. ColorCode Yellows are the spontaneous. The adventure seekers. They are often optimistic and enthusiastic. They are motivated by pleasure and fun. Yellows are persuasive and can be seen as self-centered but are often perceived as happy, charismatic, and fun.

To date no peer reviewed research has found support for Hartman's Personality Profile. It also is criticized for assigning people to one color without considering personality characteristics exist on a continuum.

Influencer's Toolbox

Identifying with the Traits

Understanding people's personalities is important but is a means to an end. Given this is a book on persuasion, let us take a look at how you identify the Big Five in others. Then we will examine how you should adjust your behavior accordingly.

Identifying Openness

You can identify those with the trait of openness by their enthusiasm for everything. They talk quickly because they have so much to say, which you can often spot on a phone call, video call, or in person. They have a lot of new ideas, but few come to fruition. They have a diverse set of interests and hobbies because they like to try them all. This often includes interests in art, music, and reading. This will often come up in conversation or be visible in their offices/backgrounds.

Identifying Conscientiousness

Those with the trait of conscientiousness are neat and efficient. This can be noticed in their clothing, car, and offices. They arrive early to meetings and video calls. They are the most likely to fall into the workaholic category as they are perfectionists and goal-oriented. They tend to be less social and more to the point, which can become apparent early in an interaction with them.

Identifying Extraversion

The trait of extroversion is easy to identify. They are the ones talking to everyone. They tend to be gregarious and the life of any party or conference call. They will instigate small talk or be willing to go along with it if others do. They are excited about ideas in a meeting or phone call but following through, without direct interaction, can be more challenging. They will likely have a lot of pictures in their office, each of which is a platform for a story.

Identifying Agreeableness

One can identify the agreeableness trait by the devotion to comfort, to some extent comfort for themselves but mainly for others. Some social overlap exists with extraversion but it comes more from a place of being interested and wanting to be liked by others. They are highly trusting, empathetic, and modest, so their backgrounds or and what they discuss rarely ever shows off. They avoid confrontation, so in meetings, you will find they go along with other people even if they are not sold on an idea; therefore, they are less excited. When they speak, they tend to use collective language because they genuinely often think of the other parties.

Identifying Neuroticism

One can identify the neurotic trait because those with it are always stressed. These people are often smart and funny, both of which can be picked up early in interactions. However, they are low risk takers and skeptical. They question everything. They can be moody, so they are the most likely to provide a different feel from one interaction to another, possibly within an interaction. They are neat and on time, similar to the conscientious types, but unlike them, they expect the same of others and are upset if others do not live up to that expectation. They usually have large egos, so opposite to those that are high on agreeableness, they make sure their voice is heard and are unlikely to go along with an idea they do not support.

Influencing with the Traits

Now that you have identified these individual traits, how do you approach each?

Influencing Openness

With people showing the openness trait, try to match their excitement. Your excitement will be contagious for them. Give them a chance to be creative and put their stamp or style on the idea but do not provide too much slack, otherwise they will make it their own and keep changing things. The goal is to excite them, engage them early, and keep them on track. These people are best persuaded by presenting them with three options to choose from: less takes away the sense of control and more gives them too many directions to go and is unpredictable. Finally, keep things on a higher level for this group; the details are less important than the feel of the decision.

For those who are low on this trait, provide them with a low-risk approach. Offer a clear recommendation rather than choices. Keep surprises to a minimum. Get them headed in the right direction, and they will likely see things through to the end successfully.

Influencing Conscientiousness

When dealing with people who are conscientious, remember they value efficiency. Get to meetings or video calls early, call on time, and have an agenda in their hands well before the meeting. Make sure to have all of the details ready for whatever ideas you suggest. They work hard and tend to respect others who do as well, so do your best to keep up with the standard they set. Do not skip personal conversations and bonding all together but do not spend too much time with small talk.

For people who are low on this trait, do not go too far into details. Give them everything they need at a high level when you are together. Focus on how a decision or idea feels and avoid specific timelines or deadlines that will feel like an unwelcome burden for them.

Influencing Extroversion

For extroverts, like those who have an openness to experience, they are easier to excite, so match their excitement and find ways to fill in the gaps between interactions. Keep things at a higher level and avoid the minutiae. They feed off your energy and those of people around them so consider more frequent calls, video calls, or meetings or consider sending videos on whatever concept you are pushing. You and your approach as much as your idea will convince them.

For introverts, send them materials in advance and connect with them one-on-one regarding whatever you are trying to influence. Avoid putting them on the spot during meetings with other people. Expect to speak more than they will but be focused during your interactions so as to see more subtle signals.

Influencing Agreeableness

To persuade the agreeableness personality, persuade those around them. They are, more than others, impacted by the opinions of others around them, so starting with this strategy is a particularly impactful tool to use for these people. Those in this group are easier to influence because they are more trusting, so remember the ethical aspects of persuasion. This group's most powerful force is their desire to do good, so if aspects of your concept will benefit others, highlight them. And this is the perfect type of person to ask for help to persuade.

Those low on agreeableness will be skeptical and second guess your idea. Do not be disheartened. Get support from others to make it easier for them to say yes.

Influencing Neuroticism

To persuade those high on neuroticism, the key aspects are having a good plan because they are smart. Make them look good because they have egos, and minimize the risk because that drives their decisions. This is the group where you use a question to raise an idea so they present it back to you as their own. You need to have all data ready for support, be on time to all meetings, and remember that all details matter with this group. They will be skeptical so do not let that put you off; rather, your passing through their gauntlet will cement the success of your idea.

Those low on neuroticism may not be as excited about the idea but will rarely lash out if they dislike it. Slow and steady wins the race with this group because they are not the group that needs to be dazzled quickly. Stay at a higher level and make the decision easy for them and feel good.

Putting It All Together

Personalities

You have now learned the basics of an individual's personality characteristics, types, and traits along with how to communicate with people with different personality traits in order to influence and persuade more effectively.

The Big Five Personality Traits

One of the best ways to understand personality is through the Big Five Personality Trait model: the OCEAN model.

Openness: Openness portrays one's openness to experience and open mindedness. On one end are the reserved who are matter-of-fact thinkers who prefer routine and dislike change. On the other end are those who are extremely open. They are open to new experiences and are often curious, imaginative, and creative.

Conscientiousness: Conscientiousness characterizes one's self-discipline and self-control. On the one end are those who are instinctive. They trust their gut, allow their emotion to guide them, and can function and succeed without much order. On the other end are the conscientious. They are self-disciplined, responsible, and organized. They are often goal-oriented and value preparation.

Extroversion: Extroversion represents how a person interacts with others and the environment. On the one end are the introverts who are reserved and prefer solitude. They are uncomfortable starting conversations, think before speaking, and become exhausted by social interaction. On the other end are the extroverts. They are outgoing and sociable, are energized in social situations, and enjoy being the center of attention.

Agreeableness: Agreeableness depicts how one approaches situations. On one end is the contrarian, who may be competitive, demanding, and skeptical. On the other end are those who are completely agreeable – always friendly, cooperative, and trusting.

Neuroticism: Neuroticism describes one's emotional stability. On one end, you have emotionally stable individuals who are relaxed, calm, and confident. On the other end you have neurotic individuals who experience dramatic shifts in moods, stress, and anxiety and are unconfident.

The Influencer's Toolbox

Identify with the Traits: If you want to successfully persuade someone, first you have to understand where they are coming from. Using the OCEAN model, you can identify which of the Big Five traits people are demonstrating.

Influence with the Traits: Once you recognize when people are showing openness, conscientiousness, extroversion, agreeableness, or neuroticism, you are in a better position to respond to them. You can approach them in the way that will best appeal to the exhibited trait.

9 Putting It All Together

By now, we hope that you have learned the steps in the Four-Step Process of Influence and Persuasion (Building Credibility, Engaging Emotion, Demonstrating Logic, and Facilitating Action). These are the cornerstones of influencing and persuading. Use them each and every time you are trying to persuade.

1. **Building Credibility:** To build credibility, you need to establish Trust and Expertise. Trust is created by balancing Connection, Value, and Reliability with one's own self-interest.
2. **Engaging Emotion:** Emotions are powerful motivators. Remember to tap into Achievement, Fear, and Obligation.

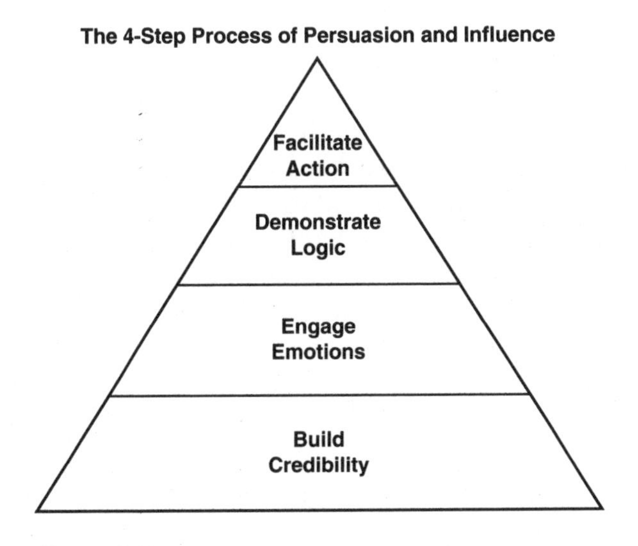

Figure 9.1

3. **Demonstrating Logic:** To demonstrate logic, communicate natural and logical consequences. Add Social Proof, which is proof from the masses, peer proof, and thought leader proof. Back it up with Documented Proof, which is your evidence.
4. **Facilitating Action:** Finally, you need to make a plea for action. Employ soft and hard closing techniques to overcome objections and lead people you are trying to influence to a yes.

There is also a fifth overarching component to the process of influence and persuasion: the **Time and Place** of the opportune moment. Be aware of the when, where, and who. These matter in finding the opportune moment to influence and persuade.

The purpose of this book was not to simply teach you this model. It was to become a master influencer, which is why you have learned a plethora of tools and tips to increase your ability to influence and persuade.

A Closer Look at the Four-Step Process

Let's look at the four-step process again in a little more detail, along with the fifth component of Time and Place.

Building Credibility

To Build Credibility you can ***Borrow Credibility***. Look for opportunities to align yourself with people and organizations who will lend you credibility while you are building your own. Borrow Credibility through your brand story, associations, partnering with experts, and showcasing your achievements and recognition.

Allowing yourself to ***Be Vulnerable*** is another good way to form a deeper connection, increase trust, develop credibility, and engage emotion. Showing a willingness to trust, by being vulnerable, makes others more apt to trust you. Consider making statements against self-interest, sharing weaknesses, or asking for help.

Becoming a Trusted Advisor is, perhaps, the gold standard in building your credibility. Trusted advisors take the time to build connections, nurture relationships, and generously share their knowledge, consistently providing value.

Engaging Emotion

One of the most important things you can do to enhance your ability to influence is to ***Manage Your Emotions***. Increase your emotional intelligence by spending time assessing yourself, practicing managing your own emotions, employing empathy, and using what you have learned to guide the emotions of others. Remember to label your emotions, take a break if you need to, be aware of other people's emotions, and consider keeping a journal of your emotions.

Another great tool in master influencers' toolboxes is ***Storytelling***. By telling stories, you engage emotion and you make information more relevant and memorable. Remember, for a story to be powerful, it has to be relevant to your listener and capture their attention.

To tell great stories, you can practice ***Scripting***. By writing, organizing, playing devil's advocate to, and practicing your stories (or pitches or speeches), you have a chance to work through the information, anticipate the conversation, foresee objections, and make your stories and pitches as powerful as possible.

Another great tool to building credibility and engaging emotion is ***Mirroring***. Mirroring builds rapport, increases liking, and engages emotion. You can even use mirroring to change the body language of others. First, copy subtle physical or verbal cues from the other party. Then, redirect the other party using your own cues.

Demonstrating Logic

Framing is another tool you can use to engage emotion and demonstrate logic. When framing your arguments, remember that people are risk averse and will give up more to avoid losses than they will to seek potential games. Also the more vivid something is, the easier people will understand it.

One form of framing, ***Anchoring***, can have a big influence on the outcome of a situation. Whenever possible, take the initiative to set the first anchor. If other parties set the anchor first, especially if the anchor is outside of the bargaining range, you may need to diffuse the anchor, provide more information, and offer a well-informed counter anchor.

Another form of framing is ***Benefit Framing***. By focusing on the advantages and benefits rather than the features, you focus on the thing other parties care about: what it does for them.

Facilitating Action

You can use several methods to get to a yes. First, you can start with a ***Small Yes***. Get the other party into an agreement mindset by eliciting yesses. Use questions to which you know the answer will be yes. Then lead people closer to the decision you would like them to make by asking questions that move them in that same direction.

To make getting a yes easier, you should be ***Providing Options***. Providing choices facilitates action. We recommend three to five choices to be ideal, depending on the complexity of the decision, with the middle option being the default (the one you most want them to choose).

Finally, you can provide a ***Safety Net***, which reduces the risk behind a decision. Think of ways in which you can add safety nets, such as guarantees, warranties, and opt-out clauses, to reduce the other party's risk the next time you want to influence a decision.

Time and Place

Make sure to remember **Kairos**. The time and place in which you deliver the message matters. Consider your state and the state of the party you want to influence. This is the difference between making a speech in front of one person or a quarter of a million.

Beyond the Four-Step Process

Throughout the book, we have provided you with a number of tools to help you understand and communicate with others better.

Pay attention to **Body Language**, that of others as well as your own. Body language is a powerful communicator. It can help you make a great first impression and help you manage the emotions of yourself and others.

To make a good ***First Impression***, be approachable, focus on the people you are meeting, make eye contact, smile, and greet them with a firm handshake.

You can use your body language to ***Manage Your Own Emotions***. Adjust your body language to adjust your mood. Feeling down? Smile. Feeling stressed, anxious, or low on energy? Adjust your posture. Not feeling confident? Try a power pose.

Use body language to ***Manage the Emotions of Others***. First, smile. Smiling is contagious and puts you and others in a more positive mood. You can combine what you know about body language and what you have learned about mirroring to break the negative poses of others by bringing them around to a more receptive nature and changing their mood.

Finally, keep the other parties' **Personality** in mind. One of the best ways to understand personality is through the Big Five Personality Traits model (i.e., the OCEAN model). Assess the other parties' Openness, Conscientiousness, Extroversion, Agreeableness, and Neuroticism and use what you know about personality to communicate with and influence individuals more effectively.

Thank you for sticking with us all the way through. We hope you enjoyed reading *Persuade* as much as we enjoyed writing it. We are confident you will be more successful if you put to use the tools and resources we provided, but please remember the responsibility that comes with being an effective persuader.

Appendix

A

A Study of Decision Makers' Decision Making

Methods and Analysis

Sample and Instrument

The primary sample for this study consisted of decision makers recruited through Amazon's Mechanical Turk. Participants in our study were asked to complete a 60-item survey in exchange for a nominal reward. A screening was employed at the beginning of the survey to confirm that participants practiced decision making within their professional role, requiring a true or false answer to the question, "I am responsible for substantive decision making as part of my occupation."

The survey collected responses regarding various aspects of influence and persuasion to test key suppositions surrounding decision making, including credibility, storytelling, statements against self-interest, the role of emotions in decision making, framing, providing rationale for propositions and requests, anchoring, the value of providing a safety net, the ideal and overwhelming number of choices, and the influence of getting a small yes.

First, the survey data were manually examined and cleaned. Second, responses were examined for completeness and clarity. In total, 939 participants began the survey; however, 90 participants were disqualified for failing one of the two attention checks, and 2 participants did not affirm they answered the survey truthfully. Finally, the data were also examined for random responses, where we found 20 additional participants who were believed to be responding randomly and were discarded from analysis. This resulted in 827 complete and usable responses. Analysis was performed using PSPP (version 1.4.1), the open-source alternative to IBM's SPSS.

Table 1 Sample Statistics

Correlations	n	%	Cumulative %
Gender			
Male	454	54.9%	54.9%
Female	366	44.3%	99.2%
Other	2	0.2%	99.4%
Prefer Not to Say	5	.6%	100.0%
Education			
Less than a High School Degree	2	0.2%	0.2%
High School Degree	35	4.2%	4.5%
Some College	67	8.1%	12.6%
Associate Degree	71	8.6%	21.2%
Bachelor's Degree	438	53.0%	74.1%
Master's Degree	195	23.6%	97.7%
Doctorate or Professional Degree	19	2.3%	100.0%
Role			
Executive/Senior Management	122	14.8%	14.8%
Middle Management	285	34.5%	49.2%
Management/Team Leader	269	32.5%	81.7%
Staff	151	18.3%	100.0%
Race			
Native American or Alaskan Native	16	1.9%	1.9%
Asian	66	8.0%	9.9%
Black or African American	176	21.3%	31.2%
Native Hawaiian or other Pacific Islander	1	0.1%	31.3%
White	549	66.4%	97.7%
Prefer Not to Say	19	2.3%	100.0%
Ethnicity			
Hispanic or Latino	187	22.6%	22.6%
Not Hispanic or Latino	616	74.5%	97.1%
Prefer Not to Say	24	2.9%	100.0%

Participants in our study ranged from 19 to 83 years old with a mean age of 39.72, were predominately white (66.4%) and male (54.9%), and well educated, with the majority of them having completed a bachelor's degree or higher (78.9%). Also, the majority of respondents indicated that their role within their respective organizations was lower or middle management (67%). Table 1 provides the frequencies and percentages of the sample statistics.

Analysis and Results

Because we were attempting to answer 10 research questions, we used several statistical methods to analyze the results, including examination of descriptive statistics, bivariate correlations, cross tabulations, the Kruskal-Wallis H Test, and Mann-Whitney U Test, one-way analysis of variance (ANOVA), and linear regression.

Hypothesis 1: Credibility, Supported

> *Perceptions of one's credibility are highly related to liking, trust, and expertise.*

To examine the first hypothesis, participants were asked to indicate, on a scale of 1 to 7, how important a number of factors are in ascertaining the credibility of a new potential business partnership. The first hypothesis was explored by examining descriptive statistics (means, standard deviations, and bivariate correlations). The data showed that all 11 factors tested were rated, on average, as at least moderately important, with means ranging from 4.00 to 5.77. Based on the descriptive statistics, we concluded that perceptions of one's credibility are highly related to factors associated with liking, trust, and expertise. Table 2 provides the means, standard deviations, and bivariate correlations for the 11 items shown to be important in assessments of credibility.

Hypothesis 2: Storytelling, Supported

> *Storytelling is widely used in communication in professional relationships, including in building relationships, engaging emotions, demonstrating logic, and facilitating action.*

Table 2 Credibility (Descriptive Statistics)

Corr.	Mean	SD	CRED 1	CRED 2	CRED 3	CRED 4	CRED 5	CRED 6	CRED 7	CRED 8	CRED 9	CRED 10
CRED 1	5.47	1.29										
CRED 2	5.23	1.33	.473*									
CRED 3	4.76	1.68	.287*	.271*								
CRED 4	5.38	1.27	.348*	.184*	.245*							
CRED 5	4.00	2.01	.357*	.303*	.471*	.295*						
CRED 6	5.26	1.43	.391*	.359*	.304*	.216*	.346*					
CRED 7	4.35	1.90	.404*	.316*	.445*	.305*	.748*	.406*				
CRED 8	5.77	1.12	.248*	.160*	.141*	.467*	.078*	.185*	.119*			
CRED 9	5.60	1.20	.330*	.174*	.167*	.486*	.145*	.212*	.179*	.478*		
CRED 10	4.94	1.57	.383*	.216*	.380*	.527*	.511*	.310*	.505*	.263*	.356*	
CRED 11	5.59	1.17	.262*	.253*	.233*	.125*	.164*	.345*	.185*	.204*	.211*	.143*

* significant at $p < .05$
CRED 1: Customer reviews on your potential business partner's company website
CRED 2: Customer reviews on an independent third-party website
CRED 3: Wrote a white paper on their proposed solution
CRED 4: Is a person you feel you would like
CRED 5: Have the endorsement of a major sports star
CRED 6: A member of the Better Business Bureau (BBB) and the local Chamber of Commerce
CRED 7: Have the endorsement of several social media influencers
CRED 8: Are someone you feel you would work well with
CRED 9: Are approachable and easy to talk to
CRED 10: Have a lot of things in common with you
CRED 11: Have the endorsements of several experts in your industry

To examine the second hypothesis, participants were asked to indicate, on a scale of 1 to 5, how often they use stories or anecdotes in a number of specific ways within their professional relationships. The scale points read: Never, Rarely, Sometimes, Often, and Always. The second hypothesis was explored by examining descriptive statistics (means, standard deviations) and bivariate correlations. The data showed that all 14 factors tested were used, on average, sometimes too often, with means ranging from 2.59 (using storytelling to manipulate others) to 3.85. Based on these means, we concluded storytelling is widely used in communication in professional relationships. Table 3 provides the means, standard deviations, and bivariate correlations for the 14 ways storytelling was used within professional relationships.

Hypothesis 3: Statements Against Self-Interest, Not Supported

Statements against self-interest communicate trust.

To examine the third hypothesis, participants were asked to indicate how likely, on a scale of 1 to 7, they would be to take a sore throat medicine based on two different tag lines on the labels, one containing a statement against self-interest and another without such a statement. The third hypothesis was tested by examining whether responses varied by the version of the survey question received by participants. The statistical methods used to test this hypothesis were the examination of descriptive statistics (means and standard deviations) and the Mann-Whitney U Test.

Examining the means and standard deviations, it appeared that decision makers placed little difference in trust communicated through statements against self-interests (5.06, $SD = 1.46$) compared with those in the control group (5.03, $SD = 1.64$).

A Mann-Whitney U Test was conducted to compare the trust ratings between those who received a message containing a statement against self-interest compared to those who received a message that did not. The Mann-Whitney U Test indicates no significant differences between these two groups ($U = 84{,}022.50$, p-value $= 0.662$) with mean ranks of 417.52 and 410.43 for groups one and two, respectively.

Table 3 Storytelling (Descriptive Statistics)

CORR	MEAN	SD	STORY1	STORY2	STORY3	STORY4	STORY5	STORY6	STORY7	STORY8
STORY1	3.62	0.99								
STORY2	3.77	.94	.441*							
STORY3	3.85	.86	.451*	.491*						
STORY4	3.61	.96	.446*	.417*	.388*					
STORY5	3.48	1.06	.419*	.437*	.413*	.385*				
STORY6	3.77	.86	.358*	.340*	.345*	.376*	.342*			
STORY7	3.75	.93	.484*	.553*	.527*	.414*	.419*	.374*		
STORY8	3.71	.91	.403*	.398*	.352*	.455*	.400*	.463*	.402*	
STORY9	3.62	.97	.432*	.539*	.436*	.438*	.484*	.363*	.555*	.396*
STORY10	3.49	.97	.398*	.403*	.356*	.385*	.400*	.313*	.381*	.338*
STORY11	3.76	.91	.430*	.448*	.443*	.416*	.431*	.404*	.441*	.453*
STORY12	3.66	.96	.431*	.474*	.410*	.465*	.397*	.368*	.467*	.395*
STORY13	3.84	.89	.415*	.403*	.407*	.396*	.390*	.390*	.474*	.420*
STORY14	2.59	1.34	.320*	.218*	.234*	.304*	.456*	.231*	.292*	.309*

CORR	STORY9	STORY10	STOR11	STORY12	STORY13
STORY9					
STORY10	.387*				
STORY11	.458*	.363*			
STORY12	.465*	.399*	.446*		
STORY13	.454*	.337*	.448*	.430*	
STORY14	.274*	.370*	.271*	.313*	.262*

* significant at $p < .05$
STORY1: Open a conversation
STORY2: Make someone feel more comfortable around you
STORY3: Demonstrate how to do something correctly
STORY4: Motivate someone to say yes
STORY5: Provide an example to reinforce your ideas
STORY6: Strengthen your working relationships
STORY7: Strongly reinforce a point you are trying to make
STORY8: Improve or strengthen trust
STORY9: Improve or strengthen commitment
STORY10: Improve understanding and comprehension
STORY11: Engage someone's emotions
STORY12: Explain your logic
STORY13: Provide evidence of your knowledge and expertise
STORY14: Manipulate others

Table 4 Statements Against Self-Interest (Descriptive Statistics)

Statements Against Self-Interest Group	N	Mean	SD	Median	Min	Max
1*	416	5.03	1.64	5	1	7
2**	411	5.06	1.46	5	1	7
Total	827					

* Group 1: (self-interest statement): Your sore throat will be gone.
** Group 2: (against self-interest): You might not like the taste, but your sore throat will be gone.

Hypothesis 4: The Linda Problem, Supported

Emotional responses outweigh logic and reason.

To examine the fourth hypothesis, participants were given a brief description of Linda and asked to determine which statement was more likely.

> Linda is 31 years old, single, outspoken, and bright. She majored in philosophy. As a student, she is deeply concerned with issues of discrimination and social justice and participates in anti-nuclear demonstrations.

Which statement is more likely?

- Linda is a bank teller.
- Linda is a bank teller and is active in the feminist movement.

To examine this hypothesis, we examine the descriptive statistics. Although the likelihood of Linda being a bank teller is far greater than Linda being a bank teller and active in the feminist movement, a full 70.4% of decision makers indicated they believed Linda being a bank teller and active in the feminist movement was more likely. In other words, it seems the hypothesis held and emotional responses outweighed logic and reason in this particular case.

Table 5 The Linda Problem

	n	%
Linda is a bank teller.	245	29.6%
Linda is a bank teller and is active in the feminist movement.	582	70.4%
Total	827	100%

Hypothesis 5: Gain Framing versus Loss Framing, Supported

Individuals are willing to do more to avoid losses than they are to seek equivalent gains.

To examine the fifth hypothesis, participants were provided with one of four versions of a survey question and asked to determine how much they would be willing to spend to seek gains versus avoid losses. The questions varied on gain/loss framing and on the gender of the consultant in the text.

- Gain Framing: "You are a business owner. You come across a management consultant who can help you grow your revenues by 5% at a time when you project your revenues to be flat. You believe this will equate to a change of roughly $1,500,000 in your projected profits. How much would you be willing to pay her/him?"
- Loss Framing: "You are a business owner. You come across a management consultant who can help maintain your current revenues at a time when you project a 5% decrease. You believe this will equate to a change of roughly $1,500,000 in your projected profits. How much would you be willing to pay her/him?"

To test the fifth hypothesis, we examined whether responses varied by the version of the survey question received by participants. The statistical methods used to test this hypothesis were an examination of descriptive statistics (means and standard deviations), ANOVA, and linear regression.

First, data were manually examined for missing data or extreme responses. There were 108 responses removed from consideration for missing data or extreme responses, leaving 719 responses for analysis. Examining the descriptive statistics, differences appeared in the evaluations by participants between gain versus loss framing and between paying him versus paying her.

Overall, decision makers valued avoiding loss (*mean* = 176,283.6, *SD* = 326,400.1) over seeking additional gains (*mean* = 176,283.6, *SD* = 188,403.4).

Decision makers in our study also showed significant differences in what they were willing to pay a woman (*mean* = 118,448.2, *SD* = 195,624.5) compared to what they were willing to pay a man (*mean* = 178,285.4, *SD* = 323,981.1).

Descriptive statistics provided the first insight into the data. However, to examine whether the differences between four groups (based on the combination of gain/loss and him/her) were statistically significant, one-way analysis of variance (ANOVA) was carried out.

Table 6 Framing (Descriptive Statistics)

Gain vs. Loss Framing		N	Mean	SD	Min	Max
Growth	Her	180	105,349.1	184,494.1	1000	1,000,000
	Him	174	133,790.8	191,822.0	1000	1,200,000
Avoid Loss	Her	181	131,474.9	205,783.2	1000	1,000,000
	Him	184	220,361.8	407,820.8	1000	1,575,000
Total		719				

Table 7 Framing (Growth vs. Loss)

Gain vs. Loss Framing	N	Mean	SD	Min	Max
Growth	354	119,328.9	188,403.4	1000	1,200,000
Avoid Loss	365	176,283.6	326,400.1	1000	1,575,000
Total	719				

Table 8 Framing (Her vs. Him)

Gain vs. Loss Framing	N	Mean	SD	Min	Max
Her	361	118,448.2	195,624.5	1000	1,000,000
Him	358	178,285.4	323,981.1	1000	1,575,000
Total	719				

Results of ANOVA show significant differences between the three groups [F (3, 715) = 6.49, p < .001].

In particular, it can be seen that the highest mean was the one for avoid loss*him, followed by growth*him, avoid loss*her, and growth*her (Table 9).

Post hoc comparisons were made using the Tukey HSD test. Post hoc analysis indicated the mean score for the Loss/Him condition was significantly different than the other three question variations. However, the differences among the other three conditions were not statistically significant.

Finally, we tested gain versus loss framing and the gender of the consultant against controls using linear regression. Controls tested included age, gender, and work experience, along with education and organizational role, which were entered into the model as dummy variables. Non-significant control variables were removed from the model iteratively. We found a significant regression equation ($F(4, 714) = 64.96$, $p < 0.001$), with an adjusted R^2 of 0.26 with gain versus loss framing and the gender of the consultant contributing significant impact on the model.

Table 9 Framing (ANOVA)

		Sum of Squares	df	Mean Square	F	Sig.
Framing	Between Groups	1.4E+012	3	4.6E+011	6.49	.000
	Within Groups	5.1E+013	715	7.1E+010		
	Total	5.2E+013	772			

Table 10 Framing (Post Hoc Comparisons)

Question Group		Mean Difference	Std. Error	Sig.	Lower Bound	Upper Bound
Growth/Her	Growth/Him	−28441.7	28258.99	.746	−101211	44327.52
	Loss/Her	−26125.8	27979.76	.787	−98176.0	45924.38
	Loss/Him	−115013	27865.80	.000	−186769	−43256.0
Growth/Him	Growth/Her	28441.73	28258.99	.746	−44327.5	101211.0
	Loss/Her	2315.92	28220.60	1.000	−70354.5	74986.29
	Loss/Him	−86571.0	28107.61	.012	−158950	−14191.6
Loss/Her	Growth/Him	26125.82	27979.76	.787	−45924.4	98176.05
	Growth/Her	−2315.92	28220.60	1.000	−74968.3	70354.46
	Loss/Him	−88886.9	27826.86	.008	−160543	−17230.4
Loss/Him	Growth Him	115012.7	27865.80	.000	43255.97	186769.4
	Growth Her	86570.97	28107.61	.012	14191.55	158950.4
	Loss/Her	88886.89	27826.86	.008	17230.42	160543.4

Table 11 Framing (Linear Regression)

	Unstandardized Coefficients		Standardized Coefficients		
Model	**B**	**SE**	**Beta**	**t**	**Sig.**
Constant	35,392.15	31,707.36	.00	1.12	.265
Gain vs. Loss	.58	.06	.33	9.51	.000
Her vs. Him	.53	.06	.29	8.33	.000
Age	2418.28	995.58	.11	2.43	.015
Work Experience	−3409.63	1113.52	−.14	−3.06	.002

Hypothesis 6: The Because Statement, Supported

> *Providing the rationale or reason behind a request or an offer increases the likelihood of compliance compared to when no rational or reason is provided.*

To examine the sixth hypothesis, participants were presented with one of three statements and were asked to indicate, on a scale of 1 to 7, their likelihood of complying with the request. One group of participants were asked a request without any rationale provided. The second group was asked a request with weak or unconvincing rationale. The third group was asked a request with strong rationale.

- Because Statement Group 1: "I would like a discount of 10% on my next order."
- Because Statement Group 2: "I would like a discount of 10% on my next order because I cannot pay full price."
- Because Statement Group 3: "I would like a discount of 10% on my next order because I have been a loyal customer for five years."

To test the sixth hypothesis, we again examined whether responses varied by the version of the survey question received by participants. The statistical methods used to test this hypothesis were an examination of descriptive statistics (means and standard deviations), the Kruskal-Wallis H Test, and paired Mann-Whitney U Tests.

Examining the descriptive statistics, differences appeared among the groups in the mean influence of the Because statement. Participants in this study reported being more likely to comply with a request where a valid reason was communicated (*mean* = 4.99, *SD* = 1.54) than when no reason was communicated (*mean* = 4.65, *SD* = 1.58); however, they reported least likely to comply when the reason provided was not convincing (*mean* = 3.96, *SD* = 1.88).

The Kruskal-Wallis H test showed statistically significant differences among decision makers willingness to comply with a request for a discount based on how the question was asked, *chi-square* = 45.92, *p-value* < 0.001 with mean rank likelihood ratings of 421.60, 340.93, and 476.16 for statements one, two, and three, respectively.

To explore the difference between groups further, we conducted pairwise Mann-Whitney U Tests with Bonferroni corrections. In the first pairwise test, we compared the likelihood ratings between Group 1 and Group 2. The Mann-Whitney U Test indicated significant differences between these two groups ($U = 29{,}653.5$, *adj.* $p < 0.001$) with mean ranks of 300.83 and 245.15 for groups one and two, respectively.

In the second pairwise test, we compared the likelihood ratings between groups one and three. The Mann-Whitney U Test again indicated significant differences between these two groups ($U = 33{,}574.5$, *adj.* $p = 0.009$) with mean ranks of 260.27 and 2.9952 for groups one and three, respectively.

Finally, in the third pairwise test, we compared the likelihood ratings between groups two and three. The Mann-Whitney U Test indicated significant differences between these two groups ($U = 25{,}670.5$, *adj.* $p < 0.001$).

Table 12 Because Statements (Descriptive Statistics)

Because Statement Group	N	Mean	SD	Min	Max
1	278	4.65	1.58	1	7
2	268	3.96	1.88	1	7
3	281	4.99	1.54	1	7
Total	827				

Hypothesis 7: Anchoring, Supported

Anchors will influence decision makers' final estimates.

To examine the seventh hypothesis, participants were asked one of two versions of an anchoring question: one with a low anchor and one with a high anchor. They were then asked to guess how long they believed was the Mississippi River.

- Anchoring Question Group 1: Do you believe the Mississippi River is longer or shorter than 587 miles?
- Anchoring Question Group 2: Do you believe the Mississippi River is longer or shorter than 1,761 miles?

To test this hypothesis, we continued examining whether responses varied by the version of the survey question received by participants. The statistical methods used to test this hypothesis were an examination of descriptive statistics (means and standard deviations), t-tests, and regression.

First, data were manually examined. There were 54 responses removed from consideration for missing data or extreme responses, leaving 773 responses for analysis. Examining the descriptive statistics, significant differences appeared in the guesses by participants who were anchored to a lower number (*mean* = 1320.95, *SD* = 1192.73) and those who were anchored to a higher number (*mean* = 1949.10, *SD* = 1239.61).

An independent sample t-test was used to compare the estimations of the two groups (a group anchored to a lower number and a group anchored to a higher number). The results showed a significant difference between groups ($t(771) = -7.18$, $p = .013$). In particular, respondents

Table 13 Anchoring (Descriptive Statistics)

Anchoring	N	Mean	SD	Min	Max
1	391	1320.95	1192.73	12	10000
2	382	1949.10	1239.61	12	10000
Total	773				

Table 14 Anchoring (Linear Regression)

	Unstandardized Coefficients		Standardized Coefficients		
Model	**B**	**SE**	**Beta**	**t**	**Sig.**
Constant	723.23	137.65	.00	5.25	.000
Anchor	641.23	87.22	.26	7.35	.000
Executive Level Role	-354.45	125.29	−.10	−2.83	.005

who were anchored to a lower number tended to estimate the river as shorter than those who were anchored to a higher number (Table 13).

Finally, we tested against controls using linear regression. Controls tested include age and work experience, along with gender, education, and organizational role, which were entered into the model as dummy variables. Non-significant control variables were removed from the model iteratively. We find a significant regression equation (F (2, 770) = 30.01, $p\text{-}value < 0.001$), with an adjusted R^2 of 0.07.

Hypothesis 8: Creating a Safety Net, Not Supported

Providing a safety net, in this case an opt out, will increase satisfaction with an offer.

To examine the eighth hypothesis, participants were presented with one of two contract offers, one of which included an opt out and one of which did not. Participants were asked to indicate, on a scale of one to seven, how satisfied they would be with the offer.

This hypothesis was tested by examining whether responses varied by the version of the survey question received by participants. The statistical methods used to test this hypothesis were the examination of descriptive statistics (means and standard deviations) and the Mann-Whitney U Test.

Examining the means and standard deviations, decision makers appeared to be slightly more satisfied with offers that provided an opt

Table 15 Safety Net (Descriptive Statistics)

Safety Net Group	N	Mean	SD	Min	Max
1*	413	3.10	1.70	1	7
2**	414	2.88	1.50	1	7
Total	827				

* Safety Net Statement Group 1 includes Opt Out
** Safety Net Statement Group 2 Does Not Include Opt Out

out (*mean* = 3.10, *SD* = 1.70) compared with those in the control group (*mean* = 2.88, *SD* = 1.50).

Because descriptive statistics showed slight differences between the groups to examine whether these differences were statistically significant, a Mann-Whitney U Test was conducted. That is, a Mann-Whitney U Test was used to compare the satisfaction ratings between those who received an offer that included a safety net and one that did not. The Mann-Whitney U Test indicates no significant differences existed between these two groups ($U = 81{,}220$, $p = .202$) with mean ranks of 424.32 and 403.68 for groups one and two, respectively.

Hypothesis 9: Ideal Number of Choices, Supported

> *The ideal number of choices depends on the complexity of the decision.*

To examine the ninth hypothesis, decision makers were asked to report the ideal number of choices when making a number of specific decisions, such as choosing a dessert from a menu, purchasing a cell phone, and choosing among job offers. Respondents were then asked to report how many choices would lead them to feel overwhelmed making these same decisions.

First, data were examined for missing data and extreme responses. Missing data and extreme values were treated with pairwise deletion to retain the maximum number of responses. To eliminate extreme responses, responses of zero and over 1,000 were first discarded. Next, we examined the Z-scores of the remaining responses, and any responses that fell outside of three deviations from the mean were discarded as well.

To test this hypothesis, we examined descriptive statistics (means and standard deviations). Overall, the descriptive statistics suggested decision makers found between five and six choices to be ideal when making most decisions. Participants in our study reported they would feel overwhelmed with decisions that included more than seven to nine choices. Our results indicated that for simpler decisions, such as choosing a dessert from a menu or and purchasing a cell phone, respondents preferred slightly more choices and can decide between slightly more choices before becoming overwhelmed. However, for more complex decisions, such as choosing a 401(k) or choosing among job offers, participants in our study prefer slightly fewer options and are overwhelmed more easily. Table 16 provides the means for the number of ideal choices and the number of choices seemed overwhelming to participants in our study.

Table 16 Ideal and Overwhelming Choices (Descriptive Statistics)

Number of Choices		N	Mean	SD	Min	Max
Choosing a Dessert	Ideal	748	5.68	5.19	1	30
	Overwhelming	754	8.83	9.10	1	80
Purchasing Toothpaste	Ideal	740	5.40	5.57	1	32
	Overwhelming	747	8.54	8.72	1	56
Purchasing a Cell Phone	Ideal	744	5.66	6.51	1	50
	Overwhelming	753	8.76	10.26	1	88
Choosing a 401k	Ideal	741	5.53	6.59	1	52
	Overwhelming	755	7.76	9.43	1	88
Choosing a Job Offer	Ideal	747	4.93	5.53	1	40
	Overwhelming	757	7.42	8.68	1	60

Hypothesis 10: Small Yesses, Supported

> *(A) Priming an individual's agreeableness will predict their willingness to comply with a request.*
>
> *(B) Priming an individual's helpfulness will predict their willingness to comply with a request.*

To examine the final hypothesis, decision makers in our study received one of two priming questions followed by a request. The priming questions were designed to prime participants agreeableness and helpfulness.

Participants were asked either of the following:

> Do you consider yourself to be a helpful person?
>
> Do you consider yourself to be an unhelpful person?

All participants were then asked the following:

> Would you be willing to provide additional feedback after the survey?

To test this hypothesis, we examined descriptive statistics (frequencies and percentages) and cross tabulations.

First, to examine agreeableness, we compared all the responses that indicated agreeably with the first question (whether they agreed they were a helpful person or they agreed they were an unhelpful person),

Table 17 Small Yesses (Agreeableness Cross Tabulations)

	Agreeable				
	Yes		No		
Willing to provide feedback?	**n**	**%**	**n**	**%**	**% Total**
Yes	403	79.3	205	64.3	73.5
No	105	20.7	114	35.7	26.5
Total	508	100	319	100	

Table 18 Small Yesses (Helpfulness Cross Tabulations)

	Helpful				
	Yes		No		
Willing to provide feedback?	**n**	**%**	**n**	**%**	**% Total**
Yes	519	71.9	89	84.8	73.5
No	203	28.1	16	15.2	26.5
Total	722	100	105	100	

no matter the version of the question. In total, 508 participants agreed with the first question (409 indicated they were helpful, and 99 indicated they were unhelpful).

Of the participants, those who were agreeable in the first question (whether they indicated they were helpful or unhelpful) were the more likely to be agreeable to provide additional feedback after the survey (79.3% complied) than those who were not agreeable with the first question (64.3% complied).

However, the question also primed whether one was helpful or not. In fact, 87.3% ($n = 722$) indicated with the sentiment they were a helpful person (either by indicating they were helpful or they were not unhelpful). Thus, to determine whether priming for a yes or for helpfulness explained this phenomenon, we compared responses for those who indicated they were helpful compared with those who indicated they did not consider themselves to be helpful.

Interestingly, among those who indicated they were helpful, 71.9% indicated their willingness to help, and 84.8% of those who indicated they were not helpful still agreed to help provide additional feedback after the survey. Thus, we concluded, in this particular case, priming for agreeableness outweighed priming for helpfulness. So, though the first part of our hypothesis was supported, the second part of our hypothesis failed to find support.

Table 19 Summary of Hypotheses

Hypothesis	Concept	Outcome
Hypothesis 1	Credibility	Supported
Hypothesis 2	Storytelling	Supported
Hypothesis 3	Statements Against Self-Interests	Not Supported
Hypothesis 4	Linda Problem	Supported
Hypothesis 5	Framing	Supported
Hypothesis 6	Because Statement	Supported
Hypothesis 7	Anchoring	Supported
Hypothesis 8	Safety Net	Not Supported
Hypothesis 9	Number of Choices	Supported
Hypothesis 10	Small Yesses	Partially Supported

Summary of Hypotheses under Consideration

Discussion

We concluded that 8 out of the 10 considered hypotheses were supported by the dataset results, and two of them were not supported by the dataset under consideration. One difficulty of studying the predictors and influencers of negotiation were the hypothetical scenarios that failed to account for the complexity of human judgement and decision making in the real world. Despite these obstacles, these results provided support for several important suppositions in the study of biases and heuristics, influence, and bargaining.

Appendix B

50 Question Big Five Personality Traits Assessment

For each of the following statements, please indicate on a scale of 1 to 5 how much you agree with the following statements, where 1 = disagree, 2 = slightly disagree, 3 = neutral, 4 = slightly agree, and 5 = agree.

1. Am the life of the party
2. Feel little concern for others
3. Am always prepared
4. Get stressed out easily
5. Have a rich vocabulary
6. Do not talk a lot
7. Am interested in people
8. Leave my belongings around
9. Am relaxed most of the time
10. Have difficulty understanding abstract ideas
11. Feel comfortable around people
12. Insult people
13. Pay attention to details
14. Worry about things
15. Have a vivid imagination
16. Keep in the background
17. Sympathize with others' feelings
18. Make a mess of things
19. Seldom feel blue
20. Am not interested in abstract ideas
21. Start conversations
22. Am not interested in other's problems
23. Get chores done right away
24. Am easily disturbed
25. Have excellent ideas
26. Have little to say
27. Have a soft heart
28. Often forget to put things back in their proper place
29. Get upset easily
30. Do not have a good imagination
31. Talk to a lot of different people at parties
32. Am not really interested in others
33. Like order
34. Change my mood a lot
35. Am quick to understand things
36. Do not like to draw attention to myself
37. Take time out for others
38. Shirk my duties

39. Have frequent mood swings
40. Use difficult words
41. Do not mind being the center of attention
42. Feel others' emotions
43. Follow a schedule
44. Get irritated easily
45. Spend time reflecting on things
46. Am quiet around strangers
47. Make people feel at ease
48. Am exacting in my work
49. Often feel blue
50. Am full of ideas

Use the following sheet to calculate your Big-Five scores.

Extroversion

1)____+ *6)____+ 11)____+ *16)____+ 21)____+

*26)____+ 31)____+ *36)____+ 41)____+ *46)____= ______

Agreeableness

*2)____+ 7)____+ *12)____+ 17)____+ *22)____+

27)____+ *32)____+ 37)____+ 42)____+ 47)____= ______

Conscientiousness

3)____+ *8)____+ 13)____+ *18)____+ 23)____+

*28)____+ 33)____+ *38)____+ 43)____+ 48)____= ______

Neuroticism

4)____+ *9)____+ 14)____+ *19)____+ 24)____+

29)____+ 34)____+ 39)____+ 44)____+ 49)____= ______

Openness

5)____+ *10)____+ 15)____+ *20)____+ 25)____+

*30)____+ 35)____+ 40)____+ 45)____+ 50)____= ______

*Reverse score items marked with an asterisk (*). To reverse score an item, if you scored yourself a 1, rescore above as a 5. For a 2, rescore to 4; 3 does not change; rescore 4 to 2; and rescore 5 to 1.

Keep in mind that these scores will range from 10 to 50. Scores below 30 indicate you are low to average on that particular trait. Scores above 30 indicate you are average to high on that particular trait.

End Notes

1. American Psychological Association. Ethical Principles of Psychologists and Code of Conduct. Retrieved from https://www.apa.org/ethics/code/ on 12/10/2020.
2. Marshall, Andrea P., Sandra H. West, and Leanne M. Aitken. "Clinical credibility and trustworthiness are key characteristics used to identify colleagues from whom to seek information." *Journal of Clinical Nursing* 22, nos. 9-10 (2013): 1424–1433.
3. Cottrell, Catherine A., Steven L. Neuberg, and Norman P. Li. "What do people desire in others? A sociofunctional perspective on the importance of different valued characteristics." *Journal of Personality and Social Psychology* 92, no. 2 (2007): 208.
4. Zak, Paul J., Robert Kurzban, and William T. Matzner. "The neurobiology of trust." *Annals of the New York Academy of Sciences* 1032, no. 1 (2004): 224–227.
5. Mikolajczak, Moïra, James J. Gross, Anthony Lane, Olivier Corneille, Philippe de Timary, and Olivier Luminet. "Oxytocin makes people trusting, not gullible." *Psychological Science* 21, no. 8 (2010): 1072–1074.
6. Saffran, Lise, Sisi Hu, Amanda Hinnant, Laura D. Scherer, and Susan C. Nagel. "Constructing and influencing perceived authenticity in science communication: Experimenting with narrative." *PloS One* 15, no. 1 (2020): e0226711.
7. Hirsch, Alan R. "Nostalgia: A neuropsychiatric understanding." *ACR North American Advances* (1992).
8. Tamir, Diana I., and Jason P. Mitchell. "Disclosing information about the self is intrinsically rewarding." *Proceedings of the National Academy of Sciences* 109, no. 21 (2012): 8038–8043.
9. Aron, Arthur, Edward Melinat, Elaine N. Aron, Robert Darrin Vallone, and Renee J. Bator. "The experimental generation of interpersonal closeness: A procedure and some preliminary findings." *Personality and Social Psychology Bulletin* 23, no. 4 (1997): 363–377.

10. Brown, Brene. (2010). The Power of Vulnerability [Video file]. Retrieved from: https://www.ted.com/talks/brene_brown_the_power_of_vulnerability?language=en on 12/01/2020.
11. Coyle, Daniel. *The culture code: The secrets of highly successful groups*. New York: Bantam, 2018.
12. Tversky, Amos, and Daniel Kahneman. "Extensional versus intuitive reasoning: The conjunction fallacy in probability judgment." *Psychological Review* 90, no. 4 (1983): 293.
13. American Psychological Association. https://dictionary.apa.org/emotion.
14. Cuddy, Amy JC, Caroline A. Wilmuth, Andy J. Yap, and Dana R. Carney. "Preparatory power posing affects nonverbal presence and job interview performance." *Journal of Applied Psychology* 100, no. 4 (2015): 1286.
15. Murray, Henry Alexander. "Explorations in personality: A clinical and experimental study of fifty men of college age." (1938). https://psycnet.apa.org/record/1938-15040-000.
16. Atkinson, John William. "An introduction to motivation." (1964). https://psycnet.apa.org/record/1964-35038-000.
17. Danziger, Shai, Jonathan Levav, and Liora Avnaim-Pesso. "Extraneous factors in judicial decisions." *Proceedings of the National Academy of Sciences* 108, no. 17 (2011): 6889–6892.
18. Goleman, Daniel. "Emotional intelligence: Issues in paradigm building." *The Emotionally Intelligent Workplace*, no. 13 (2001): 26.
19. Lieberman, Matthew D., Naomi I. Eisenberger, Molly J. Crockett, Sabrina M. Tom, Jennifer H. Pfeifer, and B. M. Way. "Affect labeling disrupts amygdala activity in response to affective stimuli." *Psychological Science* 18, no. 5 (2007): 421–428.
20. Bruner, Jerome S. *Actual minds, possible worlds*. Cambridge, MA: Harvard University Press, 2009.
21. Cicero, Marcus Tullius, and Harry Mortimer Hubbell. *De inventione*. Vol. 1. London: Heinemann, 1960.
22. King, Martin Luther. "I Have a Dream by Martin Luther King, Jr.; August 28, 1963." *The Avalon Project*, Yale Law School, avalon.law.yale.edu/20th_century/mlk01.asp.
23. Mehrabian, Albert, and Susan R. Ferris. "Inference of attitudes from nonverbal communication in two channels." *Journal of Consulting Psychology* 31, no. 3 (1967): 248.
24. Kraus, Michael W. "Voice-only communication enhances empathic accuracy." *American Psychologist* 72, no. 7 (2017): 644.
25. Carmody, Dennis P., and Michael Lewis. "Brain activation when hearing one's own and others' names." *Brain Research* 1116, no. 1 (2006): 153–158.
26. Di Pellegrino, Giuseppe, Luciano Fadiga, Leonardo Fogassi, Vittorio Gallese, and Giacomo Rizzolatti. "Understanding motor events: A neurophysiological study." *Experimental Brain Research* 91, no. 1 (1992): 176–180.

27. Benjamin Franklin. Letter to Joseph Priestley. 1772.
28. Sá, Walter C., Richard F. West, and Keith E. Stanovich. "The domain specificity and generality of belief bias: Searching for a generalizable critical thinking skill." *Journal of Educational Psychology* 91, no. 3 (1999): 497.
29. Simons, Daniel J., and Christopher F. Chabris. "Gorillas in our midst: Sustained inattentional blindness for dynamic events." *Perception* 28, no. 9 (1999): 1059–1074.
30. Drew, Trafton, Melissa L-H. Võ, and Jeremy M. Wolfe. "The invisible gorilla strikes again: Sustained inattentional blindness in expert observers." *Psychological Science* 24, no. 9 (2013): 1848–1853.
31. Lord, Charles G., Mark R. Lepper, and Elizabeth Preston. "Considering the opposite: A corrective strategy for social judgment." *Journal of Personality and Social Psychology* 47, no. 6 (1984): 1231.
32. Asch, Solomon E., and Harold Guetzkow. "Effects of group pressure upon the modification and distortion of judgments." *Organizational Influence Processes* (1951): 295–303.
33. Milgram, Stanley, Leonard Bickman, and Lawrence Berkowitz. "Note on the drawing power of crowds of different size." *Journal of Personality and Social Psychology* 13, no. 2 (1969): 79.
34. Bizrate Insights, The Impact of Customer Reviews on Purchase Decisions, 2019. Retrieved Dec. 20, 2020 from https://bizrateinsights.com/resources/shopper-survey-report-the-impact-reviews-have-on-consumers-purchase-decisions/.
35. Cialdini, Robert B., Linda J. Demaine, Brad J. Sagarin, Daniel W. Barrett, Kelton Rhoads, and Patricia L. Winter. "Managing social norms for persuasive impact." *Social Influence* 1, no. 1 (2006): 3–15.
36. Pelham, Brett W., Matthew C. Mirenberg, and John T. Jones. "Why Susie sells seashells by the seashore: Implicit egotism and major life decisions." *Journal of Personality and Social Psychology* 82, no. 4 (2002): 469.
37. Thorndike, Edward L. "A constant error in psychological ratings." *Journal of Applied Psychology* 4, no. 1 (1920): 25–29.
38. Talamas, Sean N., Kenneth I. Mavor, and David I. Perrett. "Blinded by beauty: Attractiveness bias and accurate perceptions of academic performance." *PloS One* 11, no. 2 (2016): e0148284.
39. Denes-Raj, Veronika, and Seymour Epstein. "Conflict between intuitive and rational processing: When people behave against their better judgment." *Journal of Personality and Social Psychology* 66, no. 5 (1994): 819.
40. Levin, Irwin P., and Gary J. Gaeth. "How consumers are affected by the framing of attribute information before and after consuming the product." *Journal of Consumer Research* 15, no. 3 (1988): 374–378.
41. Tversky, Amos, and Daniel Kahneman. "Judgment under uncertainty: Heuristics and biases." *Science* 185, no. 4157 (1974): 1124–1131.

42. Cialdini, Robert B., Joyce E. Vincent, Stephen K. Lewis, Jose Catalan, Diane Wheeler, and Betty Lee Darby. "Reciprocal concessions procedure for inducing compliance: The door-in-the-face technique." *Journal of Personality and Social Psychology* 31, no. 2 (1975): 206.
43. Pink, Daniel H. *To sell is human: The surprising truth about moving others.* London: Penguin, 2013.
44. Cialdini, Robert B. Pre-suasion: A revolutionary way to influence and persuade. New York, NY: Simon and Schuster, 2016.
45. Mochon, Daniel. "Single-option aversion." *Journal of Consumer Research* 40, no. 3 (2013): 555–566.
46. Iyengar, Sheena S., and Mark R. Lepper. "When choice is demotivating: Can one desire too much of a good thing?" *Journal of Personality and Social Psychology* 79, no. 6 (2000): 995.
47. Thaler, Richard H., and Cass R. Sunstein. *Nudge: Improving decisions about health, wealth, and happiness.* London: Penguin, 2009.
48. Kinneavy, James L. "Kairos: A neglected concept in classical rhetoric." *Rhetoric and praxis: The contribution of classical rhetoric to practical reasoning* (1986): 79–105.
49. Danziger, Shai, Jonathan Levav, and Liora Avnaim-Pesso. "Extraneous factors in judicial decisions." *Proceedings of the National Academy of Sciences* 108, no. 17 (2011): 6889–6892.
50. Balliet D. "Communication and cooperation in social dilemmas: A meta-analytic review." *Journal of Conflict Resolution* (2010) 54(1): 39–57.
51. Wertheim, Edward G. "The importance of effective communication." Online. USA. Northeastern University, College of Business Administration (2008).
52. Kelly, Spencer D., Peter Creigh, and James Bartolotti. "Integrating speech and iconic gestures in a Stroop-like task: evidence for automatic processing." *Journal of Cognitive Neuroscience* 22, no. 4 (2010): 683–694.
53. Ekman, Paul, and Wallace V. Friesen. "Nonverbal leakage and clues to deception." *Psychiatry* 32, no. 1 (1969): 88–106.
54. Birdwhistell, Ray L. *Kinesics and context: Essays on body motion communication.* Philadelphia, PA: University of Pennsylvania Press, 2010.
55. Ekman, Paul, and Dacher Keltner. "Universal facial expressions of emotion." Segerstrale U, P. Molnar P, eds. Nonverbal communication: Where nature meets culture (1997): 27–46.
56. Martin, Jared, Magdalena Rychlowska, Adrienne Wood, and Paula Niedenthal. "Smiles as multipurpose social signals." *Trends in Cognitive Sciences* 21, no. 11 (2017): 864–877.
57. Duchenne, Guillaume-Benjamin. Mécanisme de la physionomie humaine: où, Analyse électro-physiologique de l'expression des passions. J.-B. Baillière, 1876.

58. Malek, Nour, Daniel Messinger, Andy Yuan Lee Gao, Eva Krumhuber, Whitney Mattson, Ridha Joober, Karim Tabbane, and Julio C. Martinez-Trujillo. "Generalizing Duchenne to sad expressions with binocular rivalry and perception ratings." *Emotion* 19, no. 2 (2019): 234.
59. Todorov, A. *Face value: The irresistible influence of first impressions*. Princeton, NJ: Princeton University Press, 2017.
60. Cuddy, Amy. *Presence: Bringing your boldest self to your biggest challenges*. London: Hachette UK, 2015.
61. Kawamichi, Hiroaki, Kazufumi Yoshihara, Akihiro T. Sasaki, Sho K. Sugawara, Hiroki C. Tanabe, Ryoji Shinohara, Yuka Sugisawa et al. "Perceiving active listening activates the reward system and improves the impression of relevant experiences." *Social Neuroscience* 10, no. 1 (2015): 16–26.
62. Pasupathi, Monisha, and Jacob Billitteri. "Being and becoming through being heard: Listener effects on stories and selves." *International Journal of Listening* 29, no. 2 (2015): 67–84.
63. Open Source Psychometrics Project. https://openpsychometrics.org/. Data retrieved from http://openpsychometrics.org/_rawdata/BIG5.zip on 09/15/2020.
64. Goldberg, Lewis R., John A. Johnson, Herbert W. Eber, Robert Hogan, Michael C. Ashton, C. Robert Cloninger, and Harrison G. Gough. "The international personality item pool and the future of public-domain personality measures." *Journal of Research in Personality* 40, no. 1 (2006): 84–96.
65. International Personality Item Pool: A Scientific Collaboratory for the Development of Advanced Measures of Personality Traits and Other Individual Differences (http://ipip.ori.org/).

Recommended Reading

Books by Shapiro Negotiation Institute

Shapiro, Ronald M., Mark A. Jankowski, and James M. Dale. *Bullies, Tyrants, and Impossible People: How to Beat Them Without Joining Them.* Currency, 2005.

Shapiro, Ronald M., and Gregory Jordan. *Dare to Prepare: How to Win Before You Begin.* Currency, 2008.

Shapiro, Ronald M., and Jeff Barker. *Perfecting Your Pitch: How to Succeed in Business and in Life by Finding Words That Work.* Hudson Street Press, 2013.

Shapiro, Ronald M. *The Power of Nice: How to Negotiate So Everyone Wins-Especially You!* John Wiley & Sons, 2015.

Some of Our Other Favorites

Carnegie, Dale. *How to Win Friends and Influence People.* Simon and Schuster, 1936.

Cialdini, Robert B. *Influence: The Psychology of Persuasion (Revised Edition).* William Morrow, 2006.

Grant, Adam M. *Give and Take: A Revolutionary Approach to Success.* New York, N.Y.: Viking, 2013.

Kahneman, Daniel. *Thinking, Fast and Slow.* Macmillan, 2011.

Pink, Daniel H. *To Sell Is Human: The Surprising Truth About Moving Others.* Penguin, 2013.

Sinek, Simon. *Start with Why.* Penguin Books, 2011.

Thaler, Richard H., and Cass R. Sunstein. *Nudge: Improving Decisions About Health, Wealth, and Happiness.* Penguin, 2009.

Acknowledgments

Thank you to everyone that helped make this book a reality. There are simply too many people to name but we would at least like to highlight a few people. First of all, our families for all of their support – writing a book is a long and consuming process and without their support, this book would simply not have been possible. Second, to everyone who provided testimonials – Howie Roseman, Tony Robbins, Julie Kadnar, Jim Kahler, Alisia Genzler, and Mark Shapiro. We cannot thank you enough. And third, to Ron Shapiro, for paving the way, and being a great mentor and friend.

About the Authors

Andres Lares has been the Managing Partner and CEO of Shapiro Negotiations Institute (SNI) since 2017. Prior to this role, Andres served various roles, including SNI's Chief Innovation Officer, where he led the company's development of technology and content. For over a decade, Andres has advised professional sports teams in the NBA, NFL, MLB, and NHL on contract negotiations, trades, and other critical negotiations. He has been featured in publications including *Harvard Business Review* (HBR), *Forbes*, *CNBC*, *Entrepreneur*, and *Sports Business Journal*. Andres guest lectures at conferences and institutions around the world and teaches a course on negotiations at Johns Hopkins University.

Jeff Cochran is Partner at the SNI. During his two decade career at SNI, Jeff has trained and coached organizations of all sizes and industries, from two C-level executives in a boardroom to thousands of people at a Fortune 100 client. He has won countless awards for being the top presenter at events with hundreds of other speakers and is consistently praised for his ability to teach complex topics in a playful manner. Some of Jeff's clients include Ecolab, Verizon, Wells Fargo, PwC, Google, Bristol Myers Squibb, Hearst Corporation, and the Baltimore Ravens.

Dr. Shaun Digan is an academic researcher, writer, and educator in the fields of management, entrepreneurship, and decision making. Shaun's research has been presented at conferences and universities around the world and has been published in academic outlets including the *Journal of Small Business Management* and the *Journal of Small Business Strategy*. Shaun also has nearly a decade of experience teaching, including in prestigious institutions and programs as the University of Louisville and the Governor's School for Entrepreneurs.

Index

O

P

Q

R

S

W

Y

Z